A publication of the

**CENTER FOR RESEARCH AND DEVELOPMENT
IN HIGHER EDUCATION**
University of California, Berkeley

LELAND L. MEDSKER, Director

the creative
college student

Jossey-Bass Inc., Publishers
615 Montgomery Street · San Francisco · 1968

the creative college student: an unmet challenge

PAUL HEIST, EDITOR

BAUM

THE JOSSEY-BASS SERIES IN HIGHER EDUCATION

General Editors

JOSEPH AXELROD *and* MERVIN B. FREEDMAN
San Francisco State College

To

T. R. McCONNELL

a pioneer and leader
in studying the problems
of higher education and
college youth

PREFACE

A concern for students of superior ability and superior talent has been in vogue in American education for many years. In fact, what may appear as attention to the concept of individual differences has been basic to several aspects of program development and curricular reconsiderations. This presumed recognition of and focus on individual differences in education have led to special programs for the mentally deficient, the retarded, and the slow learner, and, at the other extreme, for the highly able, talented, and creative student.

However, the concern for individual differences along this gross continuum has been neither as intensive nor as specific as one might desire for the individual himself. This narrow conception of the meaning of human differences has been even more limiting for the highly able than for the mentally handicapped. Furthermore, concern for important differences has been far less prevalent and effective in practice at the level of higher education than at the elementary and secondary levels. However, the situation in colleges has changed gradually in the post-Sputnik years, and today quite a number of special programs or curricular innovations represent attempts to accommodate the students, if not *the* student, of exceptional academic ability and talent.

The education of young people identified or described as creative (regardless of their academic ability and talent) has probably received the least attention at the college level. Here, the general assumption usually seems to have been that the students who possess unusual talent or exceptional creative potential perceive and learn no differently from most other young people. Consequently, there has seemingly been no recognized need for greater understanding, special provisions, or individualized treatment for them.

If considered at all, the education of college youth who have high potential for creative expression, has been subsumed for the most part under programs for highly able and academically capable students. At least this seems to be the case if one is to judge by the content and emphasis of much of the literature on exceptional youth in the past twenty years. Such programs have been in the form of honors programs, gifted-student seminars, tutorials, and independent-study courses, all of which have been open to students who qualified chiefly on the basis of grades and expressed interest. For potentially creative individuals the high attrition rate, presented and examined in this book, presumably testifies to the error of assuming that their educational needs are being either met in a general sense or in programs that lump the highly able and the talented students under such gross, comprehensive classifications as the "exceptional" or the "gifted." High ability is very often a characteristic of the highly creative, but many creative people do not exhibit unusual academic ability. Admittedly, some students given to originality and creative expression can learn and often do achieve in routine college settings, but we have come to realize that general teaching methods and common curricula are sadly inadequate and fail to help these individuals to realize their potentialities.

This loss of certain students from college became very apparent during the course of several research projects conducted at the University of California's Center for the Study of Higher Education (now called Center for Research and Development in Higher Education). In one study of students in eight diverse institutions, the research staff found that persons of unusual or exceptional potentialities, as well as many less capable men and women, were leaving college after encountering unsatisfactory, unchallenging, or discouraging academic experiences. Many of them were transferring or leaving in spite of good or acceptable achievement records. In addressing himself to the topic of educating the gifted and creative, T. R. McConnell, former chairman of the Center, offered the following comments on this problem:

> At times I am not very sanguine about the desire or the ability of our educational institutions to nurture the talents of their most gifted and creative students. Too often, the college attempts to force its exceptional students to conform, not only to accepted customs and attitudes of the community, but also to conventional habits of mind. Most of us are uncomfortable with rebellious intellect and fearful of its consequences, rather than hopeful of the results of its revolt. Therefore, I suspect that all along the way we freeze out the unconventional and creative minds, retaining the dutiful, unimaginative, compliant, competent, and unresourceful grade-getters who will become, in turn, the scholars who will sanction the same behavior in future students. Now and then, fortunately for art, letters, and science, a few mavericks slip through the screen, or quietly internalize their conflict with the stereotyped academic environment while outwardly conforming well enough with the mores to meet the faculty's requirements in greater or lesser degree. But I wonder most about the creative minds who find this environment utterly uncongenial and leave it forthwith. Some of them, perhaps, will realize their potentialities outside the Academy, as artists and writers always have. But others will have been lost to science and scholarship, others who could have brought new light and given new directions to man's long and often weary quest for self-realization.*

* McConnell, T. R. "The Rediscovery of the Gifted Student." Paper

This phenomenon of failure in educational institutions has much more evidence to substantiate it than to contradict it, as several contributors to this book reveal. A number of the chapters, some particularly relevant to the problems of retaining and educating creative youth, were originally presented in the spring of 1966 as papers at a conference sponsored by the Center for Research and Development in Higher Education and Education Extension at the University of California at Berkeley.

This conference, directed chiefly to some basic problems encountered in the education of creative youth, grew out of concern over these particular problems—a concern shared over several years with research colleagues at the Berkeley Center. The general agreement was that colleges fail as often as they succeed in educating those who are between the ages of sixteen and twenty-two and are recognized as highly creative. This conclusion about failure not only referred to the dropouts but also to those students whose attainments had been curtailed by an inadequate college education.

From the information available, we had become aware that this phenomenon was not limited to average or typical institutions of higher education but existed also in elite, selective colleges, as well as in institutions with good honors programs or specially developed curricula. However, since the administrators and faculties in most institutions seemed unaware of the inadequacies and failures of their educational programs for talented and creative youth, we wondered how we could best convey such a vital message to those in a position to act on it. Our question gained in importance from our realization that experts and writers had already written reams on creativity —with relatively little effect on faculty understanding and behavior or on program changes and improvement.

With this in mind, a conference was planned with the assistance of staff members from the Berkeley Educational Extension of the University of California. Invitations were issued to speakers who, because of their varied research backgrounds, might offer different and possibly new perspectives on the problem at hand. Some

---

presented at the Pacific Northwest Conference on Higher Education, Southern Oregon College, July 1959.

representation was sought from those conducting basic research on the creative process or creative people. Other representation, also in the field of research, was drawn from the immediate context of higher education. To complement these contributions, representatives from the world of the performing arts were selected to enlarge the discussion on creativity. The result of such considerations appears in some of the following chapters that are rewritten versions of the conference papers. Several chapters have been written specifically for this book, to give additional depth to the exploration. The reader must decide whether the different perspectives and criticisms illuminate some of the prevalent problems and offer a reorientation to more appropriate educational curricula for the highly creative.

ACKNOWLEDGMENTS

Sincere appreciation is due a number of persons who have been either directly or indirectly involved in preparing this book. Five of the chapters, now considerably revised, were initially presented as papers in a conference co-sponsored by the Center for Research and Development in Higher Education and the Education Extension of the University of California at Berkeley. Jane C. Zahn, then director of the Extension program, and Thomas Baird, a senior staff member, were involved in the early decisions regarding this conference on education for creative college students. John Pearson, program director on the Extension staff, served as conference manager and expedited the "production" of the meetings for three days. James Trent, a project director at the Center for Research and Development in Higher Education, served as panel moderator for a final symposium. He was joined by Harold Webster, former Center staff member and currently professor of psychology at Brooklyn College, and three of the conference speakers in a summary review of major problems and issues.

Consultation and editorial services have been generously given by Joseph Axelrod and Julie Pesonen. Special thanks are due to both of them.

PAUL HEIST

Berkeley
April 1968

CONTENTS

THE AUTHORS

JOSEPH AXELROD is professor of world literature at San Francisco State College, currently on leave as a visiting research professor at the Center for Research and Development in Higher Education at the University of California, Berkeley.

VITTORIO GIANNINI was, before his death in 1966, the president of the North Carolina School of the Arts in Winston-Salem; previously he was a professor at the Juilliard School of Music in New York.

RALPH J. GLEASON is a columnist on the *San Francisco Chronicle,* a freelance writer, and a commentator on traditional and contemporary jazz and the arts.

PAUL HEIST is professor of higher education and a research psychologist at the Center for Research and Development in Higher Education at the University of California, Berkeley.

DONALD W. MACKINNON is professor of psychology and director of the Institute for Personality Assessment and Research at the University of California, Berkeley.

NEVITT SANFORD is professor of psychology and education and director of the Institute for the Study of Human Problems at Stanford University.

BENSON R. SNYDER is the psychiatrist-in-chief at Massachusetts Institute of Technology and a staff member of the psychiatry department at Harvard Medical School.

ROBERT WILSON is a research psychologist and chairman of the research section at the Center for Research and Development in Higher Education at the University of California, Berkeley.

I

The Focus

1

A DIALOGUE
ON CREATIVITY

During a conference on education for creativity—at which some of the chapters in this book were presented in the form of position papers—members of a closing symposium reviewed and discussed the major issues raised at the earlier sessions. Representatives from several disciplines were engaged in this spontaneous examination of the problems of educating youth for greater creative expression in our colleges and universities. Participants in the symposium were Vittorio Giannini, president, North Carolina School of the Arts; Ralph Gleason, columnist for the *San Francisco Chronicle* and authority on jazz; Donald MacKinnon, director, Institute for Personality Assessment and Research, University of California, Berkeley; James Trent, project director at the Center for Research and Devel-

3

opment in Higher Education, University of California, Berkeley; and Harold Webster, professor of psychology, Brooklyn College. Mr. Trent served as the discussion chairman.

CHAIRMAN JAMES W. TRENT: This symposium is, in a way, a test of our own creativity, since we want to present here our unrehearsed thoughts regarding education for creativity.

When I think back to my graduate-student days, I recall that a number of young scholars with the greatest creativity potential found it difficult to put up with the regimentation of graduate school. Some extraordinary people left their studies altogether. For those who remained, however, there was a hard lesson to be learned— namely, that many of the best students, in conducting their doctoral investigations, raise more questions than they answer. I suggest we undertake the present task in that light. We might view *ourselves* as successful if we raise more good questions than we can answer.

To introduce our discussion, let me state a number of pertinent questions as I see the total problem. What do we know about the sources of creativity in the lives of individuals? What are the unique characteristics of parents who raise and foster creative youth? For example, what about the autonomous, permissive mothers who, according to report, are also able to promote a certain amount of self-discipline among their children? We have frequently heard that the basis for creativity is laid in the very early environment. Is there any research evidence for this assertion? When do the most influential experiences occur if not in early childhood? What exactly is the appropriate environment during childhood? For example, is it the freedom and liberality of the home or the well-established standards in the home that are the more important influences? Then, what about later life? Is the nature and potency of the high school or college experience so great that it shapes an individual's creative development?

Also in introduction let me briefly review some of the chief characteristics often attributed to creative persons. They are independent and innovative. They play with ideas and concepts. In academic settings, they have a highly developed sense of the theoretical and the esthetic. They are open to a wide range of experience and are spontaneous, flexible, and complex in outlook. They are frequently rebels, but we hope rebels with a cause. In general, they are reasonably intelligent, although we are told that intelligence is not directly related to creativity itself. They are not necessarily the greatest "achievers," insofar as grade-point average measures achievement. Creative people are underrepresented in applied and professional fields of study. Finally, but significantly, "creatives" have different styles of performing; they are not all of a type.

What do the symposium members think of the common view that we really don't know how to foster creativity at the more advanced educational levels? Or, if you don't want to tackle that question right away, we might first consider the methodology for assessing the nature of creative students. For example, what is your opinion of the psychological measures which are used for identifying creatives? We have chiefly relied upon rankings and ratings rather than personality correlates or productivity to identify students with creative potential. This methodology, however, generates a host of problems. We might ask whether we really can identify the truly creative person, at least in colleges and universities, or whether we must wait, instead, for the creative performance or product. If we do wait for overt signs of creativity without providing special programs designed to stimulate creativity for those who have such potential, then is it true that many of our most creative students will withdraw from college or forsake the fields in which they might well belong, succeed, and make their greatest contributions?

Finally, I think we have to address ourselves to the problem of ethics. We have to ask ourselves to what extent are we entitled to foster creativity? To what extent are we privileged to design for creative students an environment and a curriculum that reflect our values—values which initially may be alien to them?

VITTORIO GIANNINI: Creative expression at any point in life is part and parcel of the individual, his past, and his inheritance. Of course, the inheritance isn't always immediately apparent. Many talented performers and composers have come from parents who manifested no artistic talent. Talent can appear any place, in any family, in any class of society. If the talented person happens to be in an early environment which nourishes his talent, he is, of course, fortunate.

As educators, however, we cannot rely on the parents. We have a responsibility to youth and we must create the institutions which offer young people the opportunity to have their talents recognized and developed. I advocate as much exposure to the arts as possible—and from the earliest time a child can learn to respond, even though he may not understand. I feel confident that if the child has talent he will be stimulated by these encounters.

Of course, it goes without saying that we must also educate the talented pupil as a total human being, in the early years as well as later in high school and college. We have generally failed to provide this type of total educational opportunity in most formal educational settings.

CHAIRMAN TRENT: No doubt, many of our colleagues would agree that much of our educational system is too formalized and stifling and that it actually squelches creativity. How can we encourage creative expression, whatever the level of initial talent, if everything in our schools is scheduled and routinized?

HAROLD WEBSTER: Let me react to that. I think we can be critical of the colleges. But at the same time, we must remember that the colleges are an expression of our social order. They have become what they are because our general society is meeting its problems in certain ways. Of late, the attention directed to the American college is partly a result of the occurrence of broader cultural and social changes. Many college students have been involved in protest activities because they want things changed. They are critics of the social order as much as they are of the colleges.

It is true that many kinds of creative talent will not be developed within the formal structure of modern higher education. Take the so-called nonstudents, for example, those who drop out but remain and live near some of our campuses; they don't like the system and frequently leave it. We needn't place the blame or burden of guilt on colleges or on college administrators or, for that matter, on politicians; we ought to place it squarely upon ourselves and other fellow members of our society.

MR. GIANNINI: I lose patience with the people who say, "I don't like the system or the society." It's easy to give destructive criticism. Some students don't like some things about their colleges; well, there will always be people who object to anything that interferes with their particular way of doing things. A certain amount of discipline is basic to everything we learn.

Of course, Mr. Webster, you are right in saying we have to improve the system continually. We must seek a kind of artistic and academic education in which we would educate everyone for a better world. But the difficulties of implementation are enormous. For one thing, we must broaden the scope of our existing curricula rather than proliferate more specialties. And to do that well, we have to know the differences that exist among human beings. We will never create a system that is right for everybody, but we can come closer than we have come. Hence, it is of utmost importance to have professors who study their students, who give them the kind of direction that seems most likely to help their individual growth. The individual personality and motivation of each student is crucial. I agree with those who insist that it is also crucial for teachers to develop their sensitivity to these differences.

DONALD W. MACKINNON: I accept the thesis that the best education for the potentially creative student is probably the same as the best education we plan for all students. But we must face the fact that— even if we could envision and realize the best of all systems in the way of educational organization and style of teaching—it would not appeal to all students. We have to realize that some are not educable, not in the way our objectives suggest.

While we express proper concern about students who drop out or become alienated, we have to recognize that sometimes, for some students, dropping out is appropriate. Dropouts are not necessarily people we should bemoan. Perhaps, many creatives are better off leaving college. They may need time away from school. To try to force them to continue in the educational system would be most unfortunate. Some people have experiences *outside* the college context which encourage the growth that we all hope college will give. This may seem something of a paradox if we are trying to design an educational utopia, but it is a fact. We all know such cases.

If we could identify the highly creative students and if we could agree on the ideal experiences to provide in college to further the development and expression of their creative dispositions, what would happen? Many of those students, because they are such individualists, would object to our proposals!

The creative person is, above all, an individual. Many of

these people express this individuality through their artistic work. And, of course, through this work they hold up a mirror to society. As Mr. Webster has indicated, a great deal of student criticism is directed at society, by way of the school.

I agree with Mr. Giannini, too, in his emphasis on recognizing the variety of human beings and being sensitive to the variety of experiences which are most appropriate and valuable for them. There is no *single* way to nurture the creative potential of all individuals; there is no easy way to educate those with the greatest potential.

RALPH J. GLEASON: I'd like to return to a remark Mr. Giannini made earlier. I'm not tired of hearing people tell me what's wrong with society or what's wrong with the educational system. To say that we are, just reinforces many students' assumption that they can't trust or even communicate with anybody over thirty.

I agree we can't dream up a system to produce creative persons, but I do have a proposal. What I would propose for the educational system (from which I was a dropout) is that it get out of the way of creative individuals. It should not tell them what they must do or the ways in which they must do it. It should provide them with the opportunity, the place, and the platform to explore their own creativity and aid them by providing proper tools whenever possible.

Mr. Giannini, you talk about discipline as being essential in one sense to the education of young people. You can't listen to musicians like Louis Armstrong, Dizzy Gillespie, and Miles Davis play and hear their virtuosity without realizing that it is a result of hours and hours of discipline. But this is self-discipline. Some of the jazz greats have locked themselves in a room and practiced for days. Sonny Rollins, a great saxophone player, told me that he never goes to sleep without putting a pencil, flashlight, and scratch pad by his bed. If he wakes up with ideas, he writes them down and pursues them the next day.

However, the main problem of educating creative people is not a matter of discipline. The main problem—at least in the areas with which I am familiar—is that by the time they reach college age, they are faced with an enormous, rigid structure and organization. This gross entity is not only in the form of buildings, people, regulations, and forms but in the overall attitude of many of those who maintain the institution—an attitude which prevents creative people from getting to those experiences most important to them. Possibly this corporate attitude reflects the society. If so, we might conclude that the results demonstrate extremely wasteful societal tendencies.

Now that's all related to the point about individual growth. The system asks creative people to spend a lot of time in activities which, at that stage in their careers, are of no interest to them whatsoever. Most jazz musicians who become virtuosos start at an early age and spend eight or ten years practicing and playing before they ever get around to reading a novel. Only after they have mastered an instrument and begin to have something to "say" on it, do they feel a need to expand in other directions.

CHAIRMAN TRENT: Let's pursue directly a question that we've only hinted at thus far. Are there different types of creativity? Is there *one* kind of creative expression on the part of, say, certain kinds of musicians and *another* shown by research scientists?

MR. MACKINNON: Doubtless, there are different types and forms of creativity. Our own investigations at our research institute have shown this. If you note the way in which individuals evaluate their own experiences, the evidence clearly shows that artists, writers, and poets have a preference for feeling judgment. Research scientists and engineers prefer analytical thinking. But it is not quite as simple as this.

Engineers and research scientists show a preference for thinking and cognitive behavior, but those who are creative in these fields will show more feeling in their development and behavior than those who are less creative. In other words, they tend to develop "opposites" in their thinking or personality makeup; they tolerate the tendencies of opposites in themselves and, in this way, fully develop more complex dispositions, various styles of cognition, and greater openness in attitudes.

Let me cite one study by Gough, a member of our staff. He examined scientists in industry and, through a very elaborate assessment program and intense analysis, he investigated their styles as research scientists. His findings indicated no less than eight different styles or ways of behaving as a research scientist. Clearly, these and other data show that differences exist not only between creative people in two different fields but also among individuals within the same field.

MR. GIANNINI: I am surprised he found only eight different styles!

MR. MACKINNON: Well, this finding, quite naturally, is determined by the method of assessment and its accuracy.

MR. WEBSTER: If creative people are this varied and complex, then there is some merit in Ralph Gleason's suggestion that the least we can do in the educational world is to get out of their way and permit them to express or develop different styles.

MR. GIANNINI: I would like to pursue Mr. MacKinnon's point a little further. Doesn't the creative impulse manifest itself in different ways, not only according to the person's field but also as a product of his particular personality?

For instance, couldn't we speculate that some personality configurations will encourage early appearance of talent while others will delay its appearance? Any number of artists have bloomed quite late in music. Giuseppi Verdi is a case in point. At nineteen, when he sought admission to the Conservatory at Milan, he was turned down. Not only was he not admitted, but the judges who examined him wrote him a letter advising him to choose another career. This man started late and continued late. Some of Verdi's greatest works were written when he was over eighty.

MR. GLEASON: Yes. One of the jazz greats, Dave Brubeck, originally prepared for future studies in veterinary medicine at the College of the Pacific. He soon discovered that he was spending all his time playing the piano. His mother was a piano teacher and he had come from a family of musicians. He considered a transfer from the pre-veterinary program to the music department, but the campus advisor with whom he discussed the move told him to stay in veterinary medicine!

Those of you who have engaged in research on creative people—have you found any evidence that persons have been supremely successful in a creative area, such as science or painting, by following the "rules"? Aren't the great people often the ones who have decided they must do their work in rather unconventional ways? Even J. Paul Getty, in his celebrated *Playboy* memoirs, talks about all the things he did that they told him not to do. He believes that's why he is successful. Doesn't it appear to you that we can't make rules or give directions to the really talented and creative?

MR. MACKINNON: I can only agree. My answer would be that those who are really creative obviously have thrown the book away. They have come up with innovations that nobody else has discovered.

MR. WEBSTER: And this presents quite a problem for teachers because, as you and your colleagues have shown over the years, creative people are frequently not too pleasant to have around. Teachers do not always welcome original and unexpected responses in class. This suggests something for teacher-education programs. Students in these programs should be taught to be more cognizant and tolerant of innovative, imaginative youngsters. If we could retrain teachers along such lines, perhaps the exceptional student would be more inclined to remain in school.

On the other hand, I wonder whether we can identify a creative person before he has produced some kind of product. Perhaps—

MR. GIANNINI: What do you mean when you say "product"? Must it always be tangible?

MR. WEBSTER: No. I have recently returned from India where a "product" might be self-actualization or self-realization, as intangible a product as there is. In India, people say they can recognize this kind of personal development and distinguish between a holy man, for example, and an imposter. Men who have lived in India all their lives say that they believe there are types of creative self-realization—that is, re-creations of the self—which do not involve material products such as we look for in this culture.

CHAIRMAN TRENT: What about the problems teachers face with innovative but troublesome students? Can we go back to that?

MR. GIANNINI: Frankly, without the creative students, I'd be bored to tears!

CHAIRMAN TRENT: Are we guilty here of what Don Jackson has called a "double bind"? Are we asking the same student to go in two directions at once? On the one hand, are we telling him, "We

want you to be a good, mentally healthy, well-behaving citizen,"
and, on the other hand, "We want you to be unique and original"?
MR. MACKINNON: I don't think that we are putting the individual
in a bind—not the creative individual. We may be inducing tensions
between two opposite dispositions or tendencies. But, if we can
identify one feature that characterizes the highly creative individual,
it is his greater capacity to tolerate conflicting values and dispositions within himself and effect some kind of integration.

Otto Rank conceptualizes two different types of men. The
first he calls the "adaptive type"—a normal, average man who has
no strong drive for individualization, experiences little conflict, and
conforms to the social norms. He is largely at one with society and
feels comfortable in it; he may be very productive and effective.
What characterizes him is this: He emphasizes adapting to the situation in the society in which he lives.

The other type Rank calls "neurotic" or "conflicted." (I
would be more inclined, incidentally, to describe this type as conflicted rather than neurotic.) This individual strikes out on his own
and attempts to formulate his own goals, ideals, and moral standards. These are generally different from the ones that are socially
sanctioned or seen as conventional. The conflicted person develops
new attitudes toward himself and toward the world around him.
Within him are possibilities of development which do not exist in
the adaptive individual. However, if he cannot resolve the conflicts
he has permitted to develop within himself, then he will continue
to be in conflict—self-critical, critical of society—feeling guilty, in-
ferior, and, often, alienated. And he may well become seriously neurotic.

I am not inclined to impute illness to Rank's second type, as
his term "neurotic" implies, although neurotic forces may be more
fully developed in these people. I prefer to think of this conflicted
condition as carrying in itself the possibilities of further development.
Some individuals will develop beyond the conflicted condition and
others won't.

The fortunate ones will move beyond conflict to the level of
the creative man, the person we recognize as the productive artist.
This is the individual whom Rank describes as the "man of will."

As a man of will, the artist has effected integration of conflicting trends in himself. Through integration or through growth toward integration, the artist comes finally to a more creative expression of his own individuality.

When we awaken students to possibilities of dealing with reality in opposite ways, we may make them, in some ways, more conflicted. But I wouldn't describe the introduction of conflict as putting the individual in a bind. It is important to develop these opposing forces. A certain psychic turbulence is necessary to the processes of synthesis, resolution, and evolving potential for further development. That is an important component of the right kind of education.

MR. GLEASON: That's right. How can there be any creativity without prior destruction, that is, destruction of old values, old systems, old ways of looking at things?

MR. GIANNINI: But to create something, it is not necessary to destroy. Why can't we build on what has gone before? Why do we need to destroy?

MR. GLEASON: But we need to clear the old out of the way, so it won't blind a person to new ideas and approaches. Let me illustrate with an actual case of a high school principal and a sixteen-year-old student—a boy who is one of the most interesting and potentially creative young people that I have encountered. He aroused the animosity of the principal because he wore blue jeans and sandals and an earring in one ear; he also had a long, Beatle haircut. The principal told this boy that he would not be permitted to attend—of all things—a Bob Dylan concert unless he removed the earring, because people would think he was a queer.

There are a couple of points here: First, why should this man—an educator to boot—think that if a student decorates his ear with an earring he will be taken as a homosexual? Granted, this behavior is somewhat unusual; but this happened in a school with a strong program of encouraging children in creative activities and in becoming individuals. Second, placing such importance on the impact of someone's mode of dress seems so wrong.

But the main point is that you simply cannot accept the tried and the tested as your goal and refuse to see beyond them. What we really want to foster are creative people—thinking, innovative persons who create problems; such persons are not willing to hold still for whatever it is that went on before that time. Granted this does not mean that we have to destroy Italian opera in order to write other operas. However, creative youth should not be bound and restricted to the tried and the tested. The creative musicians in jazz have made numerous breakthroughs into new forms by ignoring much that was accepted before.

MR. MACKINNON: Of course, it should be said that sometimes people feel they are being creative if they merely display the trappings of creativity—for example, if they dress or behave in unusual or original ways. Investigations of highly creative adult individuals by our Institute disclose that some of them are very conforming in many areas or aspects of their lives. Most of them were rather conforming with respect to dress, perhaps because it was not worth their time to do something unusual in this regard. In fact, we frequently were amused by the highly creative individuals who came to the Institute dressed more like businessmen than like—

MR. GLEASON: Forgive me for interrupting. I feel a need to explain further what I meant by "destruction." It probably was too strong a word for what I had in mind. The process we have been discussing involves the development of new values and new approaches. One must question and re-examine these, and I would agree that this process leads naturally to changes and the replacement of old values.

MR. GIANNINI: I understand what you mean, but I don't call it "destruction." I would call that "building."

MR. MACKINNON: I think you and Mr. Gleason are describing something similar to what I have noted in some of the creative people we have studied. They seem to have the extraordinary capacity to be dissatisfied with their work, and yet they don't become discouraged. They never are wholly satisfied with their last creative products, and they set themselves even more difficult tasks for the next one. They move on to greater challenge. This is wonderful. Not everybody has this ability; the creatives seem to be continuously self-critical although basically self-accepting, while retaining a sense of destiny, commitment, and involvement in what they are doing. This ability permits them to look back with dissatisfaction and simultaneously to move on courageously to even more difficult undertakings.

MR. GIANNINI: That's an interesting point. As a composer, for instance, if I wanted to write a composition greater than any other, I would spend a whole lifetime and never finish it. That is foolish. One can only do the best he can. A composer is nervous and often hesitant when he starts a work, but at the same time he wants to get to the last double bar to finish it. He keeps thinking and writing, and he frequently worries. He's never sure how he's doing. He lives with ambiguities.

CHAIRMAN TRENT: Could we pause for a moment to consider more fully the tension, anxiety, and ambiguity with which the artist must live? You imply that the creative person is living with frustration much of the time. Is it possible that some bright people who might be open to unique and new ideas can't stand such stress and strain and ambiguity? Is it possible that many creative people are not productive because they can't live with the turbulence and the dissatisfaction?

MR. GIANNINI: Well, some people can live with tension and some can't. And there's no way of helping those who can't live with uncertainty; you can't make them over. I don't think it's frustration we have been talking about. It is uncertainty. A composer is never sure how his composition will turn out, and every time a performer goes on the stage he has "butterflies." This is not frustration. An artist wants to do well and maybe he's anxious, but it's a nice anxiousness.

MR. MACKINNON: That is very interesting. Mr. Giannini calls it "a nice anxiousness." One of our striking findings at the Institute is that the most creative individuals score higher on measurements of anxiety than the less creative individuals. In other words, they display and probably live with more anxiety than the less creative. But they are not incapacitated by anxiety. They also score high on psychiatric scales assessing ego strength, control, and adaptability. The relation between psychopathology and creative behavior is not simple. But let me oversimplify and say this: The highly creative individuals are at one and the same time more disturbed, more discontented, more anxious, *and* healthier than the average man.

MR. GLEASON: As Mr. Giannini said, even veterans of many years' experience are highly nervous before they go on stage to perform. Joan Baez, the folk singer, has only within the last year been able to whip the nervous reaction that has dogged her throughout her concert career. Most people would never surmise the tension under which she works. She has learned to deal with this by isolating herself for fifteen minutes before a performance, in total silence.

Another example is Gillespie, the great cornetist, who has had a great variety of stage experience and has performed night after night under the most outrageous conditions; yet he still is nervous before he steps on stage. Jazz musicians don't know how a performance is going to go, and they want things to go well; they want to do well. As a matter of fact, communication is the essence of the performance. Almost all artists who are worth anything at all—certainly the performing artists—want to communicate to their audience. They want the audience to hear them, to appreciate them, and to love them; otherwise, most of them wouldn't be there.

MR. GIANNINI: Paderewski's manager told me that even after this famous pianist had been before the public for years and years, he never overcame his preconcert nervousness. Before every performance, his manager had to go to his hotel at about five o'clock and would often find him crying in despair, saying he didn't want to perform that night. He had to talk to him slowly and try to bring him around with whatever argument would work. And so it went before every concert. Only after the first few minutes on stage was he all right.

MR. GLEASON: Is it true in your experience that for the really great performing artists the only reality is when they are on stage performing, and all the rest is intermission? I have heard this from jazz musicians. Bob Dylan said, in a press conference in San Francisco, "All I do is to make up songs and perform; everything else is an interference." From my observations of some individual performers whom I know, this seems to be particularly true. Reality for them is on stage.

MR. GIANNINI: Yes, I believe this "true reality" on stage exists for many artists.

CHAIRMAN TRENT: Let me now ask a final question. What kinds of programs should colleges and universities adopt in order to foster and encourage creativity? Much has been written about the kind of elementary-education programs which promote creative experiences for children. But what about the college level? Is the answer to be found in the "free-university" programs, like the Experimental College run by the students at San Francisco State College? What are your reactions?

MR. GIANNINI: I think this sort of thing is important, for I believe that the students do not exist for the school; the school exists for the students. Perhaps such "free-university" programs can refocus the emphasis of college education on the students.

MR. GLEASON: To the extent that students remain instrumental in creating these new programs, something important may develop and with good effect on the total university. What is developing at San Francisco State College is fascinating. And there are now three such projects in the Bay Area.

MR. MACKINNON: Yes, at Berkeley there is the Tussman Program. I don't think the chief importance of these new programs is in the content—I mean the topics discussed and that aspect of the courses. Rather, I would stress the importance of the kind of interaction that occurs between the people in the program—the students and the instructors. That's where the answer is going to be found.

CHAIRMAN TRENT: The members of this panel have left us with a number of issues to consider. There are, first of all, many forms of creativity, and we need to be able to distinguish among these. Then, proceeding on the assumption that it is possible to foster creative endeavor, we have to investigate what particular conditions help foster the various forms of creativity. Finally, as college and university people, our specific challenge is to discover how to strengthen the conditions that encourage—and how to eliminate the conditions that discourage—creative expression among college and university students.

2

UNEASY YOUTH:
FOUR SKETCHES

Paul Heist

The path through college is far from an easy sequence of events for a great many youth. But parents and faculty often show or feign surprise to hear or read that the college years represent a troubled time for students who are bright, exceptionally talented, or highly creative. It may seem somewhat paradoxical that many students with great ability, sensitivity, imagination, and originality also have difficulty in college or are dissatisfied with their undergraduate curricula. However, staff members at the Center for Research and Development in Higher Education have encountered numerous examples of unhappy or troubled students among the potentially creative.

The stories of several creative personalities, selected from quite different campuses, will serve to place some problems of creative youth against an immediately human background; for this reason these sketches are presented before reviewing data on the loss of creative youth in American colleges or before considering aspects of their education. In each of the sketches, we introduce individuals who represent different types of exceptional talent and ability and different forms of creative expression. Although brief, the sketches also permit the reader to understand how particular college experiences did not seem to be an appropriate or adequate diet for nurturing these young men and women.

SKETCH I: Lisa

I first met Lisa while trying to gain admission to the office of a college newspaper a few years back. Seeing my difficulty, she asked congenially, "May I help?" I explained that I was looking for some recent copies of the campus paper. She thought for a moment, then, after trying the nearby door which I had already found locked, brushed her long dark hair back over her shoulders and said, "Oh, follow me."

Leading me outside and around the building, she reached up to push open a window and, in ungainly fashion, started to crawl in. Since this was more of a feat than she had anticipated, she said, with a laugh, "Won't you give me a shove?" I complied, a bit embarrassed, by trying to lend a discreet hand. Together we managed, and after a couple of minutes she came around the corner with copies of every available issue. As she handed them to me, she announced that she knew I was "one of those researchers" studying her class. She then introduced herself, and after telling her my name, I thanked her and went my way.

Later, when I related this event to the dean of students, he described Lisa's family background and spoke of her high ability, her rather unusual habits, and her excellent freshman-year record. He also predicted that she probably would not find enough challenge on the college campus to satisfy her.

At our research headquarters in Berkeley, I found information in our files that revealed some interesting aspects about the life of this eighteen-year-old girl. Lisa was from a home representing a high level of culture and intellectual concern. Her scores on several tests tagged her as an autonomous, mature, and sophisticated young woman with very strong intellectual and esthetic interests. She also had strong needs to be free, unfettered, and independent. Both her measured characteristics and the dean's prediction led me to wonder about her. If a girl like Lisa wasn't excited and challenged by this excellent college in which she was surrounded by many equally capable peers, then where would she find intellectual stimulation and adequate satisfaction?

The forecast about Lisa came true much sooner than I might have guessed at the time. In February of the same school year, I encountered her near the University of California campus in Berkeley. Seemingly pleased to find a familiar face, she suggested a cup of coffee in a café across the street. As soon as we were seated, she spoke about her disappointment with the college she had been attending, telling me that she was not going to return and wanted to spend the rest of the spring living in the Bay Area. She spoke briefly of her earlier training in painting and thought she might return to this interest. She also explained that she wanted to look at the world and the people in it and that she wanted time to think about the importance of living and about what she had to do.

Late in the spring of the same year, I met Lisa again one evening on the streets in the North Beach section of San Francisco. She told me that she had been reading a great deal, visiting various art galleries, and taking a class in anatomy drawing. She had also spent a week in the "art world" of Los Angeles. Although she was anticipating a visit with her parents during the summer months, she had no plans for the following fall.

I saw Lisa for the last time about a year later at a small, private New York art gallery, where a number of her paintings had been hung in a show. She had been studying for six months at an art school, but was not continuing classes there. We chatted about her present way of life, her dissatisfaction with education in general, her involvement with a recent civil-rights protest movement, and her concern about problems of segregation in New York City and the rest of the country. She commented at some length about her growing desire to express herself through painting and told of her plans to go to Europe to study and paint. Recently, an acquaintance of mine reported that Lisa had returned after a year abroad and was winning acclaim as a young artist in New York.

Lisa, with scores in the Scholastic Aptitude Test above 750 on both verbal and mathematical subtests and with all the measurable characteristics of recognized creative persons, is finding her way in life without completing a formal education. Anyone acquainted with her would probably agree that she is a sophisticated and educated young adult. One also might have to concede that she would have gained little from additional years of structured curricula or intensive academic pursuits. In fact, as she herself had related, she had not found college an exciting, expanding experience. In her words, "My year and a half of college was a tight, insensitive routine." Its chief challenge for her came from two or three fellow students and one class in literature.

SKETCH II: Karen

Karen was first met as a waitress in the campus cafeteria of a small liberal-arts college. While serving after-dinner coffee, she asked why my colleague and I were visiting her campus. A brief explanation satisfied her only temporarily, for at dinner the next evening she asked more questions. The following day she again caught sight of us, this time in the coffee shop, and she and a friend came over to join us. We invited the girls to be seated and encouraged them to speak about themselves and their college.

They informed us that they had both enrolled in this church-affiliated college chiefly at their parents' insistence. Karen explained that her missionary father wanted her to attend because it was his old school. Her first-choice college had been an Eastern girls' school, which she had thought would be a good place to pursue a career in the arts. She spoke of this choice as being a bit "dreamy-eyed," since her selection had made little sense to her parents. They had argued that the only proper education for their children could be found within a school of their religious denomination. More than that, her father had stated that the arts were not proper subjects to study in college, especially since they didn't lead to a respectable vocation. Nevertheless, Karen, now in her sophomore year, admitted to us that she still wanted to go to another college and often thought and spoke about transferring.

Karen was very neat and attractive, but her appearance was somewhat unique on this campus where decorum in dress prevailed. Her long hair, her low-heeled sandals, and her casual offbeat attire, reminiscent of Oriental dress, were cues to her distinctiveness. As my colleague later commented in an interview summary, she dressed and walked "with simplicity and beauty."

On a later visit, near the end of the same school year, I learned that Karen made all her own clothes—a fact which accounted for their special design—and that she had spent most of the first sixteen years of her life in the Orient. The dean of women informed me that Karen had been quite unhappy during her first year on campus and that she had sought out a faculty member during this, her second year, for help in transferring to another college or to the local state university. However, after initiating this move, Karen had felt obliged to write her parents about her plans. Her father had countered by writing to the dean's office; as a result, the dean of women had discouraged her seeking out a "controversial" faculty member as counselor and confidant. Thus, her attempt to transfer had never gone beyond serious exploration.

During her junior year, Karen was added to a supplementary interview sample and became a subject in a study of selected students on her campus. The persons in this supplementary sample were identified as "high creatives" through measured personality characteristics. In the context of this additional information and subsequent interviewing, the "pattern" of Karen's life gradually was revealed.

In spite of her parents' wishes and admonishments, Karen had decided to major in painting and sculpture with music as her minor field. The graphic-arts program at that time was not extensive enough to lead to a complete major, but she decided to settle for as much work as she could get. Because of her disappointment with "the narrowness of the music department," chiefly in the type of music permitted in the program, she attempted to round out her course work in literature and language during her junior and senior years. She also enjoyed most of the activities and sports offered in women's physical education and took the only two dance courses in the curriculum. In the interview during her junior year, she described the "sheer delight" she experienced from the movement of her body, whether playing field hockey or swimming or dancing.

During her junior year, Karen also began to express herself by writing short stories on her own. A few fellow students became aware of her talent, and at the beginning of her senior year, she was asked by the editor of the campus paper to write a column on campus life. Though sprinkled with a dry and subtle humor, her column included gentle criticisms of the student body, the administration, and college policies. Occasionally, she even wrote about the inadequacies of the education received on campus.

During a senior-year interview, Karen confessed that her biggest disappointment in school was that this "good college" did not permit a person to major in dance or even to study it to any appreciable degree. She described the dance program as "ladylike calisthenics" and said that "the developments in modern dance had never crossed the state boundaries."

Karen discovered, toward the end of her senior year, that she probably would not have enough concentrated credits to graduate. Her advisor said that when he told Karen of this deficiency, she laughed "almost hysterically" for about a minute and then shouted, *"Isn't* that wonderful!" Less than a week later, Karen's roommate awoke to find a note on her dresser. In it Karen wished her good luck, congratulated her on her graduation in June, and ended with, "I'm leaving for the real world." Beyond this point our information on Karen ends.

SKETCH III: Peter

Peter was one of the identified creative students in our files at the Center for Research and Development in Higher Education. Initially, we had become aware of him through a routine review of questionnaire information and test scores that were part of the entrance requirements at his school, one of the most selective colleges of science and technology in the country. Peter stood high among the entering students in both scholastic aptitude and previous achievement. In this class of over 150 students, his measured personality characteristics marked him as one of the five with highest potential for original and innovative thought.

Through released college records, we found that Peter had already achieved scholastic recognition before entering college, chiefly through the publication of two research reports while in high school. From his experiences since junior high days in a small chemistry laboratory in his home and from his studies in a special area of chemistry, he had become quite advanced, at least in chemistry, as compared with others in his entering college class.

The subsequent story of this young man is also one of general success if the B.S. degree is used as the criterion. Throughout most of his college years, Peter obtained excellent grades and was one of the number of creatives in his entering class who remained for four years and satisfactorily completed all requirements.

Our staff first interviewed Peter during his third year in college and twice following graduation. His overall reaction to college, as drawn from these interviews, can be summarized as general dissatisfaction. However, even though he was never very happy about his courses or the instruction, he only rarely had given serious thought to transferring. He was obviously not a perpetual malcontent or griper. His analyses of what he saw as inadequate in his education and as faults in the institution's program were rational and astute.

Peter received excellent grades in his major field from the first year on, and his peers learned to respect his scholastic achievement. Nevertheless, he reported twice that only one professor—and not in his major field—had mentioned seeing or reading his earlier research reports, although the campus newspaper had highlighted his former studies during his second year. Until late in his junior year, no one in the chemistry department had spoken with him about a future in chemistry. "In fact," said Peter, "no one ever spoke to me as if I might be a young scientist *now,* let alone treated me as if I might become a future research scientist. Nor did we get any class work in the first three years that smacked of real research or taught us how to conduct it." He went on to say, "One professor once lectured to us for several sessions about the necessity of spending years learning the fundamental material, and he argued that research in the sciences could not be understood or done until all the essential foundation work had been completed."

During his first three college years, Peter developed new interests and pursued one or two others he had developed earlier. As he received growing satisfaction from playing in a woodwind ensemble, he began to skip some classes to practice on his instrument. Late in his second year, he "discovered" philosophy and, although he had only taken one course, began to read widely in this field during his third year. During this same period, he began seriously to question his religious beliefs and wrote a series of papers in which he examined the concerns and questions underlying this change in his life.

By the beginning of Peter's senior year, he also realized that he didn't want to continue in chemistry after graduation. At this late date, he considered switching his major to physics. He explained that he had found little room for original thinking in chemistry, at least as taught in his first three years, and he had encountered much more flexibility in an advanced physics course. This decision probably was influenced by a favorite physics professor who had discussed with him the metaphysical frontiers of nuclear physics and astronomy.

To bring this story to a close, Peter had his poorest year for grades during his fourth year. During the previous summer, he had read avidly in several fields, including a variety of historical and contemporary fiction. In the course of his last year, he went back to writing poetry, which he had given up after his high school days. He finished his work in chemistry with a critical paper, chiefly directed to how this subject could be taught for the purpose of cultivating essential research skills. The following fall, the physical sciences lost an innovative and creative chemist; Peter enrolled in a distant graduate school in the field of philosophy.

SKETCH IV: Anthony

Anthony became known to us at the Center during his first semester in a fairly well-known, liberal-arts college. He had enrolled with the intention of majoring in mathematics, while also hoping to pursue a long-standing interest in music and the arts in general.

About halfway through his first semester, Anthony, who had early informed us that he preferred not to be called "Tony," expressed great satisfaction with his choice of a college and anticipated completing four years and graduating.

This young man came from a prosperous home. His father was a merchant who had moved from a small retail operation to the presidency of a wholesale firm during Anthony's lifetime. Private schools and private lessons worked no hardship on this family. Although the mother had received years of training in music, neither she nor her husband had completed a college education. However, in the home there was much good music (both Anthony and his sister were rather accomplished musicians), and on the bookshelves there was a small amount of good literature. The parents represented a mixed marriage, the father being Jewish and the mother Protestant. This fact probably accounted in part for the little religious education that Anthony and his sister had received, especially after elementary school.

During most of Anthony's first seventeen years, his family lived in an upper-middle-class, suburban community. He received his high school education in a good public institution, after trying a private school for his two junior high years. During these last six precollege years, he took private lessons, first on the piano and then for three years on the French horn. Previous to the private lessons, his mother worked with him on the piano for three or four years.

Anthony fared very well in high school in all academic subjects, and his success in and enjoyment of mathematics led to an early decision to major in this field. Yet, as intimated, he fully expected to pursue his esthetic interests and to continue to play in orchestral groups. However, his expectations in music, at his advanced level of proficiency, probably would have been unrealistic in any of a variety of selective, liberal-arts colleges. But to understand his aspirations and expectations in music, a little more should be told about Anthony's background and training.

Early in his preschool years, Anthony's mother had recognized his talent and his unusual facility for learning fundamental musical concepts. After he had picked out his first melodies on the keyboard, she began to encourage and nurture his interest. By age seven, he was composing his own little pieces, and when he was ten he performed for a half hour in a solo recital. While he was in the eighth grade in private school, he started fooling around on several other musical instruments. His classmates were amazed to find that he very quickly could play a clarinet and saxophone almost as well as students who had been studying them for several years. During the latter part of this same year, his music instructor introduced him to the French horn. Anthony soon decided that this was the instrument on which he would like to concentrate in high school.

The French horn—and, to a much less extent, the piano—became one of the chief means of expression and involvement for Anthony during the next four years. He started taking private lessons in the fall of his freshman year, but discontinued this instruction the following summer when his proficiency and understanding exceeded the teacher's. As a sophomore he received some help from his mother, who accompanied him on the piano in all the compositions they could find for the two instruments. He also participated in both the high school orchestra and band as the first-chair man on his instrument. During his last two years in high school, he again obtained private lessons by commuting to a nearby metropolitan center.

Near the end of his junior year, Anthony was one of the two young artists invited to perform as soloists with the local metropolitan symphony. This invitation was initiated by his instructor, who was convinced that his youthful virtuosity merited such an opportunity. His two performances resulted in considerable local recognition. With a musical career at this advanced level already under way, his desire to go to a liberal-arts college might have been readily challenged. A much more likely choice might have been an outstanding conservatory.

Nevertheless, Anthony's choice of college, based on his mathematical interests, had a certain logic. His mathematical score on the Scholastic Aptitude Test was above the ninety-ninth percentile, which was very much in line with the school's excellent mathematics department and the numerous bright males who came to major in this field. However, the ease with which he had succeeded in this field earlier had not served to prepare him for the calibre of the competition. Although he managed little more than a *C* average for his freshman year, Anthony was not fully aware of most of his peers' intense commitment to mathematics and science. During his second year, he began to realize that he could not pursue all of his diverse interests—practice on the French horn, play in the campus orchestra and in a small faculty-student ensemble, play the piano in a jazz group, attend symphony concerts, take time to write music, keep up with his other course work, and occasionally date his girl friend. Even then, it took time for him to see that this varied richness of activities—all of which he either wanted to continue or felt he had to—interfered with his accomplishments in mathematics and with the development of skill on his horn. By the end of his sophomore year, Anthony tried to solve his problems by giving up all his musical activities but the small ensemble, but his decision was too late to avoid failing grades in two courses and less than a *C* average for the year.

Anthony left the campus that June with a feeling of failure. He had been placed on probation but with the right to return the following semester, but he had no intention of coming back. His feelings of guilt were complicated by dissatisfaction and bitterness toward the institution, since he had failed both in achieving his academic goals and in gaining in musical stature. His thoughts were mixed and confused in his attempt to divide the blame between himself and the college.

In this depressed state, he decided not to go home and caught a ride to Chicago instead, with the idea of finding a position with a radio-station band or hotel orchestra. His search for a week led to no results, and he finally accepted a job as a bellhop in a lake-resort hotel. When his folks visited him early in July, he and a friend had decided to enlist in the United States Army, hopefully to put in their service time as band musicians. The following October, Anthony was off to take another try at his future by playing second-chair horn in an Army-band school.

CONCLUSION

The reasons why exceptional and creative college youth very frequently have difficulty finding or realizing themselves in college are examined fairly thoroughly, and from different perspectives, in most of the later chapters. However, a brief review of certain aspects of the problem, especially as they relate to the four individuals I have just described, may lay the groundwork for the research findings to follow. Since the college men and women in my sketches were all enrolled in excellent institutions that were ranked among the best in the country, most observers would probably hesitate to take a critical look at these colleges or their curricula to discover the reasons for the four students' difficulties or dissatisfactions. However, three of them did have reactions that definitely reflected on their respective schools, at least in regard to their own learning and attainments. Only Anthony, who left college after a challenging and hectic second year, placed the blame mostly on himself, however, and departed feeling quite confused. The other three were very critical of the inadequacies they saw in the existing programs and, to a lesser degree, in the instruction.

The real "stories" of these creatives are probably quite varied and also complicated by the fact that they all attended four quite different institutions. Since the problems of educating those with high creative potential are considered in later chapters, I will limit my conclusions here to a few comments and reflections pertinent to the disclosures in the four vignettes.

Lisa, Karen, and Anthony may be seen or explained as misplaced persons. When the optimal realization of individuals with exceptional ability, giftedness, or creativity is a major concern, the choice of a specific college becomes much more important than it is for average students. Although all four of these individuals appeared to use a fair amount of logic in their choice of colleges —considering what they knew of these particular institutions at entrance—at least the three labelled as "misplaced" could, with guidance, have selected a number of more appropriate and presumably more satisfactory campuses for their needs than they did. As for Peter, he speculated on one occasion that he might have fared better if he had pursued his science interests in a liberal-arts setting. The chief advantage from such a move would have been an earlier transfer to a nonscience major. As it was, he succeeded the best of the four in obtaining a fair, if not good, education during his undergraduate years. As I have mentioned, his creativity never became dormant, not throughout his undergraduate years, in spite of the institution and its nonchallenging experiences.

The other three—only one of whom came close to finishing her degree—may, as misplaced persons, be viewed as needing special settings or considerations. Only a brief analytical commentary regarding each may be permitted here.

Lisa, who later followed an early career in painting, chose a college of great intellectual and academic challenge. However, partly because of her high ability and exceptional talent and partly, perhaps, because of mediocre instruction, she appeared to remain unchallenged. The fact that this college offered a very limited fine-arts curriculum served as another contributing factor. Thus, the varied artistic experiences that Lisa required because of her strong motivation for personal expression and involvement with color and graphic media were almost completely absent on campus. Her needs for such involvement were much stronger than any satisfactions she seemed to gain in the verbal or literary sphere. She also had strong needs for diversified cultural experiences and more varied emotional and sensuous stimulation than most students. Consequently, no matter how excellent, any small college that was hidden away in bucolic and nonmetropolitan settings could never have provided a viable and sufficiently colorful program for this young woman.

Though Karen was much closer to the average in academic aptitude, her story, basically, is not too dissimilar from Lisa's. However, her college was a place of much less academic pressure and enrolled relatively few students who could have matched Lisa and her peers in ability and motivation; but the curriculum included a greater range in the graphic arts and music. Nevertheless, Karen was seldom satisfied and, like Lisa, also sought more variety in the media in which she wished to express herself. More than that, as the four years unfolded, she felt increasingly restricted and hemmed in. She once explained that her years of upbringing within a strongly religious family were probably the source of a self-containment and fortitude that permitted her to remain on this one campus for four years. Like Lisa, she also needed more and richer opportunities for expression, emotionally and creatively. In her case, a transfer after the second year to one of a number of other colleges would probably have been a sound and profitable move, since what she wanted in music and dance had to be found elsewhere than on her campus.

Anthony probably would have encountered "his problem," or brought it with him, on all campuses, large or small. But the difficulties he might have experienced would have been less traumatic in a college or university where excellence—especially in mathematics—was not determined by only extremely capable fellow students who gave most of their time to their studies. His intense need to be involved in music, his interest in different musical instruments and varied forms of musical expression (classical, modern, and jazz), and his desire to engage in music at advancing levels of artistry would have jeopardized even a keen interest in mathematics. To have succeeded and remained in the college at which he had enrolled, Anthony would have needed to realize earlier that he must sacrifice some of his musical expression, along with a number of other interests, to academic activity.

Anthony's particular college experiences, strangely enough, occurred in an institution where the music program *per se* was neither extensive nor close to the level of quality or status of the mathematics curriculum. This average musical curriculum was probably a saving grace for him. However, informal music groups composed of other excellent musicians among students and faculty drew him away from the study necessary for keeping up with his math classes. His commitment to and involvement in music make it apparent that a number of other schools might have been more appropriate for him. If his mathematics interest was genuine, in line with his high numerical ability, then a college with fewer academic demands in this field would have been suitable for him. And if music was to remain his predominant form of expression and involvement, the choice of another college would have had even stronger points in its favor.

These concluding remarks serve to highlight the complexities of college choice for mentally capable and potentially creative people. Realizing these complexities, we may well wonder how often the most appropriate choices are made by talented and creative youth, many of whom have considerably more knowledge about colleges than the mass of first-year entrants.

II

*The Creative Student
in Liberal Arts and Sciences*

3

CREATIVE STUDENTS:
COLLEGE TRANSIENTS

Paul Heist

The research projects at the Center for Research and Development in Higher Education resulted in a wealth of information about the diversity of students attending American colleges and universities. This information permitted students to be assigned to a number of categories or type-classifications, which varied according to the personality characteristics or particular criteria under consideration. For example, for some purposes students were typed by their socioeconomic background, and for another study objective they were categorized according to their degree of intellectual disposition or orientation. In a couple of extensive projects, students were classified according to their emotional stability and levels of anxiety.

Through a number of the Center studies, information was

35

also made available on many highly exceptional college students. These individuals were initially among the entrants to a small number of colleges cooperating in a special study of a single generation of students. The findings at an early stage of the Center's investigation revealed the dropouts and transfers of many capable students. This problem stimulated an interest in the fate of students with seemingly great potential—that is, students who were talented, creative, and often very bright. The staff interest in certain types of students, especially those in samples being interviewed on several campuses, was intensified by becoming acquainted with their backgrounds, thoughts, attitudes, and accomplishments; it was especially increased, however, by many of the students' atypicality and their deviant or troubled college careers.

One of the special types—if the students can be categorized as such—was the creative individual we encountered either through the interviews or other circumstances or later identified by use of criterion data. The fact that these creative students tended to disappear, along with other exceptional types, from the campuses where we first met them led to a greater concern about them and their academic activity and records. As this interest developed, specific attention was directed to the academic records and the lives of the creatives in the context of several other investigations.

During a several-year survey of the first group of National Merit Scholarship winners, our staff at the Center developed an early interest in the loss or mobility of college students of exceptional ability and talent. We (Heist *et al.*, 1961) discovered that when these 1956 winners made their initial choice of institutions, they tended to distribute themselves nonrandomly, with very large proportions of them attending selective colleges and universities with the best academic reputations. When compared with matched samples of scholarship winners in institutions ranking significantly lower in quality, those students in the selective institutions were found to be a rather special breed—more intellectually and esthetically oriented and more interested in dealing with theoretical and abstract problems and materials. In general, many of these students of both sexes exhibited characteristics associated with creative behavior.

During our followup surveys that took place in the scholarship winners' second and third years of college, a special withdrawal trend was noted. From this group of students, who seemed to be well matched with their particular schools, some outstanding men and women transferred to other institutions, while others dropped out entirely—at least for a while. A study of this early trend was not pursued as part of the continuing National Merit Scholarship project, but the finding was predictive of research results to come.

A year or two after this loss of National Merit Scholars from certain excellent colleges was observed, early findings in two other studies at the Center began to substantiate this withdrawal phenomenon. The findings in both studies, which included reputable, strong academic institutions, dramatically illustrated the concentration of exceptional students in excellent schools *and* the high incidence of withdrawal among achieving students, including a surprising number who could be categorized as individuals of high creative potential. These observations were first given supporting evidence in the results obtained in a collaborative project between the Berkeley Center and a selective school of science.

LOSS OF CREATIVES FROM A SCHOOL OF SCIENCE

In this four-year study of men in science, a surprisingly large number of persons in one class were identified as having some definitive characteristics of creative people, and many of them were among those transferring in the first two years. This unexpected finding grew out of a special followup study of early dropouts from this particular institution.

Early in this study, the AVL *Study of Values* (Allport, Vernon, and Lindzey, 1951) was administered to entering freshmen. Results obtained from this test revealed a significant difference in the *pattern* of scores on four scales between two "types" of later dropouts—those who had attained high grades and those of near-average or low achievement. Most high-achieving students were significantly above the normative mean on the Theoretical and Aesthetic value scales, especially when these two scales were viewed as a pair, and considerably below the mean on the Economic and Religious scales. More significantly, this *pattern* or combination of mean scores for this particular group of men (see Figure 1) was as extreme or deviant from the norm as any scores we had seen for any selected or unselected group of male or female college students. The mean scores for the lower-achieving dropouts were considerably closer to the normative mean, with the exception of the Theoretical value scores.

	Theo.	*Econ.*	*Aes.*	*Rel.*	
Mean Scores (Standard Deviations)	53.3	33.7	46.5	31.4	High
	(6.7)	(7.4)	(6.9)	(9.0)	
	50.9	39.9	35.5	37.3	Low
	(5.6)	(7.9)	(6.6)	(9.6)	

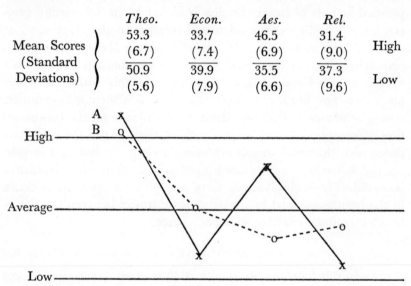

FIGURE 1. Score patterns on AVL *Study of Values* for high-achieving (A) and low-achieving (B) dropouts at a school of science.

The particular method of identifying these high-achieving dropouts as the more creative students in this one institution provides no assurance of their actual creative production, if and when the opportunity arises for them to perform as the criterion scores would indicate. However, this pattern of four scores on the AVL *Study of Values* (see Appendix) for these capable dropouts is almost identical to the one reported by MacKinnon (1960) as typifying the values of recognized creative adults in several different fields. Consequently, this school of science and the scientific field in general were justifiably concerned at losing a large proportion of capable and innovative persons.

A review at the Center of the AVL scores and the profiles of the individual science students disclosed that 73 per cent of the high-achieving dropouts matched or exceeded the creative pattern (scores on four scales) noted by MacKinnon as compared with only 20 per cent of the lower-achieving group. This finding led to an obvious question: Why was such a large proportion of bright, achieving students with presumably high creative potential leaving this impressive institution of science education, along with other students of less creative potential? To conclude that they were leaving for the same reasons would be open to serious question.

A still later review of the AVL profiles of all students in the particular class indicated that a majority of very bright, potentially creative students had withdrawn by the end of two years. Those who remained into the third year—some seventeen students with comparable profiles, but with lower verbal and numerical-aptitude scores than the creatives who withdrew—tended to complete all four years. At the end of the senior year, all but two of these remaining students were still there to graduate. These fifteen students represented 13 per cent of the graduating class.

Among the total number of dropouts at the end of four years, more than one third (38 per cent) could be typified by the creative profile (A) graphed in Figure 1. Of the total of thirty-nine entering students identified as creatives, 61 per cent withdrew or, at least, did not finish in four years. Of the 131 students not so identified by the AVL patterns, only 30 per cent withdrew or did not complete their work in four years. These results are shown in Table 1.

Table 1. Creative and Noncreative Students Who Graduated or Dropped Out of a School of Science

| | *Identified Student Types (AVL Patterns)* | | | | | |
| | Creatives | | Noncreatives | | Total | Class |
	No.	(%)	No.	(%)	No.	(%)
Graduates (4 years)	15	(39%)	92	(70%)	107	(63%)
Dropouts	24	(61%)	39	(30%)	63	(37%)
Totals	39	(100%)	131	(100%)	170	(100%)

LOSS OF CREATIVES FROM LIBERAL-ARTS COLLEGES

The loss of exceptional students, as observed in the two different samples described above, resulted in questions and tentative hypotheses about the records of such students in various educational settings. For example, the very characteristics of bright young people who have a strong liberal orientation or of highly motivated creatives who need to seek new experiences and to express themselves might be closely related to dissatisfaction with particular institutions or to faulty relationships with faculty and administrators. A free-swinging, innovative creative in most small, four-year colleges would undoubtedly engender apprehension, frequently encounter strong reactions from teachers and peers, and would often be viewed as too different. The high-ability student with these same traits, when caught up in the demanding regimen of a strong science program, might be viewed as troublesome and misplaced. For the creative student the curricula at certain institutions might also create problems. A small college offering a limited sampling of courses and restricted by inflexible policies or a science institute requiring much drill and learning of fundamentals probably would operate at cross purposes with his needs and mode of learning.

These speculations were soon amplified in the Center's study of students in a varied sampling of eight institutions. This study was initiated shortly after the loss of the creative-type person was noted in the study of male science students. Within the context of this second, larger project, a special study of creatives and their records was conducted in half of the institutional sample, or four selective liberal-arts colleges.

During the project, all these colleges lost a variety of excellent students (classified as such on the basis of their precollege records *and* the results of first-year interviews). This loss first became apparent when students in the interview sample were not available for the second-year interviews. Additional losses occurred during the third and fourth years of this long-range study. Among those withdrawing were numerous individuals with the highest ability scores, many of whom had serious intellectual interests and a high potential, quite often, for creative expression.

This finding—in line with some results from earlier studies —led to a more extensive examination of the loss of creatives. In three of the four selective liberal-arts colleges, a lengthy procedure was used to identify the most creative students by peer and faculty nominations. This identification process resulted in two levels or categories of creatives: those with highest potential and those with high potential. For the most part, persons were nominated whose creativity had been made evident, for example, in the form of short stories, poetry, paintings, and papers presented in seminars or through their thinking and styles of living. On each campus at least twenty peers (persons in the same class) were interviewed and given a definition of creativity by which to assess their classmates. Whenever a fellow student was nominated six times out of ten (listed twelve or more times by the 20 peers interviewed), he or she was placed in the highest classification. Others nominated between three and five times were placed in the high category. The faculty nominations were used largely to check teacher agreement or disagreement with the student nominations.

This procedure of identifying the creatives resulted in a total placement of only twenty-one women and twenty-five men in the top (highest) category on these three campuses, all of which enrolled many exceptional young persons. These students rated as highest on creativity also had strong intellectual orientations and very high aptitude scores. As a group, their average score on the Scholastic Aptitude Test's *total* score (verbal and mathematical scores combined and divided by two) was above the ninety-fifth percentile. But, astonishingly enough, at the end of the fourth year, only a minority of these capable persons remained to graduate from the college they had entered four years earlier.

Among the women creatives in the highest category, only two were present at their class graduation (two campuses). For those women in the high category, the loss was also very severe; only six of them graduated, although all these women (N = 23) also ranked high on a measure of intellectual orientation. The loss of creative men, categorized as both highest and high and also ranking high on intellectual orientation, was not nearly so great as it was for the women. However, in two of the institutions, the dropouts among these young, innovative males totaled more than 50 per cent.

These losses of exceptional students in institutions noted for their academic quality generated more specific questions about the types of students who tended to leave college and about the programs and the instruction offered to them. We also wondered whether these three schools actually recruited and enrolled an unusually large number of students with high creative potential—that is, in addition to those persons identified as creative by their peers in our study. We became curious about the general withdrawal rates on these campuses but, more specifically, about the loss of all other persons who might be categorized as potentially creative.

The identification of the potentially creative students among all the entering students in these colleges was accomplished by "reading" the students' pattern of scores on eight scales in the Omnibus Personality Inventory. This inventory was constructed chiefly to assess some personality characteristics or patterns of attitudes assumed to be meaningful and important in the lives of students in an academic environment (Center for the Study of Higher Education, 1962).

The specific scales on which mean scores differentiated between creative students (those nominated by peers and faculty) and samples of students in the same institutions not so identified were Thinking Introversion, Theoretical Orientation, Estheticism, Complexity, Autonomy, Religious Liberalism, Impulse Expression, and Schizoid Functioning. These scales had been included in the OPI initially to assess the following: the quality and degree of academic interest (measured by several scales), flexibility of perception, authoritarian thinking, and the degree of impulsiveness, alienation, and emotional disturbance. The scores on all scales for the nominated creatives ranged between the seventieth and ninetieth percentiles.

A combination or pattern of high scores on the first four scales (falling near the ninetieth percentile on three of them) denotes strong intellectual interests and concerns. The intellectuality of creative persons is, however, somewhat different from that of students identified as scholars. For example, the scholarly students had higher scores than the identified creatives on both Thinking Introversion and Theoretical Orientation. Although a theoretical, analytical orientation is not absent among creatives, these individuals give priority to their esthetic sensitivities and present a tolerance for the ambiguous and unstructured (the latter measured by the Complexity scale), while also exhibiting interest in dealing with ideas and reflective thought.

The combination of the Autonomy and Religious Liberalism scales serves as a dual measure of nonauthoritarian thinking. Persons scoring high on both are cognitively, if not emotionally, released from their own subcultural pasts; they are much less judgmental and exhibit greater independence in their thinking than those scoring below the normative mean. They also are freer to examine new ideas and attempt new and different experiences. Persons typified by the level of the mean scores (seventieth to ninetieth percentile) obtained by creatives on these two scales generally profess definite values and have strong feelings about certain ethical considerations, but they seldom subscribe to the beliefs and practices of the orthodox Christian denominations.

The mean score obtained by creatives on the Impulse-Expression scale represents a wholesome level of impulsiveness and an above-average need for self-expression and self-gratification. This impulsiveness was complemented by the relatively high mean score of the creatives on the Schizoid-Functioning scale, which, together with the impulsiveness score, denotes an above-average amount of psychic energy, tension, and anxiety. The score on Schizoid Functioning also implies some feelings of alienation and/or a willingness to disaffiliate from others. However, the two scores at the indicated levels do not imply emotional disturbance or neurotic tendencies.

At this point, we can return to the general identification of creative or potentially creative students among the total student sample within the three select colleges. The process of selection was based on criterion patterns for assigning students to two levels or categories of potential creativity. The criterion pattern consisted of the OPI mean scores and profiles of those students (described earlier) who were nominated or rated highest for recognized creativity in their accomplishments or behavior. The mean-score profile (A) for the males who were nominated as being the most creative (highest) is graphed in Figure 2 (the profile for the women is nearly

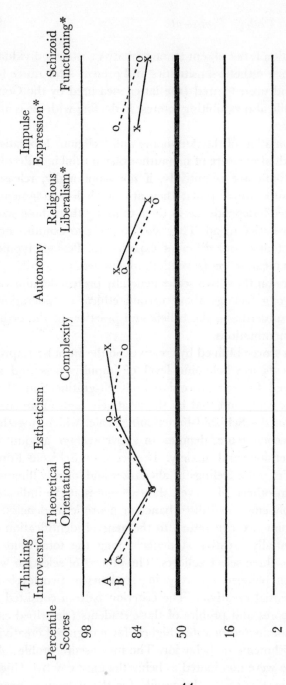

FIGURE 2. OPI (Forms C and D) scores and profiles for (A) 20 males ranked as highest on creative potential in three selective colleges and (B) 25 male and female arts majors rated as highest in creative expression by faculty members in three other colleges. On the scales indicated by an asterisk, the mean scores represent only 15 persons in two (B) colleges.

identical to the one for the males, so that these data add nothing to the story). The second profile (B) in Figure 2 represents men and women students (not previously described) who were majoring in music and the graphic arts in several other schools not included in any Center study. They were rated as high on a creativity dimension by faculty members in the departments in which they majored. The duplication in approximate scores and patterns in the two profiles substantiates the validity of the identifications, as well as the similarity of the needs, attitudes, and interests of the highly creative.

In the identification of creatives from the total student sample, those identified as having the *highest* creative potential were students who had a set of scores on the composite scales that matched or superseded the criterion profile pattern. The students categorized as *high* were those who did not completely meet all the criteria of the pattern of scores. Certain qualifications or adjustments on several scales within the criterion pattern were basic to this secondary classification. These qualifications were related to the academic major or religious belief. For example, rigid adherence to the established criteria—shown by the scores on certain scales (Estheticism, Complexity, and Religious Orientation scales) and determined by those nominated as the highest creatives—precluded the identification of some potential creatives with strong science interests or firm religious commitments. But, in summary, the use of criterion measures readily permitted the selection of *highest* and *high* creatives.

Our underlying concern about the loss of creative students prompts us to ask whether the majority of potential creatives, or students with the *measured correlates* of creativity, tend to leave college or to transfer, as did those ranked as creatives by peers and faculty? The data to be reviewed and presented in Table 2 indicate the answer to be mostly affirmative.

First of all, the comparative percentages for Colleges A, B, C, and D suggest an inferential, although tangential, question about the differences in the entering proportions of creatives among the four schools. One might inquire whether the total percentage of potential creatives in a college is related to its public image—an image which often derives from the general characteristics of an institution, its program emphases, and the characteristics of its stu-

Table 2. Percentages of Potentially Creative Students in Four Selective Colleges and the Percentages of Students Who Withdrew from Their Class before Their Senior Year

Student Categories	College A (197)		College B (390)		College C (242)		College D (587)	
	M	F	M	F	M	F	M	F
Entering students with a high potential for creativity	37	37	20	40	17	30	8	7
Creatives withdrawing	62	81	59	74	56	49	48	54
Noncreatives withdrawing	43	58	49	67	33	22	44	51
Levels of significance (Chi-square analysis)	.02		Not significant		.05	.02	Not significant	

dents. In unique and distinctive institutions, the students often have become a very important aspect of the total image, positive or negative. The syndrome of personality characteristics found in identified creatives may well be, then, a strong factor in the public image of some institutions. For example, a college regarded as liberal and intellectual and as having a large percentage of creative students may consistently attract liberal, intellectually oriented students—and a large percentage of creatives.

Differences in proportions of creative students among colleges also lead to questions about the possible influence of creative types on their peers and the psychological climate of a campus. Colleges A, B, and C could be described as having more than their share of creative youth as compared with College D. The college D figures, in which 8 and 7 per cent of the entrants are categorized as creative men and women, probably are more typical of the proportions to be found in most colleges and universities. One might even speculate that since the range of personal acquaintanceships tends to be wider on smaller campuses and since the college D enrollment is more than twice as large as those at A and C, the possibilities for stimulating interaction among creative personalities are much greater at both of the latter two schools than they are at D. However, as the data show, having more of their kind present on a campus does not lead to a lower withdrawal rate for the creatives (colleges A and C).

Judging by the total number of withdrawals from these particular classes under consideration in each school, we can see that being among the small number of potential creatives in college D does not seem to weaken the chances of graduating. The loss of creatives in college D and also B is not significantly greater than the percentage of withdrawals for all other students (noncreatives) in these schools. At the other two colleges (A and C), which enroll students of somewhat higher ability than B and D, the data indicate that *noncreatives* tend to fare better and to drop out of school in somewhat smaller numbers than the creatives. One general conclusion to be drawn from the data on these students in four colleges is that their creative potential and the opportunity for associating with other creatives do not improve the chances of completing an education—at least not on the campuses in which the students initially enroll. In other words, in somewhat different situations, whether involving a few or many creatives, they drop out at least as frequently as other students.

When the students classified as *highest* creatives are considered apart from the total of both levels of highest and high, the percentage of those who withdraw is increased in most cases (data not shown in the table). For example, the number of creative males dropping out of colleges A and C increases from 65 to 75 per cent. The number of women withdrawing from colleges C and D increases from 50 per cent to 65 and 75 per cent respectively, approximating the figures for colleges A and B for all women creatives.

One additional observation relates to the difference in withdrawal rates between the sexes. A limited range in the percentages (48 per cent to 62 per cent) exists among creative men in the four colleges. The differences, however, among the women are large enough (49 per cent to 81 per cent) to suggest the need to consider the impact of dissimilar campus environments and the varying sources and means of satisfaction to be found in these institutions. Answers to such speculations might be approached through other data and information available on the students and the colleges. For example, the results of interviewing students on these campuses indicated that women found the general social environment and academic climate more inhospitable and threatening at colleges A and B than they did at C and D, although somewhat paradoxically, colleges C and D impose more sociopsychological structure and more regulations and restrictions on student life and activities. But such "findings" will have to remain at the conjectural level, pending similar analyses in other schools.

CREATIVITY ON OTHER CAMPUSES

The data shown in Table 3 represent a first attempt at further analyses of the problem of creative dropouts, in which the same assessments of college entrants in three quite different private institutions permitted duplication of the findings for the students in the first four schools (Table 2). College N is a selective women's

Table 3. Percentages of Potentially Creative Students in Entering Classes in Dissimilar Institutions and the Percentages of Students Withdrawing before the Fourth Year
(Significant at .01 level)

Student Categories		College N (Women—122)	College R (Coed—321)	College Z (Men—178*)
Entering students with high potential for creativity	Highest	11.5	2	4
	High	51.5	7	11
Creatives withdrawing		53	73	64
Noncreatives withdrawing		28	47	36
Total proportion withdrawing from the specific classes		44	54	41

* Number represents two classes in college Z on which the essential information was available.

school with a strong emphasis on both the liberal and creative arts. College R, a coeducational liberal-arts institution, is still quite strongly affiliated with a Protestant denomination, and college Z is a selective school of science education.

The students in the three colleges varied significantly in aptitude, with average scores ranging from the sixty-fifth to the ninety-seventh percentile; the men in college Z scored considerably above the women in college N, and the latter significantly above R. The differences in ability were not in line with the differences in the proportions of students with potential for creative expression as identified by their scores on eight criterion scales of the OPI. That is, college Z, with the students of very high ability, does not have many more creatives than college R. A very high proportion (63 per cent) of students categorized as creatives entered the women's college (N). This may reflect either an extraordinary process of selection of institution by the applicants or a special recruitment and admissions policy by the school. As one might surmise, N is one of a small number of women's colleges with a rather distinctive image. If this percentage of creative girls is typical of the usual first-year classes, the special image of the college and its students should be maintained in the future, since students serve as a chief agent in propagating institutional images.

In contrast, the much smaller proportion of creatives in the coeducational institution (R) is probably close to being typical of most good denominational colleges. This college is much like college D in Table 2, not only in the proportion of creatives but in size, academic caliber of students, and type of program offered.

The data for the school of science (Z), based on the records of two classes over four years' time, indicate that a relatively small proportion (15 per cent) of persons could be labeled creative among these very bright males, all of whom entered with excellent high school academic records. But, as in college R, a majority (64 per cent) of the men identified as creatives withdrew, mostly in the first or second year. Again, the percentage of creatives leaving is much larger than the 36 per cent of noncreatives who withdrew. If we recall the breadth of cognitive-intellectual experiences supposedly sought by high-ability creatives, it is probably not too surprising that men of this orientation left a school in which the curriculum is comprised of only four science majors. In line with their broader perspectives and interest in the theoretical and abstract, the eleven out of twenty-seven creative men still present in the fourth year were concentrated in the more theoretical fields (five in physics, four in mathematics, two in chemistry, and none in engineering).

The large concentration of potentially creative women in college N provides a more advantageous sample for examining several questions. Does the apparent harmony between the creative students and the program in the liberal and creative arts relate to persistence in the college? Are the learning experiences sufficiently rewarding to hold the type of student who tends to leave a variety of other colleges? Do the *most* creative young women (highest versus high) tend to leave this school as readily as the exceptional women in selective liberal-arts colleges (Table 2)?

The data on withdrawals at college N (Table 3) reveal that little more than a half of the potentially creative women left, as compared with 44 per cent of the total class and 28 per cent of those not identified as creative. The 53 per cent of the creatives withdrawing represent 76 per cent of the total withdrawal sample. Thus, a large majority of those who left this particular selective college also might be described as the very ones who presumably would profit the most from continuing their education in this program.

The record for only the highest creatives shows that they were entirely lost from college R, as the six persons in this category all left. But in both colleges N and Z, half of the highest group withdrew and half were still enrolled during the fourth year.

Interpretations of the results of these exploratory analyses might well vary among investigators. However, the high dropout rate for creative students who were either ranked or identified by objective test scores—averaging about two out of three for all the creatives in the seven institutions compared—strongly suggests that the number of intelligent, creative youth who finish at the college of their original choice is not equivalent to the number of noncreative men and women who do.

HOW CREATIVE STUDENTS SEE THEIR EDUCATION

Since many of the students identified as creative or potentially creative *did* graduate from their respective colleges, the Center found it particularly interesting to discover how 15 recognized creatives, graduates from five colleges, reacted to their education and the schools from which they received their degrees. These students were interviewed several times over four years, and the summarized comments that follow were in response to several questions about their education and academic experiences. For the most part, this summary represents a direct use or paraphrasing of the students' statements.

It would seem safe to assume that analyses of and reflections upon educational experiences by those who completed their education would tend to be less critical than the reports from creative students who withdrew from the same institutions. Those who finished have had a broader sampling of experiences upon which to base their evaluations and criticisms. This "borrowed" perspective on the creatives' education has been limited to observations and points frequently repeated by the interviewees.

The most frequent reactions—reactions from twelve students in at least four of the five schools—dealt with a described rigidity or inflexibility of the "system." In this respect, they spoke critically of colleges as organizations and referred to the persistent webs of trivial regulations and established, traditional curricula that seemed to change very little. A majority of men and women spoke of the pressures and constraints on their time and lives. This complaint—again discussed by those from all but one campus—was chiefly the result of increasing academic demands and a vague pressure experienced and transmitted by instructors and students. This pressure was related not only to the reported amount of work assigned and the expanding reading lists but also to the rising irritation with the increasingly superficial treatment accorded subject matter in many classrooms.

These graduates also frequently discussed at some length the quality of teachers, instructional methods, and student-teacher relations. A near consensus seemed to be that they felt lucky to have one really good teacher per term. The general quality of instruction they described as mediocre and uninspired. Few teachers were "alive, hep to the real world, and understanding of students" or "thoroughly involved in the process of teaching." One talented young man who had majored in physics said, "What a profession! It's composed of squares and dullards!"

On two campuses, several exceptional students felt natural opportunities existed for student research in the undergraduate years but that teachers didn't do much to encourage an interest, nor did teachers include the students in their research.

Almost all of the fifteen students were dissatisfied that their college education and experiences did not approach their expectations. They felt they had been forced to abandon their pursuit of self-knowledge, hobbies, individual interests, and outside reading for lack of time. They frequently complained about meeting deadlines and following a schedule determined by teachers, week after week.

Most of these students found their on-campus experiences, especially in their last two years, to be "a pretty confining grind." One person referred to a "deadly routine," in which the upperclassmen traveled in narrower and narrower channels. None of the interviewees spoke of any novelty, challenge, or esthetic stimulation in their last year's programs. Some students seemed to beat the mundane routine by noncurricular involvements, but generally at a cost to their course work and grade records.

Several students indicated that what seemed to be lacking were opportunities to be involved in the wealth of living and the excitement of learning things of personal interest. To them, college education seemed an enforced detour which kept them from essential perceptual and emotional satisfactions. These feelings and frustrations perhaps were related to their attempts to bring more of "life" to themselves in the form of controversial or risk-taking experiences. With their need for expression and experimentation blocked in the academic area, they felt they had to seek other means to utilize or test their intellect, commitments, and emotions. These activities—not always appreciated by peers and superiors—included a variety of work in the arts and the leadership in protest activities against campus administrative policies. A few of these students wrote letters and columns of criticism and prepared clever, colorful posters urging campus involvement in discussion and action on issues of civil rights and national foreign policy. These activities preceded by several years the crescendo of student civil-rights activity in the South and the general protest activities on many American campuses in the early sixties.

SUMMARY

Students who drop out or transfer from the college of their original choice—the latter seemingly a growing phenomenon—have been studied in a variety of educational settings. Academic difficulty, which is an inevitable concomitant of traditional grading practices, continues to be the chief reason for much student transiency. However, many students, at all levels of ability and frequently at good levels of achievement, tend to transfer or leave college.

Several research projects at the Center for Research and Development of Higher Education have provided information about the surprising number of exceptionally able and talented young people who become dissatisfied with their first-choice college and leave. In two long-range studies, large percentages of these students who left were identified as having high potential for creative involvement and expression. This loss of creative persons from a small number of selective liberal-arts colleges led to further investigation of the situation in these institutions and others.

Observations in seven quite dissimilar schools indicated that the proportions of identified creatives withdrawing ranged from approximately 50 per cent to 80 per cent. In five out of seven of the particular institutions included in these analyses, a significantly higher proportion of the creative students on each campus left than did dropout students not identified as creative. The major conclusion to be drawn from the data is that the students who are ranked as creative or identified by measured characteristics of creativity either leave some colleges more frequently than or as frequently as all other students not so identified.

REFERENCES

Allport, G. W., Vernon, P. E., & Lindzey, G. *Study of Values—A scale for measuring the dominant interests in personality.* Boston: Houghton Mifflin, 1951.

Center for the Study of Higher Education. *Omnibus Personality Inventory research manual.* Berkeley, Calif.: The Center, 1962.

Clark, B., & Trow, M. Determinants of college student subcultures. In T. M. Newcomb & E. K. Wilson (Eds.), *College peer groups, problems and prospects for research.* Chicago: Aldine, 1966.

Heist, P., McConnell, T. R., *et al.* Personality and scholarship. *Science,* 1961, *133,* No. 3450, 362–367.

Heist, P., & Webster, H. A research orientation to selection, admission and differential education. In H. T. Sprague (Ed.), *Research on college students.* Boulder, Colo.: Western Interstate Commission of Higher Education, 1960.

MacKinnon, D. W. Identifying and developing creativity. In *Selection and educational differentiation.* Berkeley: Field Service Center, 1960.

4

THE EDUCATION OF
CREATIVE SCIENCE STUDENTS

Benson R. Snyder

What happens to "creative" students at an institution which focuses
on engineering and science? What is the effect of a demanding science curriculum on those students most capable of original and creative contributions? When we ask these questions, are the contin-
gencies for students who major in the applied sciences different from
those of students who major in physics and mathematics?*

The need for closure—that is, for making a commitment to
one of several possible solutions—may be a more crucial experience
in the undergraduate education of engineers than that of scientists.

* A version of this chapter appears in *Report on Massachusetts Institute of Technology Student Adaptation Study,* edited by me in 1967 for
the M.I.T. Education Research Center.

The student scientist may have and need greater sanction and freedom for intellectual risk taking than his counterpart in engineering. This at least raises the interesting possibility that creative solutions or formulations by engineers may involve "intolerance" rather than "tolerance" for ambiguity. Creative activity for student engineers may involve a cognitive and emotional style that differs significantly from that of developing scientists. One style is presumably not better than the other, however. Stated simply, creative activity for the engineer and for the scientist may be qualitatively quite different undertakings.

In the realm of formal education another distinction needs to be made. It is very plausible that an antagonism may exist between professionalism—the achieving of professional status in the arts, science, and engineering—and the development of creative competence in these fields. Higher education today may be focused more on the former than the latter.

A series of subsidiary questions should be kept in mind as this presentation unfolds. (1) What bearing does the institutional setting—and, in fact, the larger social system—have on the functioning of individuals with creative talent? The varied academic communities may, in all probability, provide significantly different environments for the creative artist and the creative scientist. In a university emphasizing the sciences, group approval is especially high for the innovator, the man who questions basic formulations and comes up with a new synthesis of theory. This is particularly evident when a new theory leads, in turn, to an engineering invention. On the other hand, in liberal-arts colleges there are examples of creative artists who have met with a crushing ostracism in their immediate environment precisely because of their creative efforts. (2) How does the creative individual interact with those persons who form a meaningful part of his environment? (3) Is the creative individual psychologically free to leave the group of which he is a member? Does his creative activity provoke their disapproval or praise? In other words, does the creative individual derive his major source of self-esteem from the group of which he is a member or from the sense of accomplishment that may be associated with creativity itself? (4) What inherent supports and stresses in a social system influence the development of creative talent? To what extent do certain social structures, certain value systems, certain educational encounters foster or impede creative thought?

IDENTIFICATION OF CREATIVE STUDENTS

For the purpose of this investigation, the dilemma of a definition was arbitrarily met by using an operational statement of creativity derived from three scales in the *Omnibus Personality Inventory* (OPI). The three scales of this inventory, Thinking Introversion, Complexity, and Impulse Expression, were selected as having a probable relationship to creativity and originality.*

Thinking Introversion refers to the individual's emphasis on ideas and philosophies, on thinking as opposed to action. The items on this scale refer to several major themes, the most prominent (twelve items or 20 per cent of the total) being the derivation of pleasure from actively engaging in analytic, deductive, and synthesizing thinking. A subsidiary theme is excitement or satisfaction in intellectual activity generally. The commitment to ideas is not, however, at the expense of interpersonal relationships. Though interested in ideas and thinking, high scorers are also concerned with the human condition. They apear to think of themselves as autonomous, not bound by group pressure, and prefer to arrive at conclusions independently.

The majority of the items in the *Complexity* Scale reflect a desire for, or seeking out of, new and complex experiences of a social and cognitive nature. This desire appears to be associated with a lack of interest in the conventional, regulated, simple, and certain life. The individual scoring high on this scale probably prefers trying out new ways of doing things and seems to enjoy new experiences. Ideas appeal more than facts, and "fooling around"

---

* More extensive definitions of these OPI scales were developed by three members of an MIT research group, Drs. Snyder, Kahne, and Huntington. All items making up each scale were reviewed and those inferences on which consensus was achieved were stated. The inventory was developed by staff members at the Center for Research and Development in Higher Education, University of California, Berkeley. Data furnished in the *Omnibus Personality Inventory Manual* suggested that these three scales were strong correlates of creative expression.

with ideas is not considered a waste of time. High scorers on this scale do not "need" clear-cut, unambiguous answers and certainty of outcomes. Freedom to invest time in intellectual risk taking and playing with ideas may be a crucial factor in this scale. Low scorers appear to prefer a well-ordered life with everything in its place and express a need for tangible results. There is also an implication that low scorers carefully and conservatively budget their time.

The items in the *Impulse Expression* Scale deal with apparent pleasure in either conscious thought or action; with increasing pressure for immediate gratification of impulse, and with the relative intolerance of delay that results as excitement mounts. Impulses referred to in items making up this scale are primarily aggressive or sexual. Manipulation or control of others is a subsidiary theme reflected in a cluster of seven items. Both socialized and controlled expression of impulse, together with more infantile impulse expressions, are also included in clusters of items in this scale. High scorers will probably show less reliance on a set schedule, on orderliness in dress, or conventionality in attitudes. They may also acknowledge an interest in novel, radical, or rebellious adventure with an exhibitionist flavor.

CHARACTERISTICS OF MIT STUDENTS

In September 1961, 721 members of the freshman class at Massachusetts Institute of Technology took the Omnibus Personality Inventory. Their average mean score on Thinking Introversion was 54.6 on a standard scale (where a score of 50 represents a midpoint for an average group of students). These means from MIT were compared with those obtained on the test at several other colleges and universities. The results indicated that the scores of the MIT group were closer to those of students at two small liberal-arts colleges than to those of students at two large universities or an Ivy League college for men.

The population at MIT represents considerable diversity, in spite of the emphasis on ability as the chief criterion for selection. The educational, psychological, and social experience of the students as they move through four years at the school is hardly uniform either. Different paths through the institution have different hurdles and different tasks, requiring different patterns of coping and different adaptive responses from the students.

The mean scores for the entire freshman class on the inventory showed an interesting pattern by the time these students had reached their third term and had made the selection of their major field. The mean scores on the Thinking Introversion and Complexity scales for engineering students were consistently below those means for groups majoring in science. But the Impulse Expression means for those in engineering were slightly higher than those for the science majors. Humanities and social-science majors had a pattern of scores on the three scales that was more like the one for the scientists than for the engineers.

By the third term, it became apparent that students who withdrew or were disqualified had high scores on the Complexity scale. Only the students in two science courses, the humanities, and architecture had a higher means here than those who had withdrawn or been disqualified. This particular finding of relatively high Complexity scores for the withdrawing students held up through the eighth term, or senior year. Apparently, the first-year "filter" through which the freshmen passed had more drastic affects on certain types of students than others. This provided an early cue to the fact that the institutional toll on high-scoring, creative students tended to occur early rather than late.

Certain institutional characteristics probably are relevant here. At MIT the engineering students move in and out of their field less frequently than do science majors. Social-science and humanities majors, however, show greatest degree of movement across fields.

THE FATE OF CREATIVE STUDENTS

In order to determine the fate of the creative student at MIT, a comparative study was made of two extreme groups. Students were identified who had scores that were one-and-a-half standard deviations (34 percentile point) *above* and *below* the MIT mean on the three OPI scales referred to above. The paths which these high- and low-scoring groups followed through four years were identified in the attempt to answer the following questions:

How many students left the institution? How many stayed? In what fields did they major? What was the final cumulative grade average of those who remained for the entire period?

Again, a note of caution is in order against a too hasty drawing of inferences from such data about the degrees of creativity. We simply do not know, to date, what the actual relationship is between the operational definition derived from the three OPI scales and the students' actual creative performance as undergraduates or as postgraduates. However, the study was premised on the assumption that the potential for creative expression was much greater among the high group on the scales than the low.

We turn now to a comparison of our extreme groups. There were sixty students with means below a standard score of 41 and forty students with means above 68 on the Thinking Introversion scale. There were fifty-six students with means below 40 and fifty-nine students with means above 72 on the Complexity scale. And on the Impulse Expression scale fifty-one students had means below 36, while sixty-eight students had means above 68. The percentage of students leaving the institution, either withdrawing on their own or being disqualified, was greater for the group scoring high on all three scales than for those scoring low (significant at the .01 level). The result is clear: Students scoring high on Thinking Introversion, Complexity, and Impulse Expression are more likely to leave the institution than low-scoring students.

Because, as entering freshmen, the high scorers on the OPI scales might be overrepresented among students of lesser academic ability, they could be disproportionately represented among those expected to be dropouts—namely, those entrants scoring low on the Scholastic Aptitude Test. However, an analysis of the relationship between the three OPI scores and the two SAT scores indicated quite the contrary. We discovered, for example, that a highly significant and positive association exists between SAT-M and the three scales. Rather than being low scorers, students who are high on Thinking Introversion, Complexity, or Impulse Expression also tend to be high on the mathematics subtest of SAT. The same situation holds for the only association that appears to be significant between the verbal subtest (SAT) and the three scales: High Thinking Introversion scores tend to be associated with high SAT-V scores. Detailed examination of the various matrices left no doubt that low SAT scores are not related to high scores on these variables.

At the very minimum, we are left wondering what it may be that an institution asks of these high-scoring students which they fail to do or choose not to do. Is an institutional filter operating, especially in certain fields, to select out the bright and the potentially more creative students from the college? An interesting and important alternate possibility raised by Dean Gordon Brown of MIT is that the high scorers on the OPI scales may be individuals who have adolescent expectations and attitudes about engineering or science which are challenged by the harsh reality of the various disciplines themselves. Nevertheless, if we are correct in assuming that this group of students is to be found among the intellectually most qualified freshmen, we must consider that the institution may be failing to meet the important developmental stage of adolescence in some of its most gifted students.

Students in the groups scoring low on Complexity, Thinking Introversion, or Impulse Expression tended to stay in one course for their entire enrollment at MIT when compared with the entire class. This trend toward "stability in place" was even more dramatic when these low-scoring students were compared with the high-scoring groups on these scales. The trend, as noted, was partly determined by the fact that the engineering majors stayed in one course more than any other group and had lower mean scores on two of these scales than the other groups.

There was no significant difference in the cumulative grade-point average at the end of four years between the low- and high-scoring groups on Complexity or Thinking Introversion. However, the low group on Impulse Expression had a significantly higher final cumulative average than the high Impulse Expression group. Thus, the greater the restriction of impulse, the greater the tendency for higher grades. However, the situation was actually more complicated. To anticipate our test-retest results: The one scale to show a significant increase in means over four years was the Impulse Expression scale. The correlation between this scale and the grade-point average was considerably higher in the freshman year than in any other year. Similar, though less dramatic, correlation existed between high Complexity scores and low grades in the first year; however, this correlation did not persist at a statistically significant level beyond the third term. These correlations may be taken as further evidence for the hypothesis that the first year of college may have a different set of cognitive hurdles than the last three years.

Let us summarize our observations. MIT was, and is, losing three times more students who as freshmen expressed their preference to experiment with ideas or take cognitive risks than those preferring a well-ordered life with tangible results. Such a gross statement, inferred from our operational definition of the Complexity scale, is clearly subject to question. However, we are justified, at least, in admitting continuing curiosity about just what the institution does or does not do for those entering students who take risks and appear to have an intellectual "itch." When such students stay in the institution, they achieve essentially the same final grade-point average as their more cognitively conservative classmates.

When we looked at those students who had extreme freshman scores and stayed at MIT through their senior year, still another trend became apparent. Half of the high scorers on Complexity were in science, while a sixth of all seniors were in the field of science. Our high-Complexity student, then, if he stayed in the institution, was most likely to be found in the school of science. There was one instructive exception to this fact: In an engineering course where the instructor explicitly rewarded risk taking, a greater number of students had high freshman scores on Complexity than in other fields.

We have, in the most general terms, seen what happened to the highly creative student, as we have temporarily defined him, as he entered into and moved through MIT. The major loss of this type of student occurred in the first year and a half, and those who stayed took paths through the institution that were different from their less creative peers. From the data presented so far, we cannot say whether their actual life experience at the institution differed significantly. We need to know much more than we know at present about what actually happens in the classroom, in the lecture period, in the dorm, and elsewhere to answer this question.

INSTITUTIONAL IMPACT AND ADAPTIVE STRESS

Generally speaking, a freshman arrives at the Institute and within the first week his expectations are challenged by a considerable amount of informal, if not private, information. He becomes aware that very fine discriminations are being made on the basis of the shoes that a student wears, the cut of his clothes, the style of his haircut, and the tone of his voice. The freshman also gets a great deal of semiprivate information on the social and psychological climate into which he has moved. There are strong pressures on each student to "swallow it," as one entrant put it.

These social and psychological stresses impinge on the freshman's inner sense of self. Such pressures operating toward conformity lie as much in invisible influences as in the formal curricula—probably even more in the former than in the latter. Whether he puts on the external signs of a particular identity, like a ready-made suit, obviously depends on many factors. In fact, the unique solutions that different students develop have consequences that may extend far beyond the freshman week. The continual quizzes and grading of the informal, invisible curriculum are covert but compelling. The student, with all these demands unresolved, then goes to class and hears still other voices challenging him to look at his preconceptions. The cognitive stresses of the classroom, which can often be profound and probably should be, result in range, subtlety, and complexity of stresses for a student. Consider the following example of a bright freshman who first confronts both the visible and invisible curricula.

In the lecture hall, the teen-ager hears from his professor that the course is exciting and that much independent thought will be demanded. He is urged to think about the subject, reflect on what he reads, and develop a skeptical approach. At the time of the first quiz, however, he learns that all that is required is the playback of a large number of discrete facts, and the message which many students hear is that reflection and original thought are hazardous while memorization will get the A's. The outcome of such thinking may be early cynicism about the academic enterprise and a determination to play the academic game shrewdly, with an emphasis on getting grades. Certainly, the effect of an institution's visible and invisible curricula on creative students should have high priority for further study.

What about the Institute's effect on the development of creativity? In the senior year, 213 students—30 per cent of those who had taken the OPI as freshmen—came back in their last term and retook the test. The volunteer bias of this sample was weighted by more science majors and fewer fraternity students than in the class as a whole. The general results for this senior group were that, after four years at MIT, the Thinking Introversion means went down, the Complexity means showed almost no difference between the freshman and senior years, and the Impulse Expression means increased significantly by the senior year.

The increase of means on the Impulse Expression scale may suggest that our sample of students placed significantly less reliance on set schedules and manifested fewer conventional attitudes after four years at the institution. The seniors might have been acknowledging that they wanted novel, radical, or rebellious adventures far more than when they were freshmen. Obviously, caution is in order about drawing too grand or too expansive inferences. We are not able to say whether the seniors were more freely expressing infantile impulses than when they were freshmen or whether they had developed a higher degree of socialized, controlled expression of impulse than in their first year. This is obviously a crucial question, but we are not able to answer it with the data at hand.

The drop in Thinking Introversion mean scores, though not dramatic, is intriguing. As students move on toward graduation, there may be less mental introversion and more propensity to act. The data, however, hardly warrant the judgment that MIT students were deriving less pleasure from deductive or analytic thinking or from intellectual activity in general. The drop in Thinking Introversion scores after four years may possibly reflect the students' increased socialization to a more regulated, orderly, and planned academic life, as inferred from shifts in his cognitive style and intellectual interest. Such a formulation does not necessarily contradict the noted increase in the Impulse Expression mean over the same period.

In the above studies, we have assumed that group mean changes reflect individual changes. Such an assumption, while legitimate, may be seriously misleading when the many other influences which may be contributing to that effect are considered. We have noted one such possibility—the institutional filters. Clearly needed are detailed studies of scores reflecting on *individual* change.

One such study illustrates the type of inquiry which we think should be pursued. Rigorous criteria were applied to determine significant change in the various OPI scores from the freshman to the senior year; a difference of at least two standard errors of measurement between the freshman and eighth-term scores was considered necessary for a significant change. On this basis, those students showing a significant increase or decrease in OPI scores were combined with those who were from the test-retest sample and had freshman scores more than one-and-a-half sigma above or below the first-year mean. Thus, one group contained students who had started out and remained high on a given scale or students whose scores had increased significantly on a particular scale. The comparison group consisted of students who had started low and remained low or students whose scores had decreased significantly.

The small number of students whose Complexity scores had significantly increased almost equalled the number whose scores had decreased. The former group had a final grade-point average of *B*, slightly below the latter group's final average of *A*−. We will come back in a moment to this observation. There were far fewer students with a significant change in their Complexity scores than was the case with the other two scales. While the Complexity scale permits characterization of particular groups of students at one point in time, its usefulness in change studies is limited because of the large variances in the scores.

The experiences of students during four years at this institution appear to be associated with a significant increase in Impulse Expression and with a decrease in the senior means on Thinking Introversion. Whatever the Complexity scale measures, it may reflect more an inherent psychological trait, a quality of mind, or the characteristic response of the individual to ambiguity than the qualities measured by the other scales do. Possibly, these scales—particularly Impulse Expression and Thinking Introversion—reflected the students' adaptive responses to different aspects of the educational culture in which they were living, rather than "inherent" traits.

In the senior year, the school of science had more than twice as many high-Complexity students as low-Complexity students. The school of engineering had twice as many low-Complexity students as high at the same point in time. As noted, the students scoring high on this scale had a final grade-point average slightly below that of the low-Complexity group. This evidence is further suggestive that the mastery of the separate cognitive tasks in these two fields has different emotional and social consequences. Seeking and gaining delight in complexity of stimulation and experiences may be at some cost in grades.

Finally, we remain hesitant about our interpretation of Complexity changes because of the large variance characterizing the group mean. In continuing analyses we are using scores reflecting individual change with a directional component. The application of techniques assessing individual change should reveal more appropriate information.

The trend for the entire test-retest sample to increase their scores over four years on Impulse Expression is impressive and occurs without regard to school. Fifty-three students had a significant increase while only four had a significant decrease on this scale. Those students—numbering eleven—who as freshmen had significantly low Impulse Expression scores and showed no change as seniors achieved a considerably higher grade-point average at graduation than the thirteen students who had high freshman and high senior scores on this scale. This suggests that the student who can delay his impulses at age eighteen will probably get better grades than the student with some difficulty in impulse control.

One other reservation is in order. The change on Impulse Expression may well represent emotional development and growth associated with the move from adolescence to adulthood, rather than a response to the immediate educational environment. The analyses available in this study did not permit us to determine the real reason for the change.

Let us move now from test data to accounts given by two students of their moves through college. They spoke directly to both issues that concern us in this section: the institution's impact on highly creative students and the institution's role in developing creativity in students.

The first vignette is based on an extended interview with a graduate student who was not part of the study. The second is from an interview with a student who was in the class we studied (described above). Formidable problems in confidence and anonymity arise, of course, in the reporting of such data. We chose to include the first vignette because it illustrates a point that emerged from the study sample interviews and yet does not compromise the participants. The second student gave his permission to use material from his interviews "if it would help."

A slight, almost boyish-looking man in his mid-twenties first informed us that he was working for his Ph.D. He had finished all the experimental work and writing for his thesis and only needed to complete a language requirement to graduate. He had returned to graduate school following a period of employment, during which time he had made a major original contribution to his discipline.

As an undergraduate he had majored in mathematics, but not at MIT. Even though he had done well, he graduated feeling he was second-rate since he was eighth in rank, not first, in his senior class. He was also disconsolate because his roommate and his five closest friends had received higher scores on a nationwide competitive examination. He was "only" thirtieth in the entire country on this examination. Such was his evidence for being second-rate.

He spoke of former classmates who had come from large, urban high schools and performed perfectly for their professors. They gave the answers that their teachers wanted; no one in this group, according to him, attempted to increase their knowledge or to raise new questions. He felt that all of them were lazy.

On a recent occasion when he had met his former roommate again, he decided to prod and push him to the limit. Since the roommate, a straight A student, was one of the "lazy ones," he was curious as to whether he could goad him into coming up with a new solution to an old problem. After some time, his old roommate did respond with an original answer to a difficult scientific problem, avoiding an adequate but less imaginative approach. He said, however, this simply took up too much time and energy and wasn't worth the effort. On the other hand, our mathematics major had always been excited by new formulations and had been considered a pest because of always asking questions. He suggested to us that a study of creative people could benefit greatly from an intensive analysis of very bright individuals who are *not* creative—a suggestion we have taken seriously.

Our second student, chosen from the random stratified sample of interviewees participating in a recent study, smilingly, but correctly, described himself as disadvantaged. He complained that he had gone through one-and-a-half years at MIT in a "fog." Though highly able, he had literally spent almost all of his time keeping "afloat." He had been terrified that his inadequacies would destroy him. Though his courses had been challenging and his professors had genuinely encouraged reflection, he had not had time—or, at least, felt he had had no time—to do more than prepare the work for the next day. Coming from hill country in the South, he said he had "stolen time to take in the art galleries and the symphony" and had been hungry for all he could get out of urban life. The time spent on these things, however, had actually been only a few hours out of days and weeks and months devoted to school work.

After this young man had lost his scholarship because of a drop in grades, he had enrolled in a "third-rate school," which was, he felt, only interested in his getting a working knowledge of his field and in his taking a degree. There were no demands to think about subject matter or to derive first principles. In his view, the informal curriculum required only attendance and cognitive servitude.

In this second school, however, he could quite easily do very well academically. Most important, he had had time to take a job in a laboratory to compensate for the boredom of classes. Here in the laboratory he could explore concrete, tough, and complex problems in a manner that had been impossible before. His work involved developing a small, but highly imaginative, functional piece of hardware that had important research implications. This experience gave him a sense of competence, as well as excitement, that he had not known before. As an outgrowth of his job, he eventually made a change in his major field.

This student's brief history suggests that stress and excitement can come in unexpected places and must be taken into account in the curriculum and in the planning of courses. He had, indeed, felt constrained and bored in the early period at the "third-rate" school, but he had the freedom which was not formally intended by the system to pursue a question and to become involved. On the other hand, both excitement and challenging questions were possible at the first school, but he had not had enough time to pursue them.

These two brief histories serve to highlight the picture we have drawn of an entire class moving through four years at a specific institution. Students develop a variety of strategies to deal with the almost inevitable conflict between expected present, actual present, and hoped-for future. Certain strategies, certain solutions used by students, have much higher survival value in one academic institution than another and in one academic field than another. The institution, more than the student, sets the odds on the various strategies and coping patterns that will win. Further, an invisible curriculum may play as important a role as the formal curriculum in determining which strategies and which solutions are most adaptive. Those strategies having survival value for the present do not automatically serve the student well in mastering his field, developing his intellect, or permitting or encouraging creative expression. It is precisely because of this failure that we are challenged to consider the consequences of our curricula for the development of excited, imaginative, and concerned students.

III

The Artistically Talented
and the Educational Establishment

5

NURTURING TALENT AND CREATIVITY IN THE ARTS*

Vittorio Giannini

However comprehensive the American educational scene may seem in general, there is a serious lack of schools offering artistic training to talented and creative children at an early age—a period that is extremely important for receiving professional guidance in the performing arts. The first time that most talented young people are exposed to any teaching of quality in the field is when—or perhaps we

* This paper, originally presented by Vittorio Giannini, has been revised and supplemented by Neal Snyder and Paul Heist. Dr. Giannini, who died in November 1966, was a distinguished American composer and violinist and had been a devoted teacher of composition at Juilliard and other music institutes for over a quarter of a century. The first president of the North Carolina School of the Arts, Giannini did much to develop the idea of this special school and to help bring together its highly distinguished faculty.

73

should say *if*—they have the good fortune to enroll in a college where a qualified staff and a good program in the arts are available. But college is far too late to begin, especially in music and the dance. It is too late to develop physical and technical competence, whatever the student's level of talent or creative potential may be. Only an early start and long years of hard work can produce the best results. It is also late from the standpoint of theoretical knowledge. The usual curricular requirements in college-level music departments make this quite clear. The situation in college dance and drama is generally even more dismal, although there may be some performance opportunities. Usually, however, very little instruction or only instruction by persons lacking in professional expertise is available.

CREATIVITY AND THE LIBERAL ARTS

The average liberal-arts college has a small music department with too much emphasis on rudiments. The fact that the first year of study often includes "remedial" subjects, such as *elementary* ear training, *elementary* harmony, and *elementary* sight singing or sight reading, is evidence of the deficiencies in early training or pre-college programs. It does not make sense to have elementary arithmetic at the college level for those enrolled in engineering education. Students are already expected to know a great deal about arithmetic and mathematics by the time they enter engineering school. The deplorable situation in the arts, however, is not confined to liberal-arts colleges. Even such professional schools as Juilliard, Eastman School of Music, Curtis, and Peabody find it necessary to offer introductory courses at presumably advanced levels, as well as providing elementary courses to accommodate students with inadequate backgrounds. These are essentially remedial courses. What happens to a college curriculum when it is necessary to try to crowd into four years that which should take at least eight or, perhaps, ten? To cover the necessary amount of material, much of it must be very superficially presented and superficially learned. College teachers naturally feel the need to concentrate on the higher studies and advanced work; consequently, they skim basic studies. As a result, many so-called musicians and other artists have a smattering of knowledge instead of a real understanding and command of their discipline or medium.

Students in the performing arts must become virtuosos in their particular disciplines if they wish to present first-rate performances and achieve quality of expression. And this also applies to composition, playwriting, and poetry. Persons may have great creative gifts, but they must also make instruments of themselves—the finest, the most delicate, and sensitive instruments—through which great flights of imagination and the spirit can be projected to the listener or reader. But the development of such virtuosity is very difficult with the program deficiencies and lack of experiences in early musical education, as well as in the music departments of most colleges and universities. When one also considers the requirements of other course work and the general academic pressure in the liberal-arts college, one is made even more aware that college training in the arts falls far short of the professional-school program.

It is appropriate to point out here the important but different functions of the liberal-arts school and the professional school of arts. In professional schools—to continue using music as an example—a music student is admitted on the basis of talent or skill in his chosen field and not for *general* academic performance and promise. In most liberal-arts colleges, musical talent or skill may only receive secondary attention, if any, in the admissions process. Through the use of these different criteria, the majority of entrants in the two settings are very dissimilar. As a result, a regular college orchestra of fifty or sixty may perhaps include only twenty music majors—which is all right, but not for the maintenance of high performance standards. The musical experience is, perforce, of lesser quality, but so also are the type and quality of the students' associations and intellectual exchange with their peers. Moreover, the conductor cannot expect from the nonmusic major the same standards or dedication that he can and must demand from the music major.

These two different approaches of the liberal-arts college and the school of arts appear very justifiable. We certainly have a great need for both of them if we put them in the right perspective. I do not think, however, that a great majority of professional artists in the performing arts can be trained in a typical college or univer-

sity—at least, not to a level of optimum performance. But I realize
that the liberal-arts colleges have an important function here. They
should have as an objective the exposure of all students to the arts,
with the hope of increasing their understanding and appreciation.
They could bring students to higher levels of appreciation if they
would offer fine performances by artists and if they would teach for
an understanding of dance, drama, painting, and sculpture. But
such exposure will, of course, not lead to the desired results for
everyone.

The talented youth who wishes to be a performing artist
probably requires the total art environment of a music conservatory
or a school of arts. More important, he should go where he can as-
sociate with other talented artists, where he can have the freedom
and stimulation that one needs in the arts. He should also choose a
place where he can receive instruction from top-flight performing
and teaching artists. While they are cultivating his talent, he also
can learn from them the qualities of dedication and commitment,
so he will come to understand the effort and hard work which go
into creativity and performance. Creativity can best be nurtured by
competent, sensitive teachers and through living and associating with
students of similar interests and talents. It cannot be developed spontaneously without proper attention and discipline. Cases of totally
or almost entirely self-trained and self-motivated geniuses in the
performing arts are probably a good deal more rare than in many
intellectual fields. Jazz musicians may at first seem to be a noteworthy exception to this rule, but the most accomplished actually
have had long apprenticeships, formal and informal, with older
virtuosos. An artistically inclined individual practices his art because
it is almost a compulsion, a response to the need to accomplish something to the best of his ability. Education at a school like the North
Carolina School of the Arts has been geared to encourage this kind
of accomplishment.

THE NORTH CAROLINA SCHOOL OF THE ARTS

The North Carolina School of the Arts very early achieved
a position of some uniqueness on the American educational scene.
Its first years, after it opened in the fall of 1965, were a period of
much excitement and great promise. It seems like an appropriate

time now to reflect on the underlying ideas and objectives that were basic to its early development and inception.

The plans for the school originated in 1963 through the imagination and leadership of Terry Sanford, then the governor of North Carolina. He brought the idea into being and successfully convinced the state legislature of its merit. The basic idea, according to Mr. Sanford, was borrowed from the Juilliard School of Music and the New York City High School of the Performing Arts. Located in Winston-Salem, the North Carolina School of the Arts is the only school of its kind in the South and the only school of the performing arts for junior high school, high school, and college students in the country. It has its own board of trustees and is only financially responsible to the state governor and the legislature.

The professional education the school provides is primarily for talented students in the performing arts from North Carolina, although a portion of the student body is, and will be, from other states, regions, and countries. (The opening enrollment of 229 students included 148 youngsters from North Carolina and 48 from other Southern states.) Since the school is dedicated to training artists who will be broadly educated, it devotes much attention to academic subjects. However, its chief purpose is to (1) search for and identify exceptional artistic talent within the region and (2) provide a place where this talent can be developed to the fullest by a staff of selected professional artists. Because it is a professional school in terms of both students and staff, admission is determined almost entirely from the results of an audition which every prospective student receives in the presence of instructors in his intended field. His individual potential is assessed by means of this audition.

The school curriculum consists of a sequential program as already indicated, integrated across three levels—elementary, high school, and college. Eventually, a postgraduate level will be added. Within the age ranges of these several traditional levels, candidates are accepted at any age if their degree of talent warrants admission. One of the more radical aspects of the new school's approach is that students are not forced to fit themselves into formally structured year-levels for their artistic studies; rather, they are allowed to progress as quickly as they are able and according to their desire.

In consideration of the necessarily small size of the institution

—to accommodate individual attention—officials believe that the school will be of greatest value if the majority of the enrollment is concentrated at the high school level. The present intention is to have about two thirds of the total student body in high school, with most of the rest in college and a sprinkling in the elementary grades. During the opening year of the school, there were 136 high school students, 78 college students, 9 elementary students (the youngest of whom was 12), and 4 special students. The belief is that the school can best operate with a maximum enrollment of 550 to 600 —a level toward which it is slowly growing from its first-year enrollment. The decision to maintain the school permanently as a small institution is dictated by the importance placed on teacher-student relationships for proper development of artistic and personal potential. Needless to say, any sound education program should ideally be premised on frequent contact between teacher and pupil. This fact seems especially important in the performing arts, where the student can only learn the skills, discipline, and outlook of the performer through personal coaching and contact. With a ratio of four or five students to each teacher, a program like this is very expensive to operate, the cost per pupil per year being about $4,000.

The areas or fields in which students currently may major are music, drama, and dance. Besides these three major fields or departments, there is one other department in academic studies. All students take classes in the latter area, but since the purpose of the school is to train and educate professional artists, rather than to compete with liberal-arts institutions, individuals cannot major in the so-called academic fields. Nevertheless, the name *School of the Arts,* rather than *School of the Performing Arts,* was intentionally used to indicate the importance conferred upon academic studies within the program. As stated earlier, the planning group wanted the students to become well-rounded, well-educated artists. With this added objective, teaching of the highest quality is important in the academic department as well as in the arts.

Academic subjects presently offered include English, three foreign languages, science (mathematics, biology, chemistry, and physics), history, psychology, economics, social studies, and art appreciation. During the initial year, the total curriculum was accommodated by a faculty composed of 33 instructors in the arts and 16 in academic studies. The students were distributed as follows: 127 in music, 53 in drama, and 47 in dance. In the second year there were about 150 in music, 60 in drama, and 90 in dance, with appropriate increases in faculty.

The curriculum has been developed rapidly at all three levels of instruction. The high-school course work is based, naturally, on state requirements. But the emphasis is personal, with each student's academic program tailored to his particular needs. Advanced courses with research experiences are available, as is individualized work in science and mathematics. The requirements for the bachelor-of-music degree provide an example of the college-level curricula:

Liberal Arts	48 credits
Music Theory and History	40 credits
Major Study	40 credits
Minor in a Performing Medium	4 credits
Ensemble Performance	8 credits

The school is also undertaking special programs, as evidenced by the annual summer theater in Winston-Salem and summer sessions in such cities as Siena, Italy.

From the beginning, the faculty has provided a high level of intense and rigorous learning experiences. The mornings are devoted entirely to the artistic disciplines and the afternoons to academic work, although this schedule has since been somewhat modified. The demanding nature of the program is further indicated by the fact that each student is evaluated by a jury at the end of every year. These evaluations are employed to determine whether or not a person will be eligible to continue in the school—admission does not guarantee continuous matriculation.

AN ENVIRONMENT CONDUCIVE TO CREATIVITY

Artistic talent—as well as a gift for great creative expression —if not present within the student cannot be given him. However, he can be placed in an environment of the best influences and can be taught and helped to teach himself to become an artist, as well

as to become an outstanding human being. To fulfill these goals, the
school's faculty has been carefully selected. Only persons who have
proven themselves both as first-class performers and first-class teachers have been considered, with the result that leading artists have
become members of the faculty. The music staff, for instance, includes, among others, the Claremont String Quartet, the Clarion
Wind Quintet, pianist Howard Aibel, and singers Rose Bampton
and Norman Farrow. Masters classes in this department have been
taught by such outstanding artists as Andres Segovia, Ruggiero
Ricci, and George Ricci.

It has been fairly easy to maintain the music and dance faculties, even though they are composed entirely of persons who come
from the performing world and keep up professional engagements.
Members can leave for two or more days, give a performance, and
then come back and teach. A slightly different system, however, is
necessary for operating the drama department, because performers
in a show must usually be gone for a longer period of time. Therefore, a nucleus faculty teaches history, speech, and basic acting.
When outstanding directors and actors are free, they are asked to
teach. With a faculty of this composition, some members are always
on campus while others are fulfilling engagements.

In reviewing the chief contributors to a stimulating environment, we have failed to consider one point. We should frankly admit
that one may question whether all talent in the arts can be correctly
included under the term "creativity." In music, composition is clearly
an act of creation, although—as with all other cultural products—
it varies from being highly original to highly derivative. Jazz improvisation is in the same category since it *is* composition, instanta-
neous composition. However, it seems improper to describe the
performance of composed music as an act of creation. Yet, an original, outstanding interpretation could be regarded as some form of
creativity.

Dance and drama are quite comparable when considered in
this fashion. Between choreographers and dancers and playwrights
and actors one may draw the same distinction as the one between
composers and performers. One may also suggest that improvisational

dancers and actors (as in revues like *Second City* and *The Commit-tee*) provide parallels to the jazz musicians.

Conductors, dance directors, and directors of dramatic pro-ductions should not automatically have unusual qualities of crea-tivity ascribed to them either. The best of them, generally, are clearly very creative, however. This is particularly obvious in the case of those doing outstanding work with new material.

The point of this digression has been that, although the ef-forts of the school are obviously efforts on behalf of artistic talent and competence, we cannot say with any certainty whether they *truly* serve the cause of creativity until there is evidence on the mat-ter. Apparently, we must wait several years or, at least, until numer-ous graduates are abroad in the world; then we can attempt to as-sess the creativity of their contributions and performances and perhaps inquire as to whether they feel the school aided them in developing creativity.

Even though it is too early to make any claims about the education or development of creative artists in this school, there is some early evidence of how this program has affected its students in some ways. It has certainly broadened the horizons of many. One need only picture a young violinist who, as a member of a poor rural family, has never heard of chamber music and is then exposed at first hand to the Claremont String Quartet.

The satisfaction of the students' artistic urges also seems to have helped their general motivation, so that they turn to academic pursuits with fresh attention. In the first two years of the program, the faculty has observed that, generally, the students who do supe-rior work in the academic fields also do superior work in the arts. It has been the exception and not the rule, to date, to find a highly satisfactory performance in the arts and a much less satisfactory one in the academic division. The dean of dance has commented, "I find in every single case that the best dancers are also the best students." Even students who passed their artistic evaluation during the initial audition but presented poor school records have been getting better grades in academic subjects during the first semester in which they were receiving intensive artistic training. Although the high school academic subjects are all college preparatory courses, the students do not seem to resent this work. Previous to enrolling in the school, they had to attend schools where they probably did not have much chance to play their instruments or practice under competent instruction.

The students often speak of the fun they have in the afternoon under this program. Some say, "I have all morning for my oboe,"—or whatever their specialty is—and comment that they now like to go to school. "I don't have to take a lot of junk," they say. "I have real subjects." So we see that they are not only grateful for the opportunity to practice their art but also grateful to be freed from the deadening, time-wasting, nonacademic, and barely academic courses prevalent in American schools.

The school has undoubtedly played a role in improving the emotional condition of some of its sensitive, talented students by providing an environment in which they can adjust socially. It appears to be important to their personal and artistic development to be in an environment of young people who share their aspirations. As one boy said, "I come from a small town in the mountains in North Carolina. I have always liked to play the flute. Finally, I got my mom and dad to buy me one. But I had trouble in school because nobody else liked the flute. The boys liked to play ball or tease the girls, and they used to make fun of me. After a while, I started to believe that there was something wrong with me. But now I've found out here that there's nothing wrong with me; there're a lot of guys like me."

This development or realization is very important. Even if this boy does not become a flutist, his new experiences and relationships have helped him realize that he is not odd. In experiences of this nature we see another value in this sort of school. By asserting the validity of other means of expression than words or writing, the school provides relief and satisfaction for artistic youth whose preferred idiom is an art form. It allows them a healthy involvement and a success which some might not be capable of in academic work.

Not only does the school allow a student to determine, before it is too late, whether he should strive for a career in the performing arts (and the importance of early training and early encouragement of creativity in these areas bears repeating) but it also allows him to make this decision without losing time academically. The courses he takes permit him to continue his education in other fields and thus prepare him for a transfer to another school should he so desire. Despite the rigorousness of the class work, few students, to date, have transferred or dropped out.

In an article in the *New York Times,* Howard Taubman used two adjectives that suggest the main features of the school's promise: "imaginative" and "tough-minded." It is a school, he felt, that even the best students would not find either sterile or easy-going.

6

THE EDUCATION OF
THE JAZZ VIRTUOSO

Ralph J. Gleason

I would like to begin with two quotations: A lady once approached the jazz pianist Fats Waller (legend has now made her a Little Old Lady—she was probably a rich matron) and asked, "What is jazz, Mr. Waller?" Waller, a patient man, sighed and said, "Lady, if you don't know, don't mess with it." That is quotation number one.

Here is number two: An alumnus of a conservatory, who later became an outstanding jazz pianist, recalls, "The conservatory not only did not encourage but in every way impeded my interest in jazz and in so doing hampered my musical development. For everything I know today, I am obligated most of all to myself."

The first statement is, as I have said, jazz legend. I have heard it attributed to Louis Armstrong, Lester Young, and Charles

Parker and, for all I know, someone may be writing an article at this very moment attributing it to Charlie Mingus or Miles Davis. (I should add parenthetically that if these names are unfamiliar to you, I hope to make them familiar before I conclude. The very fact of their unfamiliarity would support the theme of my general presentation.) The second quotation, which damns the formal educational apparatus, is a statement made by a Leningrad musician who is one of the growing number of young Russians playing jazz music.

The ideas expressed in the two quotations are not unrelated, and these have certainly pervaded the thinking in this country, if not the whole world over. "If you don't know, don't mess with it" is the Zen theme of antiintellectualism which has haunted jazz since the beginning and made it mysterious (redolent of arcane Negro voodoo practices in old New Orleans on Congo Square). It has been used to reinforce the attitude that jazz is primitive music, possibly not music at all, and certainly not worthy of rank with serious music.

The attitude expressed in the second quotation is the conviction that formal education offers nothing to the jazz musician. Miles Davis, a great, creative jazz improviser and a charismatic figure without peer in the music world, was a student at the Juilliard School of Music in New York for one semester. He spent most of his time downtown on Fifty-second Street in New York's jazz clubs, listening mostly to Charlie Parker, an alto saxophonist, and writing down what he heard on match-box covers. The next day in the rehearsal hall at Juilliard, he would work out the things he had written down the night before. Naturally, with his focus on music outside of Juilliard, he didn't stay long enough to get a degree. Though only time can prove me right, I believe that it is Davis' name that will live as a musical genius and not those of his classmates.

Jazz has been a bastard music, spawned in the brothel, nurtured in the red-light district, and always associated with the sporting life. In the beginning, the entire musical world, with rare exception, screamed out against it. "UNSPEAKABLE JAZZ MUST GO!" was a headline in a music magazine in the Twenties. Public figures raged against it. The word "jazz" itself—which, I might point out, really *does* have four letters—has been traced back by etymologists to sexual connotations.

Today, in a world of shifting values, jazz stands out as a unique American artistic expression, different from that of any other art form. Jazz is now worldwide in its appeal. Jazz musicians like Miles Davis, Sonny Rollins, John Coltrane, Charles Mingus, and Duke Ellington are treated like artists and cultural giants in every country of the world but America. Here, they are really second-class citizens a good deal of the time, and even when they escape this lesser status, at some specific moments, the thought always occurs that the next occasion may bring the trauma and the hurt experienced by all Negro citizens.

In almost every other form of art, certainly in the area of serious music, the American artist is largely indistinguishable from the European. The better he gets, the more he seems to be like another culture's product. The only music which is accepted as art and is indigenously American is jazz. The better a jazz artist is, the more he sounds like a Negro (if he is not already one) and the very best musicians, with but one or two exceptions, are Negroes. Negroes made this music. They created it, developed the basic styles, and are still its leading figures. All whites could be erased from the history of jazz, and the level and quality of jazz would be just where it is today.

The Negro in this country has learned the hard way that no schoolroom really holds much for him. The jazz musician was perhaps one of the first to learn this. He might have gone into other things had he been white, but, being black, he found music and/or entertainment were ways to make money and to grab the "gimmick," of which James Baldwin speaks, and then get out. Sociologists may find in time that the high incidence of superiority in Negro jazz musicians is related in some way to the high proportion forced into a few fields; the talented tenth had fewer alternatives and thus music got more than its share.

JAZZ AND EDUCATION

To consider the topic of formal education and its role in jazz, let's review a list of ten of the greatest-of-all jazz musicians. The qualifications of the persons for such a listing, I submit, would be accepted universally, even though any list of ten is a matter of arbitrary choice. The ten on my suggested list are Louis Armstrong, Duke Ellington, Charles Parker, John Birks "Dizzy" Gillespie, Miles Davis, Thelonious Monk, Charles Mingus, Lester Young, Billie Holiday, and John Coltrane. I, and others, could make up other lists of ten, all Negroes, all similarly qualified, but the general story about their education would be much the same. Here is a very brief account on each of the persons I have named.

Louis Armstrong was a son of the ghetto in New Orleans, a street urchin attracted to music. In his own autobiography he says he was drawn to music because of the whores and the pimps and their glamorous life (seen from the point of view of his own poverty). He learned his music in an orphan's home and then was taught by other musicians with whom he played on jobs. The rest came from himself.

Edward Kennedy "Duke" Ellington has appeared with numerous symphonies and given concerts in the great music halls of the world; his achievements include precipitating a cultural crisis because the Pulitzer Prize Board would *not* honor him. This artist, whose father was a house servant in Washington, D.C., did study music in high school and took private piano lessons, but he has said that he learned, really, from listening to ragtime pianists around Washington. Instead of going to Pratt Institute to study commercial design, he began his phenomenal career as a professional musician in 1918. At sixty-seven he is, I suggest, America's foremost composer.

Charles Parker, who revolutionized the art of jazz as Hemingway revolutionized the art of the novel, studied music in high school like any other kid—he took a couple of semesters of music and played in the school band. At fifteen years of age, he became a high school dropout and launched his professional career in the night clubs of Kansas City.

John Birks "Dizzy" Gillespie, who has been sent by the State Department on long tours of the Middle East and South America as a cultural representative, learned his first music from his father, who died when Dizzy was ten. He then studied in high school and later at a Negro agricultural institute. He doubled between agronomy and music and then left it all to play in Philadelphia night clubs.

Miles Davis, already mentioned, also studied in a Negro high school and then played in bands and went to Juilliard for one semester.

Thelonious Monk, a pianist, who, like Duke Ellington, has achieved the all-American status symbol of a *Time* cover story, studied privately in New York and had no formal education at all.

Charles Mingus, like the others, studied music in high school and then learned from other musicians. Later, long after his reputation was made, he studied the string bass for a while with a classical teacher in New York.

Lester Young, whose style on the tenor saxophone opened the door for much of the vital experimentation of modern jazz, was the son of a professional musician. He studied with his father and played in his band throughout his teens.

Billie Holiday, the only vocalist on my list, is a jazz singer whose style has had the kind of fundamental effect on vocal jazz that the King James Bible has had on English literature. You "hear" her today—even though she's been dead since 1959—in the work of Peggy Lee and almost every other female jazz singer. She was the daughter of a guitar player, became a prostitute at fourteen, and never took a music lesson in her life.

John Coltrane, a tenor saxophonist, is the only one on this list with any sort of real formal training that goes beyond individual lessons. He studied in high school and later at two music schools in Philadelphia, the Granoff Studios and the Ornstein School of Music.

The other examples I could add to this list are overwhelming. Certainly there are some music-school graduates who have reputations as jazz artists, and many of the younger men today have had some sort of formal training. Much of current jazz is highly complex and exacting, and the more complicated it has become, the more sound the musical training that is demanded. For example, John Lewis, pianist with the Modern Jazz Quartet and an internationally known composer, studied at the Manhattan School of Music, and Dave Brubeck studied under Darius Milhaud when he taught at Mills College. But Brubeck, a Caucasian, is a man whose jazz success, curiously enough, has not had any influence upon other jazz musicians. Burbeck, incidentally, is the only jazz musician I know of who ever studied formally with any of the great classicists.

Any close study of serious jazz men—and Duke Ellington has remarked that no musician is more serious about his music than a jazz musician—shows that they were forced to break away from traditional education in order to break through and that they naturally found their own way outside the academies, outside the orthodoxy of musical education. They created their own empirical educational system. Why did Miles Davis, one of the most creative musicians of his generation, spend his time at Juilliard playing what he had heard the night before in jazz clubs if not because the opportunities offered him in the classroom were irrelevant?

THE NEGRO MUSICIAN AND JAZZ MUSIC

When President Johnson assembled his culture session at the White House, critic Dwight McDonald attended and subsequently wrote an account of that event in which he mourned the fact that *no* American composers had been invited. At the end of this long essay, in the usual entertaining Dwight McDonald style, he added that the one bright thing about the White House affair was the delightful playing of Duke Ellington and his orchestra. Obviously, to Dwight McDonald, jazz musician Duke Ellington is not an American composer. In our society, we just do not see these musicians or recognize their accomplishments. We do not know their names.

At the University of California—as in almost all of the leading educational institutions of this country—jazz is regarded with near horror and definite apprehension. Hertz Hall is one of the most benign places I have ever sat in to hear music. I believe I am correct in saying that only one jazz concert has been held in Hertz Hall, and this concert was given last year by several young students. They played the music of Miles Davis, Sonny Rollins, Thelonious Monk, and Charles Parker, but these composers themselves—even though they have played many times in the Bay Area—have never set foot in Hertz Hall or, as far as I know, on the University of California campus. This situation is something like assigning Bach, Mozart, and Stravinsky to play in the Jazz Workshop and Basin Street West (in San Francisco) and then having their music played in Hertz Hall only by undergraduates.

In Berkeley, as in many cities in this country, the nearest major symphony orchestra periodically gives concerts for children in the elementary grades and high school, and the students are excused from their classes to attend the performances. But only when the students themselves have made a deliberate effort to bring jazz musicians to their assemblies—and occasionally to other school affairs—have they been able to hear this form of great music. It is never offered to them as part of their cultural enhancement, nor are courses on the understanding and appreciation of jazz included.

Earlier I mentioned the School of Jazz in Leningrad. There was even a School of Jazz in the United States at one time. Located in Lenox, Massachusetts, it was inspired by the Tanglewood concert series and continued for several summers. The school had the unqualified support of almost all the major jazz musicians, who took time off from concert tours and night-club engagements to work as teachers there for room and board. Applications came from all over the world, the waiting list was enormous, and yet the school died for lack of funds. It simply could not obtain enough money to stay alive. The philanthropic foundations, which reflect the attitude of the academy and the "establishment," did not see fit to provide financial help to underwrite this most interesting and exciting experiment.

In Poland, jazz is taught in the public schools, both at the college and precollege level. Polish jazz musicians alternate between giving concerts and playing in night clubs *and* teaching and performing in the schools on the State payroll. Television programs are produced on American jazz, and jazz per se is in the curriculum.

Yet, only last year in this country, the Monterey Jazz Festival failed in its offer to underwrite, to the total of a $4,000 project, a workshop in jazz education. It was to be under the direction of a music professor from a California state college, with the purpose of providing high school teachers with a three- or four-day indoctrination in ways and means of teaching jazz to their students. Lists of available recordings, recommended books on jazz, and lectures by musicologists and jazz musicians on the history and theory of jazz were to be offered. Demonstrations of teaching techniques were also to be presented by adventuresome teachers who have—on their own —worked out ways to instruct in this area, much like jazz musicians have worked out their own ways to play. The only requirement of the Monterey officials was that the workshop should give the teachers the usual credits for attendance. This instructional project was then presented on the Berkeley campus to the University of California Extension, which did not accept it. It died because no one would fulfill the necessary technical role of sponsorship. A necessary representative of the music department or of the education department could not be found to act as sponsor. Therefore, no credits could have been given.

In answer to the direct question, "Why are there no courses in jazz?", a University of California professor of music last year responded, "We do not offer courses in plumbing either." Yet the University officials are interested in the problems of attrition on campus. How do you keep students who feel little can be gained by remaining in school from dropping out? How often do curricular provisions fail to consider particular students? Sensible answers to these questions might also keep some potentially great music students at the university.

THE CHANGING PICTURE OF JAZZ

Some interesting things are being done about the breadth of music programs in some schools and at some levels. There are, for example, thousands of stage bands today in high schools across the country. A stage band is a euphemism for a jazz band. I have been told that they are called stage bands because they appear on a stage and give concerts; but they really go by this title because if they were called jazz bands, the high school music teachers would not be allowed to devote the necessary time and effort to help them. They would be discouraged just as the leaders of the jazz-band workshop at San Francisco State (which produced Paul Desmond of the Dave Brubeck Quartet, Allen Smith, and John Handy) were discouraged a decade ago.

These stage bands are providing a place to go for the young

people who want to learn something about jazz. But this approach to jazz in some high schools is only a start—and in a second-class, behind-the-barn kind of way. Still, this development in secondary schools is encouraging. And in time it is going to have a definite effect on American music, if only because of the sheer numbers of students involved.

The jazz musician is somewhat unique as a creative artist. He cannot, unlike the poet, the painter, and the novelist, practice his art in solitary fashion in the proverbial attic. Most of his playing and practicing must be with other musicians, in order to sharpen his own ideas and response. He needs support for his own playing in every possible way. Jazz musicians now rehearse together for their mutual education in a sort of underground. By sitting in on the job in practice sessions, they are defying the union, which demands they be paid for playing. Thus, they do not have the freedom to practice or learn in the only way open to them. They need places where they can gather together and work, experiment, practice, and play without interference and without pressures. But these opportunities are not available to them.

There are jazz courses in a few colleges and universities today, but most of them are not designed for the creative musician but for the interested nonmusician. In contrast, during the short life of the Lenox School of Jazz, students not only studied in classes and in private with the master jazz men but also had the rewarding experience of playing with them. This situation, for example, allowed a young trumpet player to have Dizzy Gillespie, the great jazz improviser and technician, come to him at a rehearsal and say, "Never play a *C* chord here; it sounds wrong and here's why."

But to return to the topic of university music departments. Two years ago, while discussing the possibility of a jazz course, I was asked by the head of a large music department, "Can you *teach* jazz? Can you *teach* art? Can you *teach* a man to be a great composer?" The answer is obvious, and the question would never have been raised if this dean of music understood jazz and this form of spontaneous creativity. He should have realized that it is as much an art as any other music in his department. The rudiments and basic structure of music, as well as fundamental skills, can be taught.

But, just this lack of understanding of what jazz is all about prevents essential communication. Jazz is spontaneous, and, like much of American society which it seems to reflect, it is improvisatory. The "art" of jazz and the talent, the creativity of performance, cannot be taught, but colleges could provide the situations where the talent and musicianship might be developed.

Let me pursue this theme a little further. The jazz musician stands up in front of an audience, and he "composes" what he plays as he goes along. He starts with or creates a melodic theme, goes on with a counter melody, and develops a unique composition. It is instant art, a tour-de-force performance. This improvisation is even more impressive when one considers the surroundings in which this art is practiced. The jazz musician works in saloons a good deal of the time, creating his art in front of drunks and many talking, unappreciative customers. He very seldom has even a dressing room to relax in. The backstage conditions of the old Metropolitan Opera House, which Rudolph Bing criticized so severely in an attempt to show the advantages of a new building, would be heaven to musicians working in most jazz clubs.

The jazz musician learns chiefly by doing. He finds out a few fundamentals about the instrument in which he is interested and then he just leaps in and plays. He gets help from those with whom he plays. Other musicians taught Louis Armstrong how to read music. Other trumpet players showed Dizzy Gillespie breathing tricks. John Coltrane says he learned from playing with Thelonious Monk, Dizzy Gillespie, and Miles Davis. The masters of the art pass on their knowledge to the youths coming after them.

Today jazz is a sophisticated music compared with its early folk-music beginnings. Almost all jazz musicians now read music, unlike many of the old Dixieland musicians. Many of the younger ones have had some elementary harmony and even compositional instruction—frequently through the G.I. Bill—in some commercial music studio, which gives them the same kind of education it provides for those who want to play in dance bands.

The jazz musician also learns by listening to others, in person, and on record. This is true in America and in other countries. In Leningrad, where the opportunities to hear American jazz men have been piteously few, jazz records are treasured, and tapes for repeated study are made of the Voice of America broadcasts. In Poland, when jazz was forbidden in the early Fifties, the jazz musicians held secret underground meetings to listen to tapes. This independent and free way of learning—that is, by listening, trying, experimenting, and listening again—has probably made for much more flexibility and innovation than would have been the case in formal educational institutions.

THE CREATIVE JAZZ PERFORMANCE

When a jazz musician is finding and developing his own style, he must be ingenious and versatile. He must be able to retain in his memory the chord sequences for hundreds of tunes. He must be able to play changes effortlessly and improvise on them when his turn to solo comes, without the chance to go back and correct his mistakes. In fact, many jazz musicians have made a virtue out of necessity—which is really the story of their music—and have developed a degree of virtuosity so that they can even utilize their mistakes. Dizzy Gillespie, for instance, is known to play a long trumpet phrase, a whirling dervish of notes, and then suddenly to make a mistake. Immediately his "mental computer" shifts, and what he plays after the mistake makes the mistake itself logical in retrospect.

The life of a jazz man is far from easy. Jazz musicians play the job in the honored tradition of show business. The show must go on. A while back at Stanford—which, incidentally, is the only university ever to offer a full year of jazz programs for students— the John Handy Quintet was playing. Suddenly, the bass player became ill, in the middle of the number, before his solo was due. The solo was taken by the alto saxophonist, while the bass player finished the number merely keeping time. An intermission was called and after ten minutes in the open air outside, the musicians returned and completed the program with a performance which brought a standing ovation.

Performing under stress and adverse conditions goes on in night clubs night after night. Jazz musicians play when their bodies have all but collapsed. Errol Garner recorded one of his greatest albums with one finger in a splint, held out above the piano keys like a pencil. Most musicians play through the evening on hot, cramped "stages," with smoke and foul air filling their lungs.

A few anecdotes from the world of jazz will serve most adequately to give a feel for this performing art. At the Monterey Jazz Festival a few years ago, J. J. Johnson, a trombonist, conducted a tremendously inspiring work which he had written for orchestra and trombone and scored himself. Earlier, at rehearsals the musicians who had been added to the orchestra for the occasion from the San Francisco Symphony, had been surprised to discover that Johnson had accomplished the feat of scoring his work without knowing the elementary short cuts which a formal training in composition teaches. Obviously, he had never had the opportunity to learn them, so they had showed him the tricks during the prefestival rehearsals.

Woody Herman, at the end of the Forties, recorded Igor Stravinsky's *Ebony Concerto*. It had been written especially for Herman by the composer, and Stravinsky rehearsed the Herman band for the premiere performance at Carnegie Hall. When the rehearsal was over, Stravinsky, amazed by the virtuosity of the men, said to Herman, "If only I had an orchestra like that!" Numerous jazz artists are without peer on their instruments in the whole world of music.

Some years ago, following a memorable jazz concert at the Hollywood Bowl, pianist André Previn was approached by Lukas Foss, a composer of modern classical music, who inquired whether the musicians had rehearsed the performance for a long time. When Previn said, "No," Foss asked, "But, surely, you had it all worked out?" He was aghast when Previn said, "No, it wasn't worked out at all. We made the music right up there on the spot during the performance." "But what a chance you are taking," Foss continued. "Sometimes it must be terrible." And Previn agreed. Sometimes a performance is great and sometimes it is terrible. Such alternatives are inherent in the whole concept of spontaneous improvisation, and the product of creativity, as in many another field, may be superb in one case and leave much to be desired in another.

Duke Ellington, whose concert of sacred music at Grace Cathedral in 1965 was one of San Francisco's cultural highlights for the year, has long subsidized his orchestra from his royalties and other earnings. Ellington calls the orchestra his instrument. He uses it and he needs it, he says, to hear the music he writes. And this whole musical "workshop"—this great composer and his orchestra —rattles around the world in airplanes and buses, playing night clubs, dances, concerts, and TV shows, with Ellington working all the while in dressing rooms and hotel rooms, late into the night. The new compositions resulting are then heard soon after as they are tested by the Duke's complex instrument. If we really understood what jazz musicians are doing or "saying" through their music, if we appreciated what they are contributing to the art and culture of the world, if we accepted the contributions of this basic American music, we would subsidize a man like Ellington as a national treasure.

INFLUENCES ON THE JAZZ MUSICIAN

The jazz musician is an individualist, a highly creative individualist, though he borrows and learns from all sources. For example, the Indian musicians Ali Akbar Kan and Ravi Shankar have had a tremendous influence on jazz in recent years. The works of men like Bach, Bartok, Stravinsky, and some recent European composers have had varying influences on jazz, largely because the great jazz musicians, free of academic restrictions and following their creative instincts, go where their ears lead them and listen to everything. Many jazz musicians are familiar with the broad canvas of the world's music, unlike classical musicians, whose insularity usually excludes a knowledge of jazz. Being less restricted in his whole approach and response to music and having sought a great variety of listening experiences, the jazz musician is freer to experiment and to bring new sounds and forms of expression into his performance. This has been generally true from the beginning of jazz. It is no accident, for example, that the saxophone, a bastard instrument which has not yet been assimilated into so-called serious music, has risen to such heights in jazz. The trumpet in jazz, ever since the rise of Louis Armstrong, has been used to do things that the trumpet is not supposed to be able to do. These "extensions" result in part from the freedom of the musician and his need to explore his musical medium and to follow his ear.

Jazz has operated under a great handicap in America from the time of its beginning in the South. It is Negro music, and the Negro has always been treated as a second-class citizen. In Europe, jazz received a wide reception and was more generally appreciated long before it was recognized here because the European ear was not stopped by color. European composers today are working with advanced jazz sounds and jazz ideas, and some musicians like John Lewis of the Modern Jazz Quartet insist that the only truly imaginative and vital compositional music today is coming from Europe. Lewis also believes that American classical music will die unless it opens its ears and its performance to jazz. This is a radical idea, but some truth may be in it. Jazz musicians can and do play in symphony orchestras, frequently in brass and reed sections and sometimes in other sections. However, very few classically trained musicians are of any use at all in most jazz performances.

Lou Gottlieb, a jazz-oriented graduate of the University of California's music department, once wrote that when the first great American composer came on the scene, he would be a jazz musician or, at least, a musician familiar with jazz. I would go quite a way beyond Gottlieb's conjecture. I think that the great American composers are already with us, that they are on the scene now, and that they are represented in such jazz musicians as Duke Ellington, Miles Davis, Charles Parker, and Charles Mingus. The music these men produce is the music that lives throughout the modern world, and it carries the sense of the American people to the world. I also believe that it is the American music that will last.

The great jazz artists have done what they have done with very little help, if any, from the established educational system. These accomplishments are far superior to the products of the established educational apparatus. Most university music departments are producing performers and teachers whose compositions are written, played, and heard only by other music-department graduates. Jazz has moved the center of gravity in this art outside the academy completely.

It is challenging to contemplate what might be the result of some active, planned effort to encourage, rather than to discourage, the musically creative youth in our society. It is of interest to speculate what might be the result if "jazz education" were brought within the walls of our better high schools and colleges. It may be explosive to reconsider and to design appropriate educational experiences for truly creative youth in any form of art or in any educational discipline.

IV

The Creative Student
and Academic Standards

7

SELECTING STUDENTS
WITH CREATIVE POTENTIAL

Donald W. MacKinnon

If colleges are to educate for creativity, two basic conditions must be met: They must admit students who have creative potential, and they must provide those students with the intellectual environment and the educational experiences that will develop whatever creative potential they possess. Is it true, as many people believe, that today neither of these two conditions, so crucial for education for creativity, is being met by American colleges and universities?

     This chapter asks whether, and to what extent, colleges today are meeting the first of these conditions—that is, admitting those students whose talents best qualify them to profit from curricula and educational programs designed to nurture the development of creative potential. The question as to whether the curricula and educational programs of most colleges are optimally designed today to educate for creativity, as well as ways in which they might conceivably be improved, are discussed in Chapters 9, 10, and 11.

Are colleges and universities refusing admission to large numbers of students who are especially creative or likely to become creative if they are privileged to have a college education? Unfortunately, it is impossible to say whether this is true, nor do we have reliable data from which firm conclusions can be drawn. We do have the continuing concern that admissions practices may be working an injustice in individual cases and also a mounting fear that the number of cases in which injustice is done may well be on the increase.

If we do not have the facts about the number of potentially creative students who are not admitted to college, we, nevertheless, do have an increasing body of research data which suggest that highly creative youths, as well as youths with creative potential, are not always those whose academic records insure their admission to college. It is not surprising, then, that college admissions officers are questioning their policies as never before.

The general practice has been to select and admit students on the basis of their academic records, performance on aptitude and achievement tests, good citizenship, and leadership potential, though there are certain notable exceptions, of course. In some large state-university and college systems, the only criterion for admission has been graduation from high school or graduation with some minimum grade-point average or a specified level of performance on a scholastic-aptitude test. Private institutions, especially the smaller ones, have paid more attention to individual cases, with the possibility of greater flexibility in applying the rules. Sons and daughters of important alumni and outstanding high school athletes who do not meet the usual standards have been welcomed in the past by many colleges and, in many instances, even recruited. But now, increasingly, the value to the college, and ultimately to society, of such exceptions is being questioned.

If exceptions *are* to be made in admissions practices, some would ask whether it would not be better to make exceptions for

students who, although their academic records and measured apti-
tudes and achievements leave something to be desired, have already
manifested creative behavior or shown signs of creative potential.
But the skeptic might well counter this suggestion by asking how
one can justify the admission of a student with some creative promise if he cannot or will not measure up to the academic requirements of the college which admits him. This question is all the more
germane since such an "exception" might well be made at the expense of some other student whose record leaves nothing to be desired in terms of academic achievement. The skeptic might also ask
what the reliable signs of creative potential are in a student applying for admission to college. What is the guarantee that such creative potential, *provided it can be identified,* will ever be realized?
Finally the skeptic might well question whether colleges—considering their present shockingly high rates of attrition—can afford to
admit students who, regardless of their creative potential or demonstrated creativity, have shown neither an interest in nor motivation
for conventional academic achievement.

These are matters of policy which every college and university must determine for itself. The basic question is, of course, for
what purpose does the college wish to select a student? I shall assume that colleges do not want to bar from admission students of
creative potential but instead wish to seek them out so that their
creativity may be encouraged and their creative potential developed.

Substantial evidence garnered from many studies indicates
that the best predictors of academic achievement in college are high
school grades and scores on scholastic-aptitude tests. If, on the other
hand, one wishes to predict creative achievement in college in both
artistic and scientific fields of endeavor, the best predictor is creative
achievement—either artistic or scientific—during the high school
years or even earlier. Our own studies of highly creative persons in
a variety of fields (MacKinnon *et al.,* 1961) have yielded congruent
findings: As students, they were, in general, not distinguished for
the grades they received, and in none of the samples did their high
school grade-point average show any significant correlation with
their subsequently achieved and recognized creativeness. Further,
the productive achievement of our highly creative subjects was not

something first manifested in college or afterwards; earlier accomplishments prepared for and, in a sense, predicted it.

If high school grades and scholastic aptitude scores are not good predictors of nonacademic creative accomplishment during the undergraduate years, are they any better as predictors of creative achievement *after* college? By now there is plenty of evidence that college grades are generally poor predictors of achievement or success in later life (Price, Taylor, and Richards, 1964; Taylor, Smith, and Ghiselin, 1963; Richards, Taylor, and Price, 1962) or are, at best, only inefficient predictors (Taylor, 1963). In our own investigations, college grades, in general, have not been predictive of later creativity. Indeed, the college grade-point average of a group of research scientists correlated low and negatively (−.19) with their later rated creativity as scientists. Only in the case of architects did college grades predict significantly (−.27) their subsequently rated creativeness, probably because so much of their graded work in college—the solution of design problems and the like—is exactly what they do in their architectural practice. But even in this sample the most creative architects were not generally *A* students. They averaged about *B*. They were not poor students or lazy; rather, they were extraordinarily independent as students, turning in an *A* performance in work and courses that caught their interest, but doing little or no work at all in courses that failed to stir their imagination. This suggests that if we really wish to select for creative potential we should pay more attention to patterns of low and high grades or grade records that improve as the student advances in his major field, as well as to nonacademic creative achievements during the undergraduate years. Also, we should give somewhat less weight to mere grade-point averages when selecting students for advanced graduate work.

However, with more students applying each year for admission to graduate schools, admissions committees are placing increasing emphasis on undergraduate grade-point averages and scholastic-aptitude test scores. This is true despite the considerable evidence that undergraduate grades are generally poor predictors of success in life and despite our uncertainty as to what, if anything, scholastic-aptitude test scores predict. The most widely used tests of scholastic aptitude for graduate work are those of the Graduate Record Examination. A reviewer of these tests in the *Sixth Mental Measurements Yearbook of 1965* writes:

> The paucity of validity information is especially unfortunate. In the present atmosphere, critics of testing are bound to ask whether an aptitude test is appropriate or necessary for applicants who have recorded sixteen years or so of school achievement and taken a number of similar tests in the process. Other more sympathetic critics may well wonder at the lack of continuing exploration and appraisal of a variety of factors in graduate performance, some of which they might suspect are more accessible and more important than scholastic aptitude for differentiating applicants (French, 1965, p. 729).

Reviewing findings similar to those I have presented, Holland and Richards conclude:

> . . . [Such data] imply a need to examine grading practices, since a college education should be largely a preparation for life, both in the community and in a vocation. Under current grading practices a college education is mainly preparation for more education in graduate school.
>
> . . . If a sponsor is interested only in finding students who will do well in the classroom in college, then high school grades and tests of academic potential are the best techniques available. On the other hand, if the sponsor wishes to find college students who will do outstanding things outside the classroom and in later life, then he should continue to make an effort to secure a better record of the student's competencies and achievement in high school.
>
> . . . National surveys concerned with the conservation of talent, since they use tests of academic potential almost exclusively, probably present a grossly inaccurate picture of the loss of talent for "real life"—that is, non-classroom—accomplishment (1965, pp. 22–23).

In seeking to correct the imbalance in past and current admissions practices, it is important that we not simply substitute a new imbalance for the old. Holland and Richards caution, ". . . We should not make the same mistake that purveyors of aptitude and intelligence have made in the past; that is, to rely on only one kind of measure and to exclude others (p. 21)." We should not assume that nonintellective factors solely determine creative performance.

In earlier studies at the Institute of Personality Assessment and Research on the relation of intelligence to creativity, essentially no relationship was found between these variables. Taking scores on the Terman Concept Mastery Test (Terman, 1956) as measures of intelligence, the researchers found that the correlation of intelligence with creativity in a sample of architects was −.08, and −.07 in a sample of research scientists. As a result, I suggested (1962 b, p. 493) that we may have overestimated in our educational system the role of intelligence in creative achievement. I pointed out, however, that no feebleminded subjects had shown up in any of our creative groups.

Over the whole range of intelligence and creativity, there is undoubtedly a positive relationship between these two variables. But, of course, no college population represents the whole range of intelligence, and, within that limited range, how crucial are differences in intelligence for differences in creativity? My conclusion from the studies was that, above a certain minimum level required for mastery of a field, being more intelligent does not guarantee a corresponding increase in creativeness. It simply is not true that the more intelligent person is necessarily the more creative one. We would be foolish to select students who have the lowest scores on intelligence tests for admission to college, but, on the other hand, we clearly are deluding ourselves when we favor one student over another solely on the grounds that he scores some ten to twenty points higher on some measure of intelligence.

In 1962 I cautioned against "setting the cutting point for selection on the intellective dimension too high." Today I would caution against setting it too low, for in some quarters there has been a misunderstanding of my earlier writing. The range of scores for creative architects on the Terman Concept Mastery Test was, to be sure, from a low of 39 to a high of 179; and, in another place, I did report (1962 a) that in a study of independent inventors the individual who held more patents than anyone else in the group—in fact, held more patents than any of our creative research scientists working in industry—earned a score of 6! Nevertheless, I hastened to point out that these were arbitrary or raw scores on the test and not IQs, but this fact, I am afraid, has sometimes been ignored.

One difficulty with scores on the Terman Concept Mastery Test has been the impossibility of converting them to IQs. To fill this gap in our knowledge, we have returned subsequently to our architects, mathematicians, and research scientists and administered to as many as were willing to cooperate the Wechsler Adult Intelligence Scale (Wechsler, 1955). The most thoroughly standardized test of adult intelligence, WAIS yields three measures of the IQ: a verbal IQ, a performance IQ, and an overall or full-scale IQ. This study is still in progress, but the results to date confirm the earlier finding from our samples of no relationship between intelligence and manifest creativity. I shall report here only on the full-scale IQ measures.

We have divided the samples of architects and research scientists into three subsamples, ranging from the most creative to the least creative. Each sample of mathematicians, one male and one female, has been divided into two groups, a creative group and a comparison group. At this point, our most striking finding is the lack of any significant difference in IQ among the subsamples characterized by different levels of creativeness. The mean IQs for the three groups of architects are 132, 131, and 130; for the research scientists, 132, 132, and 132; for the male mathematicians, 135 and 133; and for the female mathematicians, 129 and 133. The ranges of IQs are similarly comparable from subsample to subsample: for architects, 120–145, 117–142, and 119–143; for research scientists, 120–141, 121–142, and 114–142; for male mathematicians, 118–152 and 126–138; and for female mathematicians, 118–140 and 118–145.

The results so far are clear: Careers in such demanding fields as architecture, mathematics, and scientific research would seem to require an IQ level approaching 120. Although the range of intelligence for 140 persons in these professions is from 114 to 152, only one has an IQ above 145 and only two have IQs below

118. In other words, 98 per cent have IQs in the range of 118 to 140. The range of IQs and the mean level of IQ are not significantly different for subgroups whose levels of creative performance vary markedly. Further evidence from the sample of architects indicates that, above a certain minimum level, a higher IQ does not guarantee a corresponding increase in creativeness. In this group, WAIS IQs correlate with creativity +.19 (not quite significant at the 10 per cent level of confidence).

While many vocations may require less intelligence than architecture, mathematics, and scientific research, I believe our findings should make us think twice before concluding that by markedly lowering the level of intelligence required for college admission we shall be admitting large numbers of students with outstanding creative potential. We can, I believe, maximize the probability of admitting students with creative potential to college and to graduate training, but not if we merely replace intelligence tests with tests of personality. We must supplement intelligence and aptitude tests with independent measures of extracurricular achievement and originality and, if additional checks are to be used, with tests that tap those traits and motivational dispositions which have been shown to be positively related to creative striving and creative achievement.

I am not proposing, however, that we administer a battery of so-called tests of creativity to our applicants. In recent years, Guilford (1959) has worked on the structure of intellect, through factor analyses, and has identified several dimensions of creative thinking. His identification of divergent thinking and such creative thinking factors as adaptive flexibility, originality, and sensitivity to problems has led to the widespread hope that his tests for creative ability might provide us with reliable means for identifying creative persons. So far, however, this hope has not been realized.

In an intensive study of research scientists in the United States Air Force (Taylor, Smith, Ghiselin, and Ellison, 1961), Guilford's tests of creativity failed to predict the criterion. In our own studies, these same tests have likewise shown essentially zero correlations with the criterion. In view of such negative findings, the use of Guilford's tests for creative potential would be questionable, to say the least.

The problem is not that tests of this sort fail to tap the kind of psychological processes involved in creative thought, requiring, as they do, that the subject think of unusual uses for common objects or the consequences of unusual events. The problem, rather, is that they fail to reveal the extent to which a person faced with a real-life problem is likely to come up with novel and flexible solutions, which he will be motivated to apply in all of their ramifications. Much more promising as self-report predictors of future creative performance are autobiographical questions concerning past and present interests, activities, competencies, and achievements—such as are found, for example, in the American College Testing Program.

In a provocative paper, Gough (1965) has called attention to three misplaced emphases in college admissions: overemphasis on test-demonstrated intelligence, underemphasis on nonintellectual determinants of achievement, and overemphasis on the "one true path to grace"—grades. I believe that each of these misplaced emphases almost certainly militates against the admission to college of those students who fail to meet the conventional criteria of high grade-point averages and high aptitude-test scores—students who on other grounds, however, could well be thought to show creative promise.

In addition to our own demonstration of zero correlation between scores on the Terman Concept Mastery Test and the judged creativeness of architects and research scientists, Getzels and Jackson (1962) and Torrance (1962) have reported similar findings of essentially no relationship between IQ measures and measures of creative behavior.

At the University of Michigan, nearly ten years after Kelly's and Fiske's (1951) study of the graduate students in clinical psychology, Kelly and Goldberg (1959) found that scores on the Miller Analogies Test (MAT) earned at the time of admission to graduate training correlated only +.16 with attainment versus nonattainment of the Ph.D. degree, +.16 with the criterion of scholarly productivity (number of publications), and +.10 with the combined criterion of academic success plus satisfaction with their choice of clinical psychology as a profession.

In Gough's (1965) own study of psychology graduate students at the University of California, Berkeley, he found a correlation of +.21 between MAT scores and faculty ratings and a correlation of +.02 between MAT scores and the criterion of survival versus dropping out of the program.

Although the Medical College Admissions Test (MCAT) continues to be used by almost all American medical schools in their selection of students, clear evidence indicates either low validity or no validity in predicting performance in medical school or later medical practice. In a comprehensive survey of research with the MCAT, Gough, Hall, and Harris (1963) have shown that the test does a poor job of differentiating between graduates and dropouts and that its correlations with scholastic achievement in medical school drop from a typical coefficient of +.18 with first-year grades to +.07 with fourth-year grades.

Evidence can be garnered from many studies beyond the few typical ones reported here that the widespread confidence in the ability of intelligence tests, admissions tests, and aptitude tests to predict scholastic achievement—let alone creative productivity—is badly misplaced. Yet such tests continue to be used widely in deciding who will and who will not go to college.

There are many studies illustrating Gough's second point, that college admissions continues to underemphasize nonintellectual determinants of achievement. Our own studies of creative persons are rich in such illustrative material.

In an early study of graduate students, Gough (1953) has reported the following finding (repeatedly confirmed in subsequent studies of other groups): those individuals who are rated high on originality or score high on a composite measure of originality (Barron, 1955) reveal a characteristic pattern of scores on certain scales of the Strong Vocational Interest Blank (Strong, 1959). From sample to sample of highly creative persons, some slight variation occurs, but the general pattern is this: relatively high scores on such scales as psychologist, author-journalist, lawyer, architect, artist, and musician and relatively low scores on such scales as purchasing agent, office man, banker, farmer, veterinarian, policeman, and mortician.

If distinctive patterns of interest are indicative of originality and creative potential, one might imagine that creative persons would also show a pattern of values different from that of their less creative peers—and they do. On the Allport-Vernon-Lindzey (1951) Study of Values, all the creative groups we at the Institute have studied tend to prize most highly the theoretical and aesthetic values.

Even on the MMPI, or the Minnesota Multiphasic Personality Inventory (Hathaway and McKinley, 1945), creative males tend to show a rather distinctive profile: the highest elevation on the Mf (femininity) scale, some five to ten points above the mean on the clinical scales of the Inventory, and a relatively high score on the ego-strength scale. The high score on femininity is indicative of sensitivity, openness to inner experience, and femininity of interests; the above-average scores on the clinical scale doubtless indicate some phychic turbulence; and the relatively high score in ego strength implies a capacity to tolerate and express effectively the richness of inner life, the anxiety, and the psychic turbulence that the subject experiences.

On the California Psychological Inventory (Gough, 1964), several possible patterns of scores usually indicate more than an average amount of creative potential. One of the simplest, but one of the most characteristic patterns, is the Ai-Ac discrepancy—that is to say, a relatively high score on Ai (achievement via independence) which is higher than a still relatively high score on Ac (achievement via conformance). Such a pattern identifies an individual who is motivated to achieve in situations that call for independence in thought and action but who is less inclined to strive for achievement in settings where conforming behavior is expected or required.

At the Institute, one of our most striking and most consistent findings in the realm of nonintellectual functioning is that both creative and potentially creative persons show a clear perceptual preference for the complex and asymmetrical rather than for the simple and symmetrical. Such a preference, which can be interpreted as indicative of the subject's being challenged by disorder and incompleteness, is revealed on the Barron-Welsh Art Scale (Barron and Welsh, 1952) in the Welsh Figure Preference Test (Welsh, 1959) and on the MMPI's special scale that measures a preference for perceptual complexity.

One would expect creative and potentially creative persons to be characterized by a cognitive style different from that of less creative persons. On the Myers-Briggs Type Indicator (Myers, 1962), a test of cognitive styles based largely on Carl G. Jung's (1923) theory of psychological functions and types, creative persons tend to show a preference for the perceptual and intuitive modes. As between perceiving (becoming aware of something, experiencing the new) and judging (judging and evaluating one's experience), creative persons are on the side of perception, although they, like everyone else, both perceive and judge. In their perceptions they also show a preference for intuition rather than for sensation, which focuses upon the immediate sensory aspects of experience. In other words, they react to the deeper meanings and possibilities inherent in their perceptions and are alert to the links and bridges between what is present and that which is not yet thought of. The perceptive mode makes for a life that is flexible and spontaneous, rich and varied. The intuitive mode makes one alert to possibilities, to what may be. And the perceptual and intuitive modes are the preferred modes of the creative person.

In our studies, one of the most valuable nonintellective indicators of creative potential has proved to be a person's concept of himself, that is, his self-image or his self-percept. A test ideally suited to reveal a person's picture of himself because of its simplicity of administration and the richness of its yield is the Gough Adjective Check List (Gough, 1960; Gough and Heilbrun, 1965; MacKinnon, 1963). On this test, which presents the subjects with 300 adjectives, the only instruction is for the individual to check those words which describe himself. Creative subjects check words which are quite different from those indicated by less creative persons as self-descriptions. The test also yields scores on twenty-four different personological and motivational dispositions, many of which have proved to be valuable indicators of creative potential (MacKinnon, 1963).

The almost total neglect of such nonintellectual determinants of creative achievement in selecting students for college is a striking confirmation of Gough's charge that there has been an underemphasis on these factors in college admissions.

Whether one would wish to administer the above-described battery of tests, or even a selection of them, to students applying for admission to college, graduate study, or professional training is a moot question. But one can hardly doubt that, in assessing an individual's ability to profit from undergraduate or graduate training, an admissions officer should pay attention to where the student stands on these clearly relevant dimensions of nonintellectual functioning. If attention were paid to such factors, I think it safe to predict that the selection of students for admission to college and graduate school would be greatly improved. In addition, the third misplaced emphasis that Gough attributes to college admissions would be removed. The overemphasis on the one true path to grace would end. Students admitted to college and graduate school would no longer be limited almost entirely to the good-grade getters and the high-scorers on achievement and aptitude tests. But once again I would stress that, while attending to the important but previously overlooked nonintellective determinants of creative achievement, the college should continue to obtain as full a picture as possible of the standing of the student on the also relevant intellective determinants of personal effectiveness.

REFERENCES

Allport, G. W., Vernon, P. E., & Lindzey, G. *Study of Values: Manual of directions.* (Rev. ed.) Boston: Houghton Mifflin, 1951.

Barron, F. The disposition toward originality. *Journal of Abnormal and Social Psychology,* 1955, *51,* 478–485.

Barron, F., & Welsh, G. S. Artistic perception as a possible factor in personality style: Its measurement by a figure preference test. *Journal of Psychology,* 1952, *33,* 199–203.

French, R. L. Review of the graduate record examinations aptitude test. In O. K. Buros (Ed.), *Sixth Mental Measurements Yearbook.* Highland Park, N. J.: Gryphon Press, 1965, 728–730.

Getzels, J. W., & Jackson, P. W. *Creativity and intelligence.* New York: Wiley, 1962.

Gough, H. G. *Some theoretical problems in the construction of practical assessment devices for early identification of high-level talent.* Berkeley: University of California, Institute of Personality Assessment and Research, 1953. (Mimeographed.)

Gough, H. G. The Adjective Check List as a personality assessment research technique. *Psychological Reports,* 1960, *6,* 107–122.

Gough, H. G. *California Psychological Inventory manual.* (Rev. ed.) Palo Alto, Calif.: Consulting Psychologists Press, 1964.

Gough, H. G. Misplaced emphases in admissions. *Journal of College Student Personnel,* 1965, *6, 3,* 130–135.

Gough, H. G., Hall, W. B., & Harris, R. E. Admissions procedures as forecasters of performance in medical training. *Journal of Medical Education,* 1963, *38,* 983–998.

Gough, H. G., & Heilbrun, A. B., Jr. *Adjective Check List manual.* Palo Alto, Calif.: Consulting Psychologists Press, 1965.

Guilford, J. P. Three faces of intellect. *American Psychologist,* 1959, *14,* 469–479.

Hathaway, S. R., & McKinley, J. C. *Minnesota Multiphasic Personality Inventory.* New York: Psychological Corporation, 1945.

Holland, J. L., & Richards, J. M. Academic and non-academic accomplishment: Correlated or uncorrelated. *ACT Research Reports,* April 1965, No. 2.

Jung, C. G. *Psychological types.* New York: Harcourt, 1923.

Kelly, E. L., & Fiske, D. W. *The prediction of performance in clinical psychology.* Ann Arbor: University of Michigan Press, 1951.

Kelly, E. L., & Goldberg, L. R. Correlates of later performance and specialization in psychology. *Psychological Monographs,* 1959, *73,* No. 12 (Whole No. 482).

MacKinnon, D. W. Intellect and motive in scientific inventors: Implications for supply. In *The rate and direction of inventive activity: Economic and social factors.* A conference of the universities—National Bureau Committee for Economic Research and the Committee on Economic Growth of the Social Science Research Council. Princeton: Princeton University Press, 1962, 361–378. (a)

MacKinnon, D. W. The nature and nurture of creative talent. *American Psychologist,* 1962, *17,* 484–495. (b)

MacKinnon, D. W. Creativity and images of the self. In R. W. White (Ed.), *The study of lives.* New York: Atherton Press, 1963, 251–278.

MacKinnon, D. W., *et al. Proceedings of the conference on "The creative person."* Berkeley: University of California, University Extension, 1961.

Myers, I. B. *Myers-Briggs Type Indicator manual.* Princeton: Educational Testing Service, 1962.

Price, P. B., Taylor, C. W., Richards, J. M., Jr., & Jacobsen, T. L. Measurement of physician performance. *Journal of Medical Education,* 1964, *39,* 203–211.

Richards, J. M., Jr., Taylor, C. W., & Price, P. B. The prediction of medical intern performance. *Journal of Applied Psychology,* 1962, *46,* 142–146.

Strong, E. K., Jr. *Manual for Strong Vocational Interest Blanks for Men and Women, revised blanks, (form M and W).* Palo Alto, Calif.: Consulting Psychologists Press, 1959.

Taylor, C. W., Smith, W. R., Ghiselin, B., & Ellison, R. Explorations in the measurement and prediction of contributions of one sample of scientists. *Report ASD-TR-61-96.* Lackland Air Force Base, Texas: Aeronautical Systems Divisions, Personnel Laboratory, April 1961.

Taylor, C. W., Smith, W. R., & Ghiselin, B. The creative and other contributions of one sample of research scientists. In C. W. Taylor & F. Barron (Eds.), *Scientific creativity: Its recognition and development.* New York: Wiley, 1963, 53–76.

Taylor, C. W. Variables related to creativity and productivity among men in two research laboratories. In C. W. Taylor & F. Barron (Eds.), *Scientific creativity: Its recognition and development.* New York: Wiley, 1963, 228–250.

Terman, L. M. *Concept Mastery Test, Form T manual.* New York: Psychological Corporation, 1956.

Torrance, E. P. Highly intelligent and highly creative children in a laboratory school (Explorations in creative thinking in the early school years, No. 6). *Research Memo* BER-59-7. Minneapolis: Bureau of Educational Research, University of Minnesota, 1959.

Torrance, E. P. *Guiding creative talent.* Englewood Cliffs, N. J.: Prentice-Hall, 1962.

Wechsler, D. *Manual for the Wechsler Adult Intelligence Scale.*
    New York: Psychological Corporation, 1955.
Welsh, G. S. *Welsh Figure Preference Test: Preliminary manual.*
    Palo Alto, Calif.: Consulting Psychologists Press, 1959.

8

THE CREATIVE STUDENT
AND THE GRADING SYSTEM

Joseph Axelrod

. . . Society will need a greater number of flexible, creative people with highly developed human potential and intellectual power. . . . The educational system will have to assume a primary responsibility for fostering this kind of human development.

These words express one of the major theses in a recent study by Trent and Medsker (1967, p. 21) and also constitute a basic tenet of this book. The thesis of this chapter is that the educational system will not be able to fulfill the primary responsibility that Trent and Medsker believe it must carry unless there is drastic modification or elimination of the standard grading system. After first considering

117

the reasons for the present dissatisfaction with the grading system, we shall present an analysis of the grading system as a harmful agent, both directly and indirectly, in the education of the creative student.

Distrust of the common assumptions behind the standard grading system has sharply increased in recent years on American campuses. The evidence shows that both students and faculty have lost faith in traditional grading practices. A study involving over 2,500 Berkeley students indicates that half of the respondents did not believe grades reflected even "fairly well" an individual's accomplishments in a course. Surprisingly, even the students with the highest grade-point average—that is, those who were most rewarded by the grading system—did not think well of it. The *Muscatine Report* voices particular concern about the opinion of this honors group, "When two-fifths of an honors level student sample expressed such significant disbelief in the system which rewarded them, it is surely time to reconsider not only the grading system itself, but the increasing emphasis which we are pressed to place upon it (1966, p. 95)."

The attitude of many "successful" college graduates toward the grading system—the criterion of success being acceptance by a prestige graduate school—is reflected in an interview with a Stanford premedical student who later gained admittance to one of the country's top medical schools. In response to a question about the things that annoyed him in his undergraduate years, the student said:

The system at Stanford as far as grades go . . . I don't think these things are conducive academically . . . I've talked to professors about this and they don't seem to know any other ways . . . But I think without grades I could have done a lot more in school than I did . . . It's a funny thing—you have to decide whether you're going to play the game. And if you want to go to medical school, for instance—Even if I had these beliefs that I *wasn't* going to study for grades and all, I'd still have to play the game and get good grades, or else my application would come in with another guy's whose grades are a little better . . . so I am sort of being forced into playing a game which I was not sure I really liked—in fact, I *know* that I didn't want to play (Korn, 1967, p. 285).

Countless cases of such individual complaints can be cited. But what is even more important is the increase in group protest on American campuses about courses and grades. In Peterson's (1966) 1964–1965 survey of 849 accredited four-year institutions, 27 per cent of the colleges reported that student protests had taken place over issues involving courses, tests, and grades. The same survey showed 38 per cent of the colleges reporting student protests over the issue of civil rights; and Joseph Katz, in citing these data, comments that while students in 1964–1965 appeared to be "mobilized in larger numbers over political issues than over education ones," he and his colleagues at the Institute for the Study of Human Problems believe the trend is now moving the other way: "It seems that larger numbers of students have become involved in educational issues and that these students are more representative of the broad mass of students (1967, p. 574)."

Student dissatisfaction with grades is coming to be more and more outspoken. Many students express the belief that the entire grading system is a "joke" which they could not possibly take seriously were it not for its effect on draft status and entrance to graduate school. Thus, the following comment about the grading system, which appeared in the spring 1967 *Supplement to the General Catalog* issued by the Associated Students of the University of California, Berkeley, is typical of a large segment of student opinion: "If the consequences of this system were not so potentially serious for you (draft board, graduate school, etc.), it could be regarded as somewhat farcical. . . . After all the proposals for reform in grading during the Muscatine Committee's deliberations, we are left with the same iniquitous system (Morton, 1967, p. 7)." It is not only the students who are dissatisfied with the grading system but also the faculty. Most faculty members reading the *Muscatine Report* would certainly feel some empathy with the professor who testified, "Grading is a nightmare. I have found that I cannot mark with any pretense in fairness several hundred essays in the time allotted me. . . .

I have therefore taken to objective examinations demanding factual answers, which I dislike extremely but consider less unfair than badly market essays (Muscatine, 1966, p. 96)."

With faculty and students expressing such dissatisfaction, it is perhaps astonishing that the movement toward reform in the grading system has been so meager. Reduction of the five letter grades to two (*Pass* and *Fail*) has been introduced at a number of colleges during recent years; but except for a few campuses, the *Pass-Fail* option is used on so restricted a basis that it constitutes almost no reform at all. Even where it is being more widely used—for example, for all courses during the freshman year—it seems to be far from the breakthrough which many dissatisfied faculty have been awaiting on the grading problem.

The newest version of the *Pass-Fail* system of grading is, by the way, significant enough to be mentioned here. Its uniqueness lies in the fact that each course carries variable-unit credit. For each course, the student receives either a zero (i.e., no credit) or any number of credits from one to six. When it opened in the fall of 1967, the College of Creative Studies at the University of California in Santa Barbara adopted this variable-unit credit system and explained it as follows in its brochure: "A student may plan to do only 3 (or 1 or 2 or 4 or 5) units of work for the course by arrangement with the instructor; but in every case the instructor reserves the right to make the final determination of the unit value of the student's work in the course. Each unit of credit is counted toward graduation: 180 units of credit (under the quarter system) will qualify the student for graduation." Such developments are not to be minimized; they should, however, not blind us to the fact that very little reform in the grading system has taken place in recent years, except on a handful of campuses in the nation.

Some of the reasons are quite clear. For one thing, selective-service classification of students, along with its tie-in with grades, has made it difficult for faculties to consider tampering with the system. Two strong interlocking pressures—the draft and admission standards at the upper-division level and in graduate schools—have been powerful forces in maintaining the status quo. A second reason is also clear: Dissatisfied as faculty members may be with the present system, the Berkeley study shows how difficult it is to attain agreement on any system to replace it (Muscatine, 1966). A third reason, which will be discussed presently, can be found in the intimate relationship between standard teaching procedures and the traditional grading system. In another paper (Axelrod, 1967), I tried to show that since these two elements are part of a single "system," any attempt to reform one must be accompanied by appropriate changes in the other; otherwise, the reform will undergo gradual but continuous erosion until it disappears. Thus, like a healthy but foreign organ rejected by a body that needs it, a reform in grading has not succeeded on some campuses, and other campuses are understandably cautious.

RELATIONSHIP OF GRADES TO ACHIEVEMENT AND TALENT

Research findings clearly justify the distrust which both faculty and students have expressed toward the traditional grading system. Course grades have not been found to constitute a reliable index to any dimension—past, present, or future—of a student's work or life, except other school grades. All the data confirm the view, stated in *The American College* (Webster, Freedman, and Heist, 1962, pp. 816–817), that a student's grade-point average is an inadequate measure of educational growth; see also the studies by P. B. Price, J. M. Richards, and C. W. Taylor cited in Chapter 7.

If course grades in general do not accurately reflect educational growth, the relationship between grades and creativity is even more distant. In Brown's discussion of his Vassar study, in which the faculty nominated ideal students, he cites the work of Getzels, who goes so far as to maintain that both high scores on standard tests and high course grades result more from narrowness and conformism than from original and creative thinking. Commenting on this observation, Brown states, "In fact, creativity is penalized since the creative student is apt to give a highly original meaning to the question which in a machine-scored test or in the presence of a 'by the book' teacher will not be scored correctly or appreciatively (1962, p. 539)."

In Brown's own study, the faculty members at Vassar nominated sixty-seven students as "ideal," indicating in each case the basis for their choice. The nominees were classified according to their grade average, with a score corresponding to an $A-$ as the dividing point. Fifty-seven per cent of the nominees were above this dividing line and 43 per cent below. (The study was repeated the next year with about the same proportions above and below the $A-$ line.) To be nominated, a student apparently had to be in the upper half of his class but clearly did not have to be of A calibre. Indeed, Brown (p. (542) reports that in some instances, though negative nominations were not requested, faculty members indicated why they had not selected some students with unusually high averages. In these cases, according to the teachers, "the grades were achieved by techniques of manipulation, overconformity, or brute effort without any saving grace or real intellectual interest."

In Miller's (1967) review of the literature on this subject, every study he cites, with one exception, shows that grades and creativity are not positively related. The single exception is a study of engineering graduates from Purdue University; here, there is a significant relation between engineering graduates who register patents and their college grades. Data on other groups show that students who receive the better academic ratings turn out, according to their scores on personality tests, to be more conforming, compulsive, rigid, and insecure than the students receiving the lower ratings. According to Miller, the sets of personality traits for achievers and for creative students have radically different configurations.

The causes for this phenomenon are undoubtedly complex. But one fairly direct and observable cause is quite clear. The more creative and the more independent a student is, the more attention he demands from his professor. Most professors who give standardized courses prefer to do them efficiently in a rather standardized way and do not give individual attention to such a student. Indeed, they regard his demands as a sign that he is a prima donna and a troublemaker. Having already created an unfavorable impression, the creative student often makes matters worse by his performance on standard classroom tests that depend on rote memory. This is not where his strength lies. Moreover, the creative student does not respect such tests and, hence, does not take them too seriously. If he voices this attitude to the professor—which he often will not hesitate to do—he exasperates him even further.

Holton asserts that many paper-and-pencil tests are expressly designed as high fences: "The horde that is turned away may be suspected not only of being too stupid to pass, but, much more importantly, too bright for the comfort of the examiner (1963, p. 3)." To illustrate his comment, Holton quotes from an autobiographical note of Albert Einstein, who believed that learning cannot be promoted by means of coercion and a sense of duty. "This coercion," Einstein wrote, "had such a deterring effect that, after I had passed the final examination, I found the consideration of any scientific problems distasteful to me for an entire year." Faculty members on American campuses who allow this view (that learning cannot be promoted by coercion) to influence their teaching and grading are often put on the defensive by "tougher" colleagues. They are not only accused of being "soft" but—and this is the acme of insult for an academic man—of lowering academic standards. Their only answer is that the "tough" professor's way of keeping standards high very likely does his students more harm than good. But such a response only emphasizes the chasm between the two types of professors. Freedman's experience with both kinds (and his studies of their students) leads him to the following observation: "No one wishes to range himself on the side of opposition to high standards, but one cannot help wondering whether the emphasis on excellence that is so powerful an influence in academic circles these days may not serve . . . to reinforce feelings of guilt and inadequacy rather than to stimulate outstanding performance or achievement (1962, p. 871)."

Even where the emphasis on excellence does not have these harmful effects, there is another risk: professors or schools that are excessively "tough" may penalize many of their best students. Paul Heist has called to my attention the case of two seniors, majoring in science at two different institutions. The first student, Baker, was about to complete his undergraduate program at a large, elite public university that accepts only the top eighth of high school graduates. The other, Brown, was completing his work at a small, highly prestigious private college that is known for its "toughness." Both students were thinking about going to graduate school. Here are five scores for these two senior men:

		Baker's Scores (Elite public university)	Brown's Scores (Elite private college)
a.	SAT—Verbal	600	680
b.	SAT—Math	720	750
c.	SAT—Total	1320	1430
d.	Intellectual Disposition (O.P.I.)	6 (below average)	3 (above average)
e.	Grade-Point Average	A	B—

If Baker and Brown were now to apply for admission to the same graduate school, who would be considered the more desirable candidate? Brown *ought* to be the more desirable because of his significantly higher SAT verbal score and the appreciably higher index on a measure of intellectual disposition. "This latter difference," Heist explained, in discussing the eight categories or indices with me, "denotes a means-end orientation on the part of Baker as compared with strong potentialities for independent scholarship on the part of Brown." But in all probability, Baker's straight-*A* grades as an undergraduate at one of the nation's most elite universities would prove powerfully persuasive to many an admissions committee. Were the choice to be made between these two, it is thus quite possible that Brown would be rejected by the graduate school of his choice, with the result that society might be the loser.

Where would the blame lie for such an outcome? With the graduate school admissions committee? Perhaps. But, surely, if one finger were to point in their direction, another should also point at the faculty responsible for Brown's college education; clearly, their assumptions and practices regarding grade distribution curves—and perhaps also the quality of their instruction—are reflected in Brown's grade-point average.

In any case, the faculty and administration at Brown's school became alarmed at the large number of students at their institution who, though highly selected at entrance, were not doing well in their studies and were leaving school; and they finally decided to seek professional help. Many of the teachers came to suspect that, given the very high selection of their freshmen at entrance, the solution to their problem would not be found by searching for deficiencies in their students. They were thus led to consider the principle set down by Summerskill in his report on college dropouts: "Since the objectives of colleges are to educate and graduate the students they admit, academic failure must be viewed as a failure on the part of the institution as well as on the part of the individual student. When a student fails on purely academic grounds, he testifies to inadequate admissions procedures or inadequate instruction (1962, p. 637)." Since Brown's school has extremely selective entrance standards, it follows from Summerskill's dictum that the faculty must have been responsible, at least in part, for the large number of students who were "not doing well."

Analyzing the problem for the college president and the department heads, Heist pointed out that the large majority of their entering freshmen made aptitude scores which—compared with those for the general population of high school graduates—placed them in a narrow distribution above the ninetieth percentile. This was a group, then, which in the past had been chiefly or entirely rewarded for their educational attainments. Very few entered college with any anticipation of receiving *C* or *D* grades—for them, an obviously negative experience. "For some students of high ability, low grades serve as a positive stimulant, but for others," Heist said, "studies have shown that an early series of low grades seems to result in the opposite effect." Such students, threatened with loss of face and even possible failure (as they or their parents and companions would define it), react in ways that often result in a form of underachievement or of "beating the system."

What solution was recommended to the college? The details are too complex to present here, but one dimension of it relates to grading patterns: "It is proposed that a rigorous grading system . . . merits serious reconsideration when the students involved are all mentally very capable and of a calibre that would qualify them as candidates for honors programs at most institutions of higher education. . . . It would seem difficult to rationalize the use of a grading system (or grade distribution) that is employed at . . . the majority of colleges and universities."*

EFFECTS OF THE SYSTEM ON THE INSTRUCTIONAL PROCESS

The case of Baker and Brown illustrates how the traditional grading system may directly penalize the creative student. Other effects of the system are, however, more insidious. It also works *indirectly* to discourage creativity among students and to keep from the creative student some of the recognition he might otherwise gain.

As an indirect cause, the grading system operates in two ways. It contributes, first of all, to the growing impersonalization in faculty-student relations. Impersonalization on college campuses today has many causes (and the basic ones lie outside the educational system altogether, stemming from the general dehumanization which is characteristic of our society at large), but one of its causes within the educational system is the ambiguous role of the professor, who must be both teacher *and* judge.

In his role as a teacher, the professor tries to establish a personal relation with his students; but in his role as judge, charged with rewarding and punishing students, he is pushed in the opposite direction. One is able to teach a friend—indeed, it may not really be possible to teach anyone who is not a friend—but one does not comfortably give a friend an *F,* certainly not in an age when an *F* may help lead to induction into the army and possibly, therefore, to death on the battlefield.

Many college teachers, having been caught in this conflict in their first years of teaching, have grown wary of showing (or of encouraging) any sign of friendship, or even friendliness, between themselves and their students. It may be all right with other professors' students, but not with their own. And this plain fact is undeniable: It is easier—and no doubt fairer to everyone—when grad-

---

* I wish to thank Paul Heist for having called my attention to the cases of Baker and Brown and for having made available to me his confidential correspondence with officials at Brown's school.

ing time comes around, if the teacher has been impersonal with *all* his students. Thus, as Riesman (1964) says, the grading relationship tends to "contaminate" the teaching relationship.

The student who suffers most from this contamination is the creative student. Of all student types, he is frequently the one who needs the personalized teacher-student relationship the most, both in order to bring out his own gifts and to meet his own emotional needs.

In addition to its contamination of the teacher-student relationship, the grading system harms the creative student in a second, even more insidious, way. This stems from the need, felt by almost every professor operating under the standard grading system, for collecting hard evidence about student performance so that he may rank his students justly and supply grade lists which approximate the bell-shaped curve. The influence of this factor on the teaching-learning process is far greater than most professors suspect. At its simplest level, it determines—partially, at least—the assignments students are asked to turn in. In many courses, daily or weekly written assignments, term projects, and questions in final examinations, tend to be prestructured and mechanical, yielding not only an appropriate spread from *A* to *F* but also the "evidence" that justifies the lower grades, in case a student or an administrative officer raises any question about them.

Moreover, this sort of objective evidence is often important to the faculty member, quite aside from the desire to protect himself. The more he feels compelled to be just and equitable in so vital a matter as grades, the more he must resort to written assignments and examination exercises that are prestructured and mechanical, and thus capable of being graded objectively.

Let me illustrate this point from personal experience. I served as a member of a general-education staff in a humanities course for many years. During one of the staff's frequent discussions about the desirability of including in our course some projects requiring students to "create" an actual object in the arts, one of my colleagues (whom I shall call Dr. Jones) proposed a project that— though it is too complex to describe here in detail—was close in spirit to a painting-by-number kit. He argued against a "free" painting assignment on various grounds. One was that it would "encourage charlatanism"; his assignment, on the contrary, would frustrate the charlatan, he said. He argued further that "attention to detail" and "patience" were both important aspects of the creative process, and demonstrated, quite ably, that his proposed assignment demanded great attention to detail and great patience.

Jones also argued that since the completed object would be appropriate in a dormitory room, students could put it to immediate use. I asked him how the student who found the end-product worthless might react, and he replied that a student, of course, had the right to hold such an opinion and that, fortunately, his grade would not be based on his *own* opinion. But Jones' most eloquent argument rested on an indisputable advantage: His proposed assignment was easy to grade objectively. He pointed out that it was impossible to judge a "free" painting, as there are no standards upon which critics generally agree. Of course, several of us on the staff argued that Jones' project would have the very opposite effect from the one intended: Instead of encouraging students to be creative, it would emphasize the merely technical elements, the crafts side of the creative process.

While those of us who opposed Dr. Jones prevailed in this discussion, two questions that he raised we were not able to answer to the satisfaction of his supporters: (1) How was a faculty member to protect himself against the student who is a charlatan if the assignment is absolutely free? (2) If a "freer" project than Jones' were adopted, how would the grading problem be handled? "Wouldn't the result just be chaos?" his supporters asked.

The Jones proposal illustrates how the grading system operates as an indirect *cause* for the emphasis that many college teachers place on the measurable external and mechanical aspects of learning. Though less obviously, the controversy between Dr. Jones' supporters and his opponents also illustrates the other side of the coin: The traditional grading system must also be seen as a *consequence*. Its deeply rooted place in our educational scheme is not only a cause but also a product of the standard conception of teaching, the model most common on the majority of college campuses.

Since Jones' conception of good teaching was of this standard type, the traditional grading system made perfect sense to him. Much the same point of view was expressed by many faculty members during the Berkeley debates that are summarized in the *Muscatine Report*. It is excellently stated by the faculty member who argued as follows:

> It would be deplorable if the rather harsh, critical environment appropriate to an educational institution gave way to a congenial, unevaluative one, in which scholars went about their business and students were simply welcome to pick up what they liked. . . . The most effective way of inculcating habits of self-criticism in one's students is as a critic, and only secondarily as an example. . . . But unless one is forced to do this, one will tend to avoid it. . . . And this is my main argument for grading: it forces teachers to evaluate their students' work and to justify those evaluations in detail—activities which neither party particularly enjoys (Muscatine, 1966, p. 95).

It is clear that for this professor, criticism and evaluation of student work do not take place as part of the *teaching* process itself, as he conceives it; for him, these elements would be largely (or perhaps entirely) absent if the grading system did not "force" teachers, as he says, to include them. His opposing terms are (a) a "rather harsh, critical environment," which he finds appropriate, *versus* (b) a "congenial, unevaluative one." Apparently "critical" must go with "harsh"; "unevaluative" must go with "congenial."

There are, however, some social groups—notably certain family groups—whose atmosphere can be characterized as not harsh but congenial and not unevaluative but critical. Is such an environment possible in the educational world? The faculty member we have just quoted must answer, "No." He finds that it is precisely the grading system—with its judgmental climate and its strong (and often irrevocable) rewards and punishments—which "forces" the teacher to perform his role as critic. I believe this is incorrect. It is not the role of critic which the grading system forces the teacher to play, but the role of judge. Moreover, the relationship he must establish with his students *as* judge (if he is to play that role well) will inevitably reduce, I believe, his efficacy as both teacher and critic. Even under conditions where the traditional grading system has been severely modified, even in an environment which attempts to be congenial *and* critical without being judgmental, grading problems of a serious nature persist. Again, let me illustrate this point from my own experience.

Last year, I directed an experimental program for freshmen which used only *Pass* and *Fail* as its course grades. I should like to discuss the cases of two creative students, Elaine and Bill, who represented a difficult grading problem for me even under the *Pass-Fail* system.

But, first, a few words about the program itself are necessary. The Freshman-Year Experimental Program at San Francisco State College was established in 1966 to combat the impersonalization which is so characteristic of the large urban campus. The fifty freshmen entering the program (it was open to any admitted freshman who applied until the fifty places were filled) were assigned to a small group of faculty members, who were responsible for their entire instructional program. They took all their courses together, sometimes meeting as a full group but more often in smaller numbers. The courses per se were not unique, but they were taught rather differently. The program tried to establish a learning climate in which learning and teaching were seen merely as aspects of a single process of inquiry. Students were supposed to work *with* the instructor, participating in the organization of their studies, the formulation of assignments, and even in setting standards. Of course, this process varied in the different courses, as each instructor had the right to express his individual needs and approaches. The program also tried to avoid being completely book-centered and concept-oriented. It required students to participate in certain projects which took them away from the classroom to the city or to the community at large.

We knew that if we had to operate under the traditional grading system, the teaching-learning relationships we were trying to establish would become contaminated. Hence, we requested permission to award only two grades: Those, as stated earlier, of *Pass* and *Fail*. To avoid their being considered a formality, we tried to make them as meaningful as possible; thus, although we greatly minimized such matters as due-dates and deadlines we set certain requirements as a basic minimum for a *Pass* grade.

In my course in English composition, the students understood that no one would receive a *Pass* if he did not hand in a term paper that combined work in the library ("book research") with work in the community ("people research"). Of the fifty students in the program, six or seven were considered by the faculty to be outstandingly creative. Of these, three turned in no spring-term paper for the English course. One turned in no paper at all; the other two, Elaine and Bill, turned in "something" at the end of the semester, but it was not the usual term paper.

Bill, a young writer and about seventeen years old when he entered the program, had received my permission to go to Big Sur for a few weeks during the semester in order to work on his spring-term project. (In the fall semester, he had done *two* term projects and turned in excellent reports. One focused on a campus residence hall, where he was then living, and the other dealt with a tutorial experience in Chinatown in which he had participated.) What he turned in as his spring-semester term paper consisted of a half-dozen sheets. There were three poems arising out of experiences at Big Sur and two fragments of prose, one of them highly imaginative, experimental, and quite exciting. His covering letter to me ran as follows:

Here's my term paper. This group of small writings is my term paper.

Now possibly you believe this does not represent broad reading but, you see, it does. I have gone deeply into the subject this semester and loved every minute of it. This is the most and the best I can do for now.

You will also find my term paper in *Another Side of Bob Dylan*, in William Carlos Williams' poem "The Late Singer," in Golden Gate Park, on Potrero Hill, and thousands of other places and things.

Thanks for all the help you've given me.

Elaine, also a seventeen-year-old, was an intellectual, activist student whose term project in the fall semester, like Bill's, involved participation in an English program for Chinese families who had recently arrived from Hong Kong. She had written an excellent project report. In the spring semester, however, she refused to write a report. Here is her letter explaining her position:

I am a product of the kind of education which the Experimental Freshman-Year Program was reportedly trying to alleviate. I don't think I'm completely "gone," but I still have vestiges of the "no-production-except-under-pressure" syndrome. And so I must confess that I put off until the last minute a formal compilation of my research on child art—which is my English project.

Until today, I had planned to hand in this term paper merely because I felt I would fail English if I didn't. Since I had already done the reading and the field work itself, the paper was just a required exercise which I was putting off for no other reason than that I tend to procrastinate.

But during this morning's discussion with Ed, it occurred to me that if I finally did get the paper written and turned in only because it was something I was "supposed" to do, then I would be guilty of continuing the very process which E.F.P. planned to stop.

Sid said something today which I really believe to be true, and it is that just because the teacher never sees any tangible, material proof that the student did any work over the semester, he cannot assume that there was no education taking place. To this, Ed said, "But what about the student who, after the first few sessions, doesn't show up again until the end of the semester with nothing to show for his absences? In a *Pass-Fail* program such as this, shouldn't this student receive a *Fail?*" Sid's answer and mine was an absolute No. That's the point. There should be no *Fails* at all.

Anyway—I won't be handing in the English term paper. I have compiled some excerpts from my journal which are directly related to my field work, and that is enclosed. I have sent you this because I feel you'd be interested in seeing the pattern of my "people research."

If you'd like, I can provide a list of my reading, although my point is that this should not be necessary.

I don't mean for this letter to be an apology or a plea for a *Pass* in English. I'm writing because I believe you want to know what I honestly feel. It is this respect for the student's attitudes and ideas which, to me, has been one of the most important parts of E.F.P., and I want to thank you for that.

Accompanying Elaine's letter was a document consisting of a dozen typed pages. On these were entries from her journal, which all students in the program had been requested to keep, although, as they had been told, they would never be asked to turn it in. Elaine's entries, which began on February 14 and ended on May 13, gave facts and reactions relating to an art class that she had started in the spring semester for children at the Mission Tenants' Union in an "underprivileged" area in San Francisco. The last paragraphs of her final entry are worth quoting:

Next week will be my last class. I am really sorry that I won't be able to continue coming during the summer. I'll be back here in the fall, but I have to go home and get a job for the summer.

What did I give to the kids in the art class? It's hard to write about. I know they're sorry I'm not coming back. The week after Easter when I didn't hold a class, Brenda said to me, "Don't be gone again, I missed you." Was the art class more than just something to take up time on Saturday afternoons? The kids could come and make a good mess without being scolded. And I provided a way of working with things—paper, paints, clay—which was different from what they get in school (where you have an "art period" for one hour a week).

And what am I taking with me? When Ernie asked me this question the other day, I said, "Some beautiful paintings"—but I know that is not what he meant. Except that I can point to the pictures around my room and I can point to what I felt when I was working with the kids on Saturdays.

When Bill (the guy who tried to talk about Black Power) got going on the Mission Project, he kept saying, "Get down to the real things, man, give them real things." And so I felt inadequate, because hunger is real and unemployment is real, and what was I doing about that? But the paintings on the wall are also real, and on Saturdays, this is what I gave to the kids, and this is what I am taking away with me.

It would be difficult to argue that Elaine should not have received a *Pass* in the course, even though, technically, she did not meet the course requirements. (Indeed, there would have been a scandal if Elaine had received a *Fail,* since she was one of the two or three most outstanding students in the program.) And what about Bill? If Elaine received a *Pass,* should not Bill also?

Early in the new program, the Omnibus Personality Inventory had been administered to the students. Bill had refused to take it, and I had not forced the issue. He did take it, however, the following spring. The scores indicate that Bill tends to be tolerant of ambiguities and uncertainties, is fond of novel situations and ideas, and prefers to deal with complexity rather than with simplicity in his environment. He shows an interest in artistic matters and activities, literature, philosophy, and history and seems to prefer abstract, reflective thought rather than practical, concrete problems. His scores also indicate that he responded to the items in an open way, unlike subjects trying to make a good impression.

Elaine's scores show that she values sensations, has an active imagination, and expresses her impulses either in conscious thought or overt action. Her scores on the autonomy scale suggest that she tends to be independent, nonjudgmental, and realistic. Like Bill, she has a great deal of interest in artistic matters and activities and prefers to deal with complexity rather than with simplicity in her experience. She likes to seek out people and to enjoy diversity, ambiguity, and new situations and ideas. Her scores also show an open approach to the OPI items.*

* I want to thank Dr. Roger Cummings of San Francisco State Col-

The faculty's end-of-the-year evaluations on Elaine's and Bill's official records read, in part, as follows:

For Bill:
A highly talented but still rather undisciplined young writer. We have advised him to pursue his work in fiction and poetry. We believe he will make a successful major in Creative Writing.

He is highly independent and his work in the program courses is highly uneven. He did extremely well in assignments that he undertook. When he felt an assignment was not particularly "valuable" to him, he simply did not do it.

It is difficult to know what his future will be. It is possible he will end up as a fine writer.

For Elaine:
The faculty considers her to be among the two or three most outstanding students in the program. She engaged in a number of highly significant community projects in connection with her courses, and her reports of her work in these projects reveal both the conscientiousness and the sensitivity she brought to them.

She was a leader in class discussions, always contributing original and stimulating ideas. If it were possible to equate the calibre of her work with a letter grade, it would almost certainly be an *A*.

CHAOS IN GRADING CRITERIA

The cases of Elaine and Bill illustrate a conflict we faced in the relatively simple situation set by the requirements of the *Pass-Fail* grading system. The conflicts are far greater when conscientious professors attempt to meet the requirements of the traditional grading system. It is especially difficult to know whether to give a student an *A* or a *B* when these letters have no consistent meaning. A grade of *B* means, of course, that the student who earns it is considered above average in one or more respects; but since "average" is no more defined than are the particular respects in which the student is above it, the real meaning of *B* remains a mystery. It may signify

---

lege for having analyzed the Omnibus Personality Inventory scores and prepared the statements which are summarized here.

solid achievement, or it may not signify achievement as much as promise. It may represent incipient genius or muddleheaded independence. It may be a penalty to the brilliant student for work inattentively done or a reward to a mediocre student for work conscientiously done.

The chaos in grading criteria is immeasurably great on American campuses. Some years ago on a fellowship from the Fund for the Advancement of Education, I spent a year investigating some problems dealing with evaluation, testing, and grading. I interviewed faculty members at four colleges and universities to discover, among other things, how discrepant their grading criteria were. I have reported elsewhere (1964) on this project, but I would like to present here parts of two interviews I held with two faculty members, as they illustrate points that are especially relevant to this discussion.

One of the faculty members I interviewed—I shall call him Dr. Harrison—told me that he was "proud" (that was his word) of having given one of his best students a *C* as his course grade. He explained that the level of Powell's performance in the course had been equal to that of other students to whom he had given *A*'s.

"I don't understand," I said. "Why didn't you give him an *A* if he deserved it?"

"Powell didn't deserve it," Dr. Harrison said. "He didn't work hard enough."

"But you just said his work was of *A* calibre."

"It was," Harrison replied, "but, you see, he hardly had to lift a finger to turn out that kind of performance. He did everything *effortlessly.*"

As we discussed Powell's case, Dr. Harrison became angry when he described the boy's "casual attitude" toward his class. He blurted out: "No student of mine is going to get away being a lazy slob if I can help it! *I won't let him get away with that!*"

In the conversation that followed, it became clear that, although Harrison had never really formulated his criteria for grading, his grades were based only to a certain extent on a student's level of achievement at the close of a semester; to a far greater extent they were based on what he estimated to be the amount of time, effort, and energy the student spent in working for the course.

During my interview with him, I attempted to explore his general philosophy further. I do not wish to oversimplify his point of view, for he was not a simple-minded person; but his attitude on this issue can be summarized approximately as follows. He believed that hard work is in itself a good, that learning *is* hard work, that hard work is necessarily painful (though it may result in pleasure in the long run), and that like all other painful activities, it is naturally avoided by everyone whenever possible unless external pressures compel one to pursue it. As we continued to talk, I could see why Harrison could not have given Powell an *A*. His particular beliefs about effort and suffering made it impossible for him to give *A*'s to any students but those who had experienced pain, discomfort, and sacrifice during his course.

This case illustrates how particular beliefs about the nature of work can affect the grading of a creative student. A different attitude toward grading is illustrated by the case of Dr. Kaye, a professor of philosophy at a large, public institution located not too far from the college at which Dr. Harrison teaches.

During the course of an interview I had with Professor Kaye, I met Morton, his teaching assistant, who impressed me as a brilliant young man. After Morton had left the office, Kaye told me that he was one of the most "creative" (the word was his) graduate students and teaching assistants he had ever encountered. After saying that there was an interesting story behind Morton's entrance into graduate school, he proceeded to tell me about him.

As an undergraduate, Kaye said, Morton had been a "peculiar" student. "On the one hand," he explained, "I identified him clearly as a potential *A* student—but he was doing only mid-*B* work in my class, or lower." Curious, Kaye took the trouble to discover that this was the situation in all of Morton's classes. His other instructors also felt there was "something there," but did not bother probing further since Morton was doing *B* or *B—* work. They simply put him down as another student "not working up to capacity." And, as Kaye said, since Morton did not present a problem to anyone, why should the faculty worry about him? "We had enough on our hands with student discontent and everything else!"

Kaye himself, however, could not let the matter go. "I had a series of conferences with Morton," he told me, "and I saw there was some kind of problem. On occasion, he showed such great flashes of brilliance—and they were exciting when they happened. I realized then that the level of Morton's work was being kept down by some sort of unreal view he had of himself. He thought of himself as just a *B—* student, you know, *incapable* of ever getting an *A.*"

"This distorted view of his own potential," I commented, "I suppose he probably got from his teachers in the first place."

"Well, in any case," Kaye continued, "I was feeling experimental that semester, and I thought, 'Oh, what the hell; I surely can't do any harm.' So I gave Morton an *A* in the course he was taking with me, even though he didn't deserve it. I thought maybe if I gave him an *A,* I could help him see himself as capable of *A* work."

"You mean you gave him an *A*—even though he hadn't done *A* work in the course?"

"That's right. He didn't deserve it. But I did it anyway."

"But you see," I said, "it worked!"

"Who knows *what* works?" Kaye said. Maybe it was a girl friend! But in any case, he was eventually admitted to graduate school and is now one of the finest minds around here."

"What if your plan hadn't worked?" I asked. "Would you have felt guilty?"

"*Guilty?* How do you mean?"

"Well," I said, "you know—at having lowered the standards of the university."

"Oh—that!" Kaye's gesture reduced my question to nonsense. He pulled off his shelf a copy of the *Dialogues of Alfred North Whitehead* and held it so I could see the title. "Do you know this?" he asked, and without waiting for an answer, he said, "Listen to this passage."

I am profoundly suspicious of the 'A'-man. He can say back what you want to hear in an examination, and . . . you must give him

his 'A' if he says it back; but the ability, not to say the willingness, to give you back what is expected of him argues a certain
shallowness and superficiality. Your 'B'-man may be a bit mud-
dle-headed, but muddle-headedness is a condition precedent to
independent creative thought in the first stage. Of course it may
get no farther than muddle-headedness. But when my colleagues
chaff me for giving more 'A's than they are willing to do and tax
me with tenderheartedness, I reflect that I would rather not have
it on my head that I was the one who discouraged an incipient
talent (Price, Ed., 1954, p. 46).

THE HIGHEST GRADES TO THE WRONG PEOPLE

In the preceding sections, I have argued that American college and university education in general, and the education of creative young people in particular, would be greatly benefited if the
standard grading system were eliminated or drastically modified. I
have tried to point to direct and indirect effects of the grading system that foster miseducation and my thesis has been strengthened
by the fact that creative students in American colleges and universities seem to be more harmed by miseducation than other types of
students.

With the focus specifically on grading practices, the basic
question of this paper, thus far, has been: What can we do for the
creative student to help him realize his potential? That question
now suggests the next: If he *could* realize his potential, what would
he do *for us?*

The answer can actually be stated in one sentence: We ought
to help him realize his potential because he may be able to help us
save our civilization. This is so dramatic a statement, the reader will
probably hear it only as a piece of rhetoric. I mean it to be something more. Let me see if I can present the case. The argument
consists of these steps: (1) Many or most of the *A* students—that is,
the "achiever" type—are able to handle well the essentially technical
problems that characterized our society during its developing stages;
(2) the problems that face leaders in the highly developed society
that America is today are not essentially of this technical sort; (3)
many, probably most, achiever-type students who move through

college and university into positions of leadership are not capable of coping with this new kind of problem; (4) the people who might be capable of coping with them—the "creatives"—are not, by and large, moving through our educational system into positions of leadership; (5) we ought, therefore, to restructure our educational processes and redefine "success" in them so that many more creatives will seek and achieve success (Maddi, 1966; Keniston, 1967).

In filling in the steps of this argument, we should begin by characterizing the "creative" individual. Since this has been done in other chapters of this book, perhaps all we need here is to repeat James Trent's brief definition, which appeared in chapter 1.

> Creative people are independent and innovative. They play with ideas and concepts. In academic settings, they have a highly developed sense of the theoretical and the aesthetic. They are open to a wide range of experience and are spontaneous, flexible, and complex in outlook. They are frequently rebels, but we hope rebels with a cause. In general, they are reasonably intelligent, although we are told that intelligence is not directly related to creativity itself.

Next, we must briefly characterize the achiever type—the successful student who is currently moving through college and university programs into leadership positions in our society. Unless he is also a creative individual, he operates most comfortably in highly structured situations. He enjoys solving problems, but he enjoys most, and solves best, a certain kind of problem—one that is largely *prestructured* (the overall framework, major elements, and direction of solution are already formulated or suggested at the time it is presented); one that is known to be *solvable* (there is virtual certainty that an answer, and a fairly unambiguous one, will probably come at the end of reasonable time and effort spent in the problem-solving process); one that is expressable in *quantitative* or semiquantitative terms; and one that is *immediately applicable* to some visible situation and can do someone some "good" (or, if an enemy, some harm).

The typical *A* man is *not* necessarily a conformist. He may challenge those in authority or depart from "safe" behavior. But he usually does this when there is no risk to his image or goals. In his personal relationships with students and faculty (and perhaps also with family and friends), he tends to think more legalistically than many of his classmates, and he tends to see these relationships less multidimensionally. He has clearer rules for resolving conflict. Moreover, the actual number of conflicts in his life is reduced by the predominance of certain values: practical goals, strong motivation toward tangible rewards, and unquestioning outward acceptance of the authority of others—even as he dreams of the day he will be the one wielding authority. A system of higher education which fosters this achiever type—that is, which applauds these individuals and places them in positions of leadership in government, business, industry, and education—appears to have been clearly appropriate in a developing society where the basic problems were technological. In a highly developed society, however, placed in positions of leadership, such men are uncomfortable with the most important problems facing them. These problems are not prestructured; they are not known in advance to be solvable; they are not expressible in purely quantitative terms; they do not have local and immediate applicability. These problems, in fact, demand the most creative minds the nation's colleges and universities can educate.

Under the standard grading system, then, the colleges and universities are giving the *A*'s to the wrong kind of person. One of the purposes of higher education is the preparation, as the college catalogs put it, of tomorrow's leaders in the community, nation, and world. The kind of person who receives the *A*'s today is just the right man—for yesterday. He is just the wrong man for tomorrow.

REFERENCES

Axelrod, J. What do college grades mean? A survey of practices at four institutions. In H. A. Estrin & D. M. Good (Eds.), *College and university teaching*. Dubuque, Iowa: Brown, 1964.

Axelrod, J. An experimental college model. *Educational Record,* Fall, 1967, 327–337.

Brown, D. R. Personality changes in college students. In N. Sanford (Ed.), *The American college*. New York: Wiley, 1962.

Freedman, M. B. Studies of college alumni. In N. Sanford (Ed.), *The American college*. New York: Wiley, 1962.

Holton, G. Testing and self-discovery. *University College Quarterly,* 9 (November 1963), 3–9.

Katz, J. (Ed.) *Growth and constraint in college students*. Stanford: Institute for the Study of Human Problems, Stanford University, 1967.

Kenison, K. Sources of unrest on the campus. In A. W. Burks, D. Cayer, & T. H. Wilson (Eds.), *The American university and the world of scholars*. New Brunswick: Committee on International Programs, Rutgers, 1967.

Korn, H. A. The incomplete liberalizing impact of higher education: Case studies of two pre-medical students. In Joseph Katz (Ed.), *Growth and constraint in college students*. Stanford: Institute for the Study of Human Problems, Stanford University, 1967.

Maddi, S. R. Fostering achievement. In G. K. Smith (Ed.), *Current issues in higher education, 1966*. Washington, D.C.: Association for Higher Education, 1966.

Miller, S. *Measure, number, and weight: A polemical statement of the college grading problem*. Knoxville: Learning Resources Center, University of Tennessee, 1967.

Morton, J. (Ed.) *SLATE supplement to the general catalogue, spring 1967*. Berkeley: Associated Students, University of California, 1967.

Muscatine, C. *Education at Berkeley*. Berkeley: University of California, 1966.

Peterson, R. E. *The scope of organized student protest in 1964–65*. Princeton: Educational Testing Service, 1966.

Price, L. (Ed.). *Dialogues of Alfred North Whitehead*. Boston: Little, Brown, 1954.

Riesman, D. Foreword in R. Heath, *The reasonable adventurer*. Pittsburgh: University of Pittsburgh Press, 1964.

Sanford, N. (Ed.) *The American college*. New York: Wiley, 1962.

Summerskill, J. Dropouts from college. In N. Sanford (Ed.), *The American college*. New York: Wiley, 1962.

Trent, J. W., & Medsker, L. L. *Beyond high school.* Berkeley: Center for Research and Development in Higher Education, University of California, 1967.

Webster, H., Freedman, M., & Heist, P. Personality changes in college students. In N. Sanford (Ed.), *The American college.* New York: Wiley, 1962.

V

Directions Toward Solution

9

EDUCATING FOR CREATIVITY: A MODERN MYTH?

Donald W. MacKinnon

My title implies that I sincerely doubt whether we are doing all that we can by way of fostering the creative potential of our students. However, I also question whether we have any firm evidence that other forms of education being proposed in such great numbers today would succeed any better than our present practices, simply because most methods have not been tried and tested in any systematic study of their effectiveness.

The field of education is strikingly like that of psychotherapy. Not only do both aim to improve the objects of their efforts—students in one case, patients in the other—but in the past both have been rather indifferent about testing the effectiveness of their theories or their practices. The reasons for such strange neglect have been mainly the same in both fields.

Educators and therapists are alike in their concern for others. All too often they feel that this concern makes whatever they do or propose to do for their charges right. Their missionary zeal for their theories and their practices makes them impervious to the demands for proof of their efficacy. One or two striking positive observations far outweigh in their thinking a host of negative instances, many of which are probably not even observed by them. Thus, the need for rigorous checking of their claims is often not even recognized. When, several years ago, a colleague of mine sent Freud reprints of papers which reported controlled laboratory investigations of the Freudian concept of repression, the great psychoanalyst responded: "I have examined your experimental studies for the verification of the psychoanalytic assertions with interest. I cannot put much value on these confirmations because the wealth of reliable observations on which these assertions rest make them independent of experimental verification (MacKinnon and Dukes, 1962, p. 703)." The attitude of educational reformers toward the innovations which they have proposed or instituted has, in general, not been much different from Freud's.

The second reason why both educators and psychotherapists have traditionally been disinclined to test the adequacy of their theories and their practices has been the enormous difficulty that any valid test would impose upon the investigator. Such studies obviously must deal with a great complex of variables over extended periods of time. It is a brave, or foolhardy, researcher who undertakes such difficult studies when simpler and shorter experiments are at hand with the possibility of neater research design and the certainty of yielding unequivocal findings. And so, over the years, we have repeatedly witnessed the proposal of new theories and practices by educators and psychotherapists who make exorbitant claims for their effectiveness—claims which subsequently seem never to be quite fulfilled although never submitted to an adequate systematic check. In the course of time, new theories and practices come upon the scene and take the place of the older ones, only to experience, sooner or later, the same fate.

EDUCATION FOR CREATIVITY AT THE COLLEGE LEVEL

One reason for questioning whether colleges are educating for creativity is that, until the last few years, they did not even show an interest in it. This lack of concern merely reflected the values and interests of society at large. Even within psychology, creativity was a long neglected topic. The present concern—which at times appears to have become a fad—was stimulated by J. P. Guilford's presidential address on "Creativity" to the American Psychological Association in 1950. But it was not until the late 1950's and the early 1960's that the implications of the research on creativity for education began to appear in print. Almost without exception, the conclusions seemed to be that those with creative potential are neglected, if not discriminated against, at all levels of American education.

However, these studies leave something to be desired. Both Torrance's (1959) study of elementary school children and Getzels' and Jackson's (1962) investigation of students in the sixth grade through high school took as a measure of their subjects' creativeness their performance on so-called tests of creativity—a highly questionable procedure since the relation of test performance to demonstrated creative behavior was not known. My own studies (MacKinnon, 1962 a and b) and those of my colleagues (MacKinnon *et al.,* 1961) at the Institute of Personality Assessment and Research used as subjects mature, practicing members of several professions—research scientists in industry, mathematicians, architects, and writers—and thus had the advantage of a much more acceptable criterion of creativity. We used the judgment of their peers, who evaluated the demonstrated creativeness with which our subjects practiced their professions.

Our studies, however, suffered from the fact that whatever conclusions we drew about our subjects' earlier educational experiences were taken from their retrospective descriptions of their experiences at home, in school, and in college, as well as of the forces, persons, and situations which, as they saw it, nurtured their creativeness. We must remind ourselves that these descriptions are subject to the misperceptions and self-deceptions of all self-reports. Even assuming that the testimony of these creative persons is essentially accurate, this is no assurance that the conditions in the home, school, and society, the qualities of interpersonal relations between instructor and student, and the aspects of the teaching-learning process, which would appear to have contributed to creative development a generation ago, would facilitate rather than inhibit creativity in today's far different world and educational climate. It just may be that if there is any modern myth about the role of colleges and universities in nurturing creative potential, it may be that we are *not* educating for creativity. If that should turn out to be the case, I would have to take my share of responsibility for having fostered it.

The concept of educating for creativity necessitates our thinking of it not as a fixed trait of personality but as something that changes over time, waxing and waning, being facilitated by some life circumstances and situations and inhibited by others. While such an assertion would be accepted by almost everyone, much less agreement can be found for statements which specify the types of situation or life circumstance that facilitate or inhibit creativity. Such disagreement merely underscores the continuing need—despite a considerable body of studies—for research to determine what kinds of situations contribute most significantly to the encouragement of what kinds of creativity in what types of individual. The problem almost certainly has to be phrased in this manner, for it is unlikely that all persons will find the same situation equally conducive to creative effort.

THE CREATIVE SITUATION VERSUS THE INDIVIDUAL

Questions concerning the facilitating or inhibiting effect of environment on creativity can be directed both to the individual's past and to his present life. Our concern here is with what we may call "the creative situation" as that situation exists or can be made to exist in the college or university community. And our problem is to discover those characteristics of the circumstances of living and of the social and educational and work milieu in the college or university which facilitate rather than inhibit the appearance of creative thought and action in students. More specifically, what can colleges and universities provide for their students in the way of experiences that will help to develop whatever creative potential they may possess?

The difficulties in answering this question are several. Although our findings on the characteristics of highly creative persons seem now to be reasonably well established, their implications for the nurturing of creative talent are far from clear. Even if we think we know what kinds of experiences a college should provide, there is no guarantee that they will have the same consequences for all students. The wide range of individual differences surely must mean that there is no single method for nurturing creativity; ideally the experiences which we provide should be tailormade, if not for individual students, at least for different types of students. We should remember that the same fire that melts the butter hardens the egg.

Just as grades and the academic record have been emphasized in determining admission to college (see Chapter 7), all too often in college a continuing high level of academic achievement is the prerequisite for admission to special programs, honors seminars, independent study, and research projects that among other goals have the objective of encouraging the student to think and reason creatively. At least an overall *B* average is the usual requirement for such educational experiences. There is reason to believe, however, that independent students frequently are denied those very educational experiences from which they would profit most because as independent students they are not always among the grade getters. College programs for the talented in the past have been invariably programs for the *academically* talented.

In our study of creative architects, we found that in college they had usually made *A*'s in courses that interested them but had done little or no work in courses that failed to stir their imagination. In general, their attitude appears to have been one of rather deep skepticism. They had been unwilling to accept anything on the mere say-so of their instructors. Nothing could be accepted on faith or because it had behind it the voice of authority. Such matters might be accepted, but only after the student had demonstrated their validity to himself. They had been spirited in their disagreement with their instructors, but one gets the impression that they had learned the most from and had their creative potential the most stimulated by those who demanded the highest standards of excellence. There is much to indicate that they had not been easy students with whom to work. One of the most difficult, but, as it turned out, one of the most creative had been advised by the dean of his school to quit because "he had no talent"; another, who had been failed in his design dissertation attacking the stylism of the faculty, had taken his degree in the art department.

It is quite clear that students of such calibre and independence as these are often enough excluded from special programs and honors seminars just because they are not "good grade getters."

Our several researches have consistently shown that creative persons are independent, and that this independence, already manifested in high school, usually increases in college and thereafter. Since creative persons share, then, the fundamental characteristic of not being particularly interested in achieving in situations which demand conforming behavior but, rather, are strongly motivated to achieve in situations that demand independence in thought and action, they would seem to be the ideal candidates for doing independent study and research. I must confess, though, that I have never been successful, even in recent years, in petitioning for exceptions to be made for just such students. I am not suggesting that the academic achievers with high grade-point averages should be excluded from opportunities to do independent work, for clearly they need this, too, and perhaps especially so since their independence of spirit needs particularly to be fostered. But I would especially urge the admission of bright and independent students whose grades are below the usual requirements for such special courses.

Of course, no instructor who has to deal with classes of students will find it easy to welcome nonconforming behavior, and this is especially so for the young, relatively inexperienced teacher. It is not nonconformity for nonconformity's sake (which ends by being conformity in reverse) that is deserving of respect or even of acceptance. Rather, it is truly independent behavior (which is an expression of the wholehearted commitment of the student to truly creative goals) that is deserving of acceptance even though it may well conflict with the goals set for the group.

For the most part, though, students with creative potential

will not so much actively disrupt group activities as they will passively, and at times stubbornly, resist efforts to integrate them into the group. Not infrequently students of creative potential, concerned with their own experiences of both inner life and outer world, more introvert than extrovert, and more isolate than social, will pursue projects of their own making.

Here one comes up against the paradox and the problem that at just the time when increasing emphasis is being placed on the identification and development of creative talent, which demands that the student be given more individual treatment, if not attention, the instructor ratio in most universities and colleges is almost certainly bound to worsen as a result of the explosion in population.

A partial answer may lie in the use of automated teaching techniques which have the merit that they permit the student to pace himself. The very personality of the potentially creative student is almost ideally suited to self-instruction. At this suggestion, I can hear loud protests that it is just the creative student with his disposition to separateness and aloneness who, for his own sake and for his healthy psychological development, needs the special personal attention of his instructors and more association with his peers if he is to develop into a well-rounded person. To this I can answer only that many of the highly creative persons we have seen are not especially well rounded. They have one-sided interests, sharp edges to their personalities, and marked peaks and dips on their personality-test profiles. We cannot help our able students to become creative if we always insist upon their being well rounded.

Here we come face to face with a sharp conflict of values in our society and schools today: the emphasis, on the one hand, upon "togetherness" (the integration of the individual into the group and its activities, good group dynamics, and smooth interpersonal relations) and on the other hand, the emphasis on the nurturing of creative talent. All our evidence points to the incompatibility of these opposed values and goals.

It is conceivable, of course, that outstandingly creative persons develop their strong desire to be alone and to have time apart from others for contemplative thinking as a result of being forced into group activities. If such were indeed the case, we might be depriving our able students of considerable motivation for creative activity if we were to free them from participation in group activities and grant them more time for their individual interests, including the pursuit of learning. This, I must say, seems unlikely to me, and so I continue to think that one of the best methods for nurturing creative potential is to de-emphasize group participation with its demands for conformity and to provide maximum opportunity for the able student to work out his own interests.

In summary, I firmly believe that those instructors who are genuinely interested in nurturing creativity must be prepared to grant greater autonomy to their more promising students and even reward them for behaviors which at times may be disturbing to group harmony.

LESSONS FROM THE CREATIVE HOME

The independence of our creative subjects appears to have been fostered by parents who, very early, showed an extraordinary respect for their child and confidence in his ability to do the appropriate thing. The parents' expectation that their offspring would act independently but reasonably and responsibly appears to have contributed much to the child's sense of personal autonomy, which, as he grew older, developed to such a marked degree.

We should note, however, that these parents did not leave the life space of the child unstructured. Within the family clear standards of conduct and ideas existed as to what was right and wrong; at the same time, however, there was an expectation, if not a requirement, of active exploration by the child along with the internalization of a framework of personal conduct. Discipline was almost always consistent and predictable. In most cases there were rules, family standards, and parental injunctions which were known explicitly by the child and seldom infringed. Thus, there appear to have been both structure and freedom that carried with them expectations of reasonable and responsible action.

This parental policy, I submit, is a far different thing from the kind of permissiveness which is frequently demanded by children and so often granted by parents today. Extreme permissiveness means the absence of standards and a lack of structure of the child's life space, with the consequence that he does not know who he is, where he stands, or what he can or should do. Small wonder, then, that alienation and anxiety are so often his fate.

I am inclined to believe that the college or the university which can create an atmosphere similar to that of the early homes of our highly creative subjects would, by that alone, contribute importantly to nurturing the creative potential of its students. Such an atmosphere is far different from that of the unstructured campus which some seek today—a campus on which no rules regulate the manner, time, and place for the activities appropriate to college life.

Another aspect of the early life space of our creative subjects is especially worthy of notice. In addition to their parents, they had a larger familial sphere—grandparents, uncles, aunts, and others who occupied prominent and responsible positions within the community—to draw upon as diverse and effective models with whom they could make important identifications. And whatever the emotional relation between father and son, whether distant, harmonious, or turbulent, the father generally presented a model of effective and resourceful behavior in some type of exceptionally demanding career. What is perhaps more significant, however, is the high incidence of distinctly autonomous mothers who had active lives and interests and sometimes rewarding careers of their own.

LIBERATION AND BREADTH OF EXPERIENCE

The college might similarly foster the creative potential of its students by offering a plentiful supply of diverse and effective models—teachers who are themselves effectively creative persons.

But, more specifically, what can instructor-models offer to nurture the creative potential of their students? For one thing, they can offer a deep appreciation of the theoretical and aesthetic ways of thinking, for these, we find, are the two values most highly prized by outstandingly creative persons. A student is on firmer ground when dealing with facts and things than when grappling with theoretical concepts and issues, and many will be tempted to remain in such safe territory. But if their creative potential is to be realized, they must be encouraged to think abstractly and to concern themselves with concepts and issues construed in abstract and symbolic terms. In research, and especially in basic research, the individual must venture into the realm of abstract thinking. Thus, one of the great advantages in participating in research as an undergraduate is the emphasis upon developing theoretical interests.

Of course, there is nothing magical about mere participation in research; its consequences for the student depend upon the conditions under which it occurs. If the professor reserves the real thinking for himself and treats the student largely as a laboratory assistant or technician, the gain will be minimal to the student, who might better spend his time in more conventional course work. On the other hand, the professor can greatly encourage the development of the student's theoretical interests if he treats him as a full collaborator in all phases of the research, especially in its conceptualization and planning; it is even better if he encourages the student to formulate his own problem and to design his own research. Such a professor, that is, one who places high value on theoretical issues, provides the student with a model with whom he can identify, and thus gives him confidence to develop his own theoretical interests.

From association with this type of a professor—more appropriately designated a guide or mentor, a true exemplar—the student experiences something of the delight and joy and fresh insights which come from thinking abstractly and exercising one's skills. He is motivated to acquire through study and hard work the theoretical know-how, knowledge, and competencies which, alone, provide grounds for the confidence to set himself ever more challenging problems in his field of interest.

Although some have stressed the incompatibility and conflict of theoretical and aesthetic interests, it would appear that he who would nurture creativity must foster a rich development of both, for the truly creative person is not satisfied with the solutions to his problems unless they are also aesthetically pleasing or—to use the mathematician's term—unless they are elegant. He demands of his work that it be simultaneously true and beautiful. The aesthetic viewpoint permeates all of the work of the creative person, and it should find expression in the teaching of all skills, disciplines, and professions if creativity is to be nurtured.

Among the more salient characteristics of the creative person are a breadth of cultural and intellectual interests, an openness to his own feelings and emotions, a sensitive intellect, and an understanding self-awareness.

The implications of these findings for the nurturing of creativity are rather clear, it seems to me, and especially so for vocational training. We should not train our students narrowly or only for the practice of a profession. What I am suggesting is that the traditional distinction between liberal-arts colleges and professional schools needs to be broken down so that we no longer think of the former as colleges which do not prepare their students for any particular career and the latter as schools which train their students for the practice of a particular vocation. If, like John Arnold, one thinks that liberal-arts colleges seek to produce generalists, and professional schools seek to produce specialists, then the need is for professional schools to see that their students are more broadly trained so as to become generalists as well as specialists and for liberal-arts colleges to see that their students acquire some specific knowledge or expertise as well as a general education.

We find that regardless of whether our creative subjects were educated in liberal-arts colleges or trained in professional schools, or had the benefits of both kinds of learning, they, more than their less creative peers, reveal an awareness both of the inner self and the outer world and are inclined to express most aspects of their inner experience and character. In other words, they admit into consciousness and behavior much that others would repress, and thus integrate reason and passion and reconcile the rational with the irrational.

I believe we would all agree that most professional training is not designed to foster such liberation of the human spirit as characterizes our creative subjects. And I think we would also agree that just because a course is taught in a liberal-arts curriculum does not guarantee it will have a liberating influence on the student. Any course, no matter what its content, can be taught in a rigid and stultifying manner, or it can be designed to encourage awareness of one's impulses and a freeing of one's imagination. I would argue, however, that increased aesthetic sensitivity, self-awareness, and imaginativeness are more likely to be engendered by a study of the arts, the humanities, and the social and behavioral sciences than by professional training. In such areas of human experience the student can more easily be brought to an awareness of the meaning and uses of analogy, simile, and metaphor; to a feeling for the symbolic equivalents of varied experience and the delights and possibilities in imaginative play; and to an appreciation of the place of human experience in the cosmic scheme.

I would, therefore, suggest that in professional education the creative potential of students can perhaps best be fostered by broadening their experience in fields far beyond their specialities, Instead of viewing such wanderings as distractions, we would do well to think of them as providing the student with that variety and richness of experience without which the highest levels of creative achievement are unlikely to be reached.

Although especially perceptive and open to experience, the creative person, like everyone else, must also judge and evaluate his experience, but it is clear that his preferred mode is that of perceiving rather than judging. The difficulty with judging is that one may come to prejudge, thus excluding from perception large areas of experience. Since critical judgment is emphasized so much in higher education, we need to emphasize the opposite if we are to foster creativity. We will do well to discuss with our students, at least occasionally, the most fantastic ideas and possibilities. Of course, discipline and self-control are also necessary. One must learn to exercise them to be truly creative, but it is important that they not be overlearned. Furthermore, there is a time and place for the learning and use of discipline and self-control, but having been learned, they should be used flexibly, not rigidly or compulsively.

In our researches we have found that creative persons not only are open to experience but are intuitive about it. We can train students to be accurate in their perceptions and logical in their reasoning—and these too are characteristics of the creative person—but can we train them to be intuitive, and if so, how? I would suggest that we can do so by emphasizing the transfer of training from one subject to another, by searching for common principles and relations among quite different domains of knowledge, by stressing thinking in terms of analogies, similes, and metaphors, by seeking the symbolic equivalents of experience in the widest possible number of sensory and imaginal modalities, by engaging in imaginative play, and by learning to retreat from the facts in order to see them in larger perspective and in relation to more aspects of this larger context.

You will note that I have discussed the implications of our studies for the creative education of students as though they are rather obvious. These suggestions seem reasonable to me, but I would remind you that they are only questionable hypotheses to be tested. I have not so much described new practices as I have pointed to a few out of many more that I believe should be extensively employed. They surely have been used by some instructors, at least part of the time, with some students in some colleges—but how widely or how consistently or how effectively nobody knows. For that reason it remains a question in my mind whether educating for creativity is or is not a modern myth.

REFERENCES

Getzels, J. W., & Jackson, P. W. *Creativity and intelligence.* New York: Wiley, 1962.

Guilford, J. P. Creativity. *American Psychologist,* 1950, *5,* 444–454.

MacKinnon, D. W. The nature and nurture of creative talent. *American Psychologist,* 1962, *17,* 484–485. (a)

MacKinnon, D. W. The personality correlates of creativity: A study of American architects. In G. S. Nielsen (Ed.), *Proceedings of the XIV International Congress of Applied Psychology, Copenhagen, 1961.* Vol. 2. Copenhagen: Munksgaard, 1962, 11–39. (b)

MacKinnon, D. W., *et al. Proceedings of the conference on "The creative person."* Berkeley: University of California, University Extension, 1961.

MacKinnon, D. W., & Dukes, W. F. Repression. In L. Postman (Ed.), *Psychology in the making.* New York: Knopf, 1962, 662–774.

Torrance, E. P. Highly intelligent and highly creative children in a laboratory school (Explorations in creative thinking in the early school years, No. 6). *Research Memo.* BER-59-7, Minneapolis: Bureau of Educational Research, University of Minnesota, 1959.

10

PERSONALITY DEVELOPMENT AND CREATIVITY IN THE SOVIET UNION

Nevitt Sanford

I have argued that education for creativity is not essentially different from good general education, which promotes the development of the total person. I have also argued, like the other contributors to this book, that individual development depends upon the total educational environment—the general society as well as the immediate academic environment. From this viewpoint, one main task of educational research is to discover how the interacting features of this overall environment influence the development of different aspects of the whole person. In the years following World War II, considerable attention and some research have also been directed to examin-

161

ing procedures for encouraging and furthering the greater realization of our talented and potentially creative youth. Ultimately, the answer we need will come from educational experimentation, which demonstrates that given procedures, deliberately undertaken, produce specified and desirable effects.

Meanwhile, we may learn a great deal from natural experimentation. We may find, for example, an institution in which a well-defined Procedure A is being carried out and another institution in which Procedure B is clearly exemplified; we may then compare the effects of the two, once we have assumed or determined that other things are equal or as nearly so as possible. Or, since any particular procedure, as well as the individuals in it, is likely to be influenced by system-wide processes, we may study the ways in which Procedure A varies from one educational system to another. Or we may compare whole systems in terms of their varying impact upon participating individuals and thus gain some understanding of human development in educational settings. Although much more complex in both study and analysis, the cultures and educational systems of nations may also be compared for their different effects on the lives of students and citizens.

From this viewpoint, a comparison of some educational practices in the Soviet Union with those in our own society might throw some light upon the development of creativity in the individual. In the fall of 1958, my wife and I made a trip to Eastern Europe, where I was to study in a preliminary way the education and the development of youth in a type of social system radically different from our own. I could hardly hope to learn very much in a month, but at least I might gain some valuable impressions and obtain some leads for future studies.

I wanted to learn what I could about the Russian objectives of education in the broadest sense: the kind of individual citizen desired, the attention given to general development and creativity, the means chosen to put into effect for realizing these objectives, and the success of the system in achieving its stated ends. I felt that a special inquiry into the education for human development and creativity, as well as into the problems of juvenile delinquency, would be valuable, both as a means for revealing the system of education and for possibly shedding light upon what are recognized as world-wide problems. (Juvenile delinquency, however, will be examined only superficially in this chapter.)

Probably my major preconception upon starting this exploratory survey was an awareness of how difficult it is to control human behavior or to mold human personality according to specifications. In our country we attempt—or at least profess—to stress individuality as the major developmental goal, and we worry—not without good reason—about conformity. In the Communist countries the major aim, of course, is "collectivism" and the preparation of youth for participation in the system. One might well suspect, as I did, that they produce far more individuality than they like, or than they know. During the summer of 1958 in the United States, I had met two young Russian men who, even though they must have been selected for their loyalty to their country and its system, appeared as individualistic as personalities as one could wish.

UPBRINGING AND PUBLIC EDUCATION

As I was given to understand, the term "public education" in the U.S.S.R. refers to all those institutionalized activities—such as propaganda for parents, nursery schools, Young Pioneers, and the Komsomol—that are designed to produce good, loyal, and hard-working Soviet citizens. The acquisition of knowledge, particularly scientific knowledge, is something else. In this respect, I reviewed and discussed with the Russians some of the issues and topics that others had covered and reported. My particular concerns, as already indicated, were with education for citizenship—or what the Russians sometimes call character education—and with education for creativity.

At a meeting I attended at the Philosophical Institute in Moscow, I was immediately reminded of a seminar held in New York during the summer of 1958. Organized by the American Friends Service Committee, the seminar had had as its guest an articulate doctoral candidate in philosophy from Moscow. He had told the group that the fundamental aim of the whole Soviet system was "the renovation of man." Asked by an Indian student about the "model" for this renovation, he had been unable to give a really clear answer. Naturally, in Russia I took various occasions to raise this same question, especially at the meeting held at the Philosophical Institute, which, I believe, has the task of providing the philosophic—that is to say Marxist—rationale for the Communist regime.

This meeting—organized by my friend, the same Ph.D. candidate I have mentioned—deserves reporting in some detail, both for the light that it sheds on Soviet conceptions of developmental goals and for its revelations of what it is like to talk with a group of Russian intellectuals. My friend had brought together his department chairman—who served as chairman and major spokesman at the meeting—several other professors, and four or five younger men, all personal acquaintances of his. All understood English. Apples and mineral water were laid out for refreshment. At the beginning of the meeting, the one woman in the group passed the apples to the guests. "Ah," said the chairman, "her name is Eve," and the whole company was delighted.

As soon as the conversation got under way, I took the opportunity to refer to the renovation of man that my Russian friend had emphasized at the seminar of the previous summer. "That is right," said the chairman, "and that is not only what we *aim* for; we *already* have it." To this I replied that I was indeed happy to be talking with a group of renovated men. This sally was greeted with much good-natured laughter. The chairman explained that he did not claim this status for himself, since he was too old to have had the benefits of the new upbringing, but that he really believed the young Russians were different. "The renovated man," he continued, "is a collectivist." I then tried to get the group to say just what "collectivist" means and just how the collectivist individual can be distinguished. The conversation that followed was not unlike that of a group of American ministers and psychologists who are asked to say what is meant by a "good Christian."

One notion that did emerge, however, was that the collectivist individual is oriented toward the group: His behavior is largely determined by his membership in the group, he thinks of himself as a member of the group, and he exhibits a sense of responsibility to the group. Stressing that collectivism is opposed to individualism, the chairman cited a new restaurant in West Germany as a good example of individualism. At this restaurant, he explained, tables were set up for no more than four people. He also cited existentialist philosophy as an example of a particularly dangerous individualistic trend.

I argued that all this was superficial, that a man might feel uneasy in groups, prefer his own fireplace, and treasure his own privacy but still be effectively devoted to socialism and the brotherhood of man. This statement brought out a second point—that collectivism does indeed have a deeper meaning, that it is not just "groupism" but is expressive of a genuine concern about human brotherhood and human welfare, and reflects a genuine capacity to sacrifice self for larger social purposes. In short, collectivism stands for a group of virtues that would characterize the "good" man anywhere in the world. When I pointed out that we in the West have the same ideals, the argument immediately shifted. "Yes," the Russians countered, "but it is impossible to attain these ideals under capitalism."

And so it went. We had more than two hours of lively discussion and argument, interrupted from time to time by the laughter that jokes or witticisms produced. Throughout the discussion I was unable to detect the slightest deviation from Marxism, nor could I evoke any disagreements among the Russians themselves. I was told that there *had been* disagreements about the Soviet educational reforms, but no one at this time cared to take exception to the chairman's statement of the official position. Members of the group seemed complacent about how the public-education system was working in Russia and expressed no dissatisfaction about their rather deficient knowledge of the American educational system—or, for that matter, of America in general.

However, a bit of light on developmental goals did come out of our conversation on the proposed, and then widely discussed, educational reform whereby the high school period would be extended for two years and each Russian student would be required to spend this amount of time working with his hands in either factory or field. Apart from various other presumed advantages, this program was said to be designed to toughen young people; teach them the value of work; keep them in close touch with the realities of life;

cultivate a sense of solidarity with the great mass of people who work with their hands; and, of course, prevent or curb adolescent delinquency, stylism, or outcroppings of Western-type sophistication. The student, for example, who was eventually to go into philosophy would be a better philosopher for having gone through this program.

Later, as I thought over these remarks, I reflected how these objectives had much in common with such American work-study programs as the one at Antioch College and how the opposition to the program—as my hosts at the Philosophical Institute had explained it to me—was much like the familiar American opposition to required work-study programs.

I obtained more information about educational objectives in Russia from the reports of research by people in the Pedagogical Institutes. For example, Professor Bojowich at the institute in Moscow was doing experiments, very much in the manner of Kurt Lewin, to determine some of the conditions that favor the development of responsibility and self-discipline. Thus, a child is asked whether he would rather play or make toys for other children. If he would rather play, then experimentation is undertaken to find out what would induce him to make toys for other children. Do appeals to his sympathy or the use of social pressure help him change his mind? Again, if a child agrees to make toys for other children while he is at home, what will favor his holding to his bargain? Research also shows that he will do better if he is given a definite time for the completion of the task. Other studies were also proceeding. At Kiev a big project was directed to studying how life in a boarding school may reduce egotism and social withdrawal. Other research was devoted to the effects of experiences in "a collective" upon the accuracy of judgments about the self.

In the Soviet Union, psychological research is to a very large extent instrumental to pedagogical aims. Where character education is concerned, the questions seem to be essentially these: (1) How can a wide variety of virtues—qualities that would be virtues in almost any society—best be developed and (2) how can it be demonstrated that collective means—that is, experience in collectives—are best for promoting the desired objectives?

I have suggested above that "collectivist" is a term the Russians use to describe anything that is good and that "individualist" is anything which is bad. This fact came out most clearly at Kiev. One of the professors was studying the formation of inner requirements—how the parents' requirements become the child's requirements. In other words, he was studying what the American psychologist with some psychoanalytic orientation would call "superego development," or what others would simply call "socialization." The Kiev professor called the establishment of inner requirements the attainment of "true collectivism"; disruptions of this process he termed "individuality." Naturally, I pointed out that in the West we see the matter almost the other way round, that the establishment of inner requirements is regarded as fundamental to true individualism. We shared a moment of amusement, and good will, when I went on to say that the Russians and the Americans, having adopted and "sloganized" the ideals of collectivism and individualism respectively, proceed to attach to them or to derive from them every conceivable virtue. We agreed with some warmth that collaboration among psychologists in the East and West would have to begin with a great deal of attention to the redefinition of old terms or, perhaps, with the agreement to abandon them in favor of new ones.

In this same connection I recall a remark of Professor Ananiev, director of the Psychological Institute in Leningrad. When I said that I assumed there were developmental goals which could be conceived independently of any social ideology or any system of social organization, he replied, "Of course. That's why we can cooperate."

To attempt a summary: It seems fairly clear that a wide variety of developmental goals can be and are conceived within the framework of collectivist ideology. Different professionals seemed to place somewhat different evaluations upon different virtues, but none of these workers had any great difficulty in showing how his favorite virtue could be consistent with collectivism. These virtues on the whole do not seem to be very different from those admired in various other countries of the world. If one suggests, as I did, that the Russian accent on integrating the individual into the group might lead to a loss of individuality—and thus a loss in originality and independence of thought—he will be met with a flat denial. On the contrary, he will be told that collectivist upbringing, in its proper sense, is the best way to promote creativity and uniqueness of personality.

Perhaps this belief should not surprise us. What the Russians want in the individual is what will promote the cause of socialism, and since nationalism is still very much alive in the Soviet Union, this means, most essentially, what will strengthen the Soviet state. What seems to be wanted above all are the capacity and the inclination to work hard in the interest of fully accepted group goals. However, the intelligence and knowledge that have been brought to bear on the problem help the Russian thinkers to recognize that blind loyalty or the total submergence of the individual in the group simply won't do. They also seem to recognize that the virtues which will strengthen the Soviet state are genuine and catholic virtues, much the same as those that would strengthen any other state.

THEORY IN RELATION TO PRACTICE

So much has been written about Pavlov's psychological and physiological theories and their place in the general Marxist-Leninist-Stalinist doctrine that I do not need to go into the matter here. However, a few impressions and comments may be in order.

For one thing, the Russians take theory very seriously. Practice, though it might actually be governed by common sense or be based on a few empirical rules of thumb, will almost always be brought into line with approved theory. For example, a nursery school teacher, who might be doing exactly what a Western teacher with good instincts and a fondness for children would do, will very probably be able to explain her program in the terms of Pavlov and Lenin.

Of course, the rationalization of practice in the proper theoretical terms is not difficult because the general principles of Pavlov, Lenin, and Marx—like those of Aristotle, Freud, and Dewey—must be "interpreted" and "applied"; hence, it is easy to find statements in their works that justify current practice. Just as the Soviet leaders, while regarding Marx as the great fountainhead, have been able to turn many of his ideas upside down, so have they been able to modify and change Pavlov's theories. Soviet psychology, in fact, could be transformed until it was indistinguishable from the major trends in American psychology without offering any serious threat to Pavlov's status as a hero. Important theoretical statements would still be prefaced by, "As Pavlov said." Even now the American psychologist may hold long discussions with the Soviet psychologist about the organism and the environment, determinism versus free will, the role of social forces in determining individual behavior, and experimental versus clinical methods without finding cause for disagreement.

Russian psychologists and social theorists are very much like self-made men. Their reading of Western literature seems to have an undirected or hit-or-miss aspect; things are often perceived out of (what we would regard) as their natural context. I discovered, for example, that a psychologist might mention as important or as typically American a work I had never heard of or he might introduce as central to our thinking an idea that had some currency thirty years ago but that has now been displaced. More importantly, however, Russian psychologists are likely to regard as distinctive Soviet creations those ideas or propositions which have been fundamental to Western psychology almost from its beginning. All this, of course, is largely a result of the isolation in which they have lived and worked. An advantage, however, of their special position is that it has favored their often coming up with a decidedly fresh and interesting approach.

When I say that theory is taken seriously, I mean not only that people, professional or other, feel the need of reconciling their practice with "correct" theory but that theory is valued for itself. It seems that the Russians participate more fully in the European tradition of system building than in the American tradition of empiricism. I became aware of the desire of professional people to put things into a large conceptual framework or to have a system that would somehow take account of everything. Thus, their capacity to reject completely a different school of thought such as Freud's is to be understood, I think, not only as a subservience to the Marxist-Leninist framework in general but also as an expression of the inclination to build tight, rigid systems characteristic of the "school men" in psychology from the beginning.

Of course, the key concepts—materialism, objectivity, collectivity, and historical development—have acquired much emotional value and, accordingly, have deteriorated in respect to meaning. This deterioration is to be noted not only among scientists and professionals but also among ordinary individuals with intellectual aspirations. If, for example, I demanded no definition of terms, theoretical discussions were likely to be quite vague; insistence upon clarification of concepts led to circular and time-consuming discussions. In neither case was it possible to come to any very sharp statements of theoretical issues or to discover any purely psychological ideas that do not already have a place within American psychology as a whole.

Of course, one cannot evaluate theory without examining practices and seeing what conceptions and propositions have ascendency. But, first, let me remark that it is not the Russians' psychological or social-scientific ideas or theories that are most distinctive, that constitute the major barriers to cooperation with them, or that most determine policy on the domestic and international scenes; rather, it is certain quasi-philosophical ideas and modes of thought that grow out of Russia's history and present culture. I refer, of course, mainly to her sense of mission with respect to world socialism, her consequent orientation to the future, her willingness to use almost any means to achieve the desired end, and her belief that through proper indoctrination one can know the progressive course of history and so align himself with it.

Judging, however, from what I saw of practice, I should say that the following are among the most important theoretical conceptions:

1. Because the individual is largely a product of his social environment, it is up to those who are responsible for his development to see that he has the right social environment and to intervene actively by presenting the right stimuli for the formation of the right habits. This is fairly straight, but fairly loosely interpreted, Pavlovian—and common-sense—learning theory. If the individual is to feel comfortable and function well in a collective upon which he can depend, he should have rewarding experiences from the earliest possible time and to the fullest possible extent. And, similarly, if

certain kinds of behavior or the development of certain tendencies in the personality are to be discouraged, these should not be rewarded or should even, in some suitable way, be punished; the most valuable form of punishment is, of course, the disapproval of the collective upon which the individual has learned to depend. Although it is desirable, as well as possible, for the individual's habit system to become autonomous—in the sense that it can function independently of the immediately present social group—it is wise to have the right habits continuously reinforced by example and group pressure.

2. The positive must be accentuated. This contrasts to all the psychoanalytic theories or "self" theories which argue that difficulties in adjustment or personal development are to be overcome by some sort of probing into the nature of the problem, by attaining self-insight, or by integrating some unrecognized tendency into the conscious self. The Russian approach is to strengthen those aspects of the person that are unimpaired, to find something that can be appealed to in a positive way, to divert a strong motive into constructive channels. As suggested above, much research is devoted to discovering the conditions of desired behavior, and the psychologists and educators I met showed great resourcefulness in finding ways to make their appeal attractive to individuals. Much of the work with which I became acquainted seemed to resemble rather closely that of the more able American psychotherapists or social workers who do not adhere to either psychoanalytic or psychodynamic theory.

3. Individual personality development, as well as the behavior of people in social situations, is to be explained and guided by Pavlovian theory. I found nothing to suggest that where upbringing and public education are concerned the individual does not matter. On the contrary, the main argument put to me was that experience in the collective is best for the individual. To put this in terms familiar to the American psychologist, the Russians would claim that the collective is best for the development of the superego and the ego. As indicated above, a great deal of research has been devoted to showing that an individual trait like self-insight is developed through experience in the collective. What would happen if it turned out

that such a desired trait were best developed by other means, I do not know.

The amount of attention given to the individual doing either research or working with young people in educational and correctional settings was to me a little surprising. I had both read and been told that in Russia punishment is designed for the crime rather than for the individual and that it is the "objective" act which matters and not the intention or motivational setting. In Poland I was also told that this attitude toward crime had prevailed in that country until 1956 but that they were now trying to return to the Western approach and develop means for individual treatment. Presumably the objective approach still prevails in the U.S.S.R. As far as I was able to discover this indeed remains the case where the administration of justice is concerned, but wherever I talked with people who were immediately concerned with children or young people—regardless of whether it was in a nursery school, a correctional setting, a public high school, or a university—the approach to the troubled or underdeveloped individual was much as an American would expect from an experienced and warmhearted worker at home.

THE RUSSIAN SYSTEM IN OPERATION

Probably the outstanding fact about Soviet society is that it is planned. In the field of our present interest, fairly clear conceptions exist as to what is desirable in behavior and in character development, and a vast institutional machinery has been set up in order to achieve these ends. Thus, parent education, nursery schools, elementary schools, the Young Pioneers, and the Komsomols all have the same general objectives, and all are supposed to operate according to the same general principles. The whole scheme is continually set forth for everyone by means of press, radio, and television.

What particularly strikes the Western social scientist and arouses mixed feelings in him is the degree to which scientists and experts participate with authority in the planning. One soon becomes familiar with the fact that psychological research is instrumental to pedagogical work and that the psychologists themselves have a large hand in determining what the pedagogical work is going to be. The directors of research institutes are, normally, also members of planning and controlling commissions. Collectivism in practice primarily seems to mean two things: (1) a great uniformity throughout the whole society in respect to what is believed to be right and wrong and (2) the use of the collective—the social group or organization—as the means for inducing individual conformity to the approved standards.

With respect to the first part, the authorities seem to have been quite successful, through the years, in creating for the individual the impression that what is right is what everyone does. There would seem to be a minimum of subcultural, social-, class-, or age-group differences over norms of conduct. Although national cultures have been preserved to some extent and religion is far from having been eliminated, one certainly does not get the impression in European Russia that the individual is troubled very much by conflicting values or social norms. One expects husband and wife to agree on how to bring up their children, just as one expects parents to agree with their neighbors, the school authorities, and the leaders of their children's organizations. This is not to say that the uniformity is complete, but it is probably greater than in any other industrialized country of the world.

It is because the norms are so generally accepted that social pressure toward conformity with them is so effective. The individual can anticipate with accuracy what other people will notice and take exception to. And it is this circumstance that seems largely responsible for the aspect of puritanism in Russian behavior and attitudes that so many observers have noted. It is not that the standards themselves—hard work, devotion to duty, cleanliness and orderliness, no display or foolishness, no public manifestations of sexual interests—are uniquely Russian or uniquely Communist; rather, it is that such standards must be strictly adhered to if one wishes to avoid public censure.

The relative absence of age-group differences in standards is particularly striking to someone from the United States. The standards of the various "peer groups" among the youth seem to be, by and large, the same as those of the adults and the general society. (The exceptions, among university students and groups of adolescents, will be commented upon later.) This adherence means that "collectives" of the various age groups can be effectively utilized by the society in putting across its major values. The youngster's wish not to be different and to be fully accepted among his peers, far from contributing to the creation of "peer cultures," is a powerful force toward integration into the major society.

The work of the Young Pioneers, which most authorities seem to regard as the most important agency for public education, can be largely understood, it seems to me, if we consider what our Boy Scouts and Girl Scouts would be like if these organizations had the active and enthusiastic support of every influential group or individual in our society and if they were subjected to no criticism by intellectuals or young people who refused to fit in. The activities of the Young Pioneers, and perhaps to a greater extent those of the Komsomols, must seem worthy to the young people not because they are told they are worthy in occasional speeches but because they are not differentiated from the obviously important ones of adults. The youngsters not only learn skills and crafts that will certainly be utilized later but also have the satisfaction of seeing the sale of their work, either on the market or elsewhere, contribute directly to the total national production.

The very general agreement about what is "good" and what is "bad" not only results in a kind of blanket protection of children and adolescents from harmful or potentially harmful stimuli but also in the almost universal endorsement and practice of activities that can only be described as wholesome. This, as we have seen, is fully justified in psychological theory. It is also fully justified on political and economic grounds, and it is hard to know which justification comes first. According to Pavlovian theory, the psychological dangers of comic books, magazines, movies, radio, and TV programs that devote themselves to sex and aggression are obvious. (Indeed, no psychological theory denies such dangers; the most any would do is suggest that the dangers are often exaggerated.) These pastimes, along with other interests such as jazz, certain kinds of dancing, and clothes and appearance are also expensive. The government probably has a hand in denigrating these pursuits since they contribute nothing to the national objectives. Also, these things are "Western" and hence suffer disapproval on political grounds. But whatever the reasons, the protection of children and young people is marked, and, as I will undertake to show later, it is effective.

It may be remarked in passing that overcrowding in housing, and particularly in sleeping arrangements, could also be very dangerous to children according to Pavlovian theory. Although a truly enormous effort goes toward correcting the appalling housing shortage, I didn't hear anyone remark on the psychological dangers to children from this situation.

Nevertheless, it seems impossible to overestimate the amount of attention given to wholesome or constructive activities for the young. I was told on various occasions that "Our young people have plenty of outlets." Indeed it is hard to see how they could have more opportunity for sports, crafts, music, the arts, and group activity. Whether their appetite for less wholesome pastimes is effectively suppressed by the approved activities would be another question.

In practice the use of the collective in developing desirable attitudes and character traits is not as mechanical or as neglectful of individuality or individual differences as one might suppose. The visitor to an institution for children or young people could not help but be impressed by the prevailing humanistic spirit of the leadership and the apparent happiness of the youngsters. At first glance, one might wonder whether some major features of "official" doctrine were not being ignored in practice. Not so. Even though the directors and teachers that I met were usually such fine human beings that one would expect them to be successful in their work no matter what their theoretical orientation, they enthusiastically described the basis for their work in Marxist theoretical terms, and proceeded to illustrate what they meant. (This is not to contradict what was said above to the effect that the same practices might be based on a different theory or that the practice might have come before the theory.)

There was a great deal of resourcefulness in using theory to further social purposes and the development of the individual. For example, the director of a nursing home that I visited was definitely out to show me that collective upbringing of babies and young children was as good as that found in a normal home, if not better. (All the babies and children here were boarders—either orphans or offspring of mothers who were ill or otherwise temporarily unable to take care of them.) A definite regime existed for all children of a given age or stage of development (they seemed to be very familiar with Gesell's work here), but allowances were made for the exceptional child. The whole regime was justified on the theoretical ground stated above, however.

The adults at the nursing home picked up and comforted the infants a good deal, as well as played with them individually. As soon as the babies were able to move around, they began doing things in groups—all the kinds of things that children do in our well-run nursery schools. But in room after room, each with eighteen children—sometimes all of one age and sometimes by design a mixture of age groups—there were a few children playing by themselves. Being able to play alone was regarded as an important achievement, so long as this did not impair the child's ability to play in the group. The directors claimed that they could tell the difference between solitary play springing from the child's imagination and solitary play based on some failure in adjustment to the group. The relative order and constructiveness of the activities in each room among children who were not fearful or subdued but relaxed and happy were impressive. Either the teachers or the director herself intervened promptly and firmly to settle arguments or to correct egocentric behavior, such as grabbing. It was up to the adult to intervene in the interests of good conditioning—as the theory says; and the children—as if they too were advocates of the theory—responded by acting as if they had been reassured.

The same kind of well-run nursery school is certainly not uncommon in the West. Perhaps the most significant thing in Russia is that the nursery school is only the first of the "collectives" in which the child has experience and that each succeeding one will be run in accordance with the same general principles.

My best view of the system at work with older children was obtained at the boarding school that I visited in Moscow. Here there were about 200 children in the first to ninth grades. Most had come from broken or otherwise unsatisfactory homes, but some had come from families who had applied because they thought this was the best kind of school for their children. Once again, the director and the teachers impressed me by their warmth, enthusiasm, fondness for children, and knowledge of their work. Yet, I could see most vividly in operation the various devices for inducing the individual to feel that he is dependent for his major satisfactions upon the group and responsible to the group in his actions. There were not only the various group activities, such as exercise out of doors regardless of weather at seven in the morning, but also an elaborate system of group rewards. The "best class" or the "best group" in various activities was recognized by a display of the group picture or by a banner on the door of their room.

This same general scheme is used throughout Soviet society, with what later effects one cannot tell; but there was no doubt that the children at the boarding school took their group activities very seriously—the scheme being nicely calculated to make each child feel that his own rewards depend on the group and that the rewards for the group depend upon him. At the same time, equal attention seemed to be paid to individual accomplishments. For example, various forms of recognition for the "best boy" or the "best girl" were observed in various lines of endeavor. "Socialist competition" has, of course, long been a feature of Soviet society, and we see this competition at work here. Recognition of an individual's accomplishments comes from the group of which he is a part, and recognition of any smaller group comes from a larger group of which it is a part. Thus, in the last analysis, each child is early made to feel an integral part of the workings of the whole society.

Student government was also heavily accented in this boarding school. Indeed, I was told that *all* discipline was in the hands of the children and that adults did not interfere. Each group had its council, and since each group competed with the others for the rewards of good behavior, the councils would see to it that bad behavior was discouraged and good behavior encouraged. Children were "in charge" of this or that activity—the dining room, dormitory inspection, and so forth—and assigned individual and group marks upon which awards were to be based. Occupation of these administrative posts was rotated from week to week, as was membership on the group councils. In my talks with the children who were in charge of various activities, I found that they took their duties very seriously and were modestly proud of their position and work. An American might suppose that behind the scenes adult authority or an adult final court of appeal holds sway. But in the present instance and other similar ones, I concluded that adult control was at a minimum. This control could be slight because the children have been prepared in nursery school for this kind of life. The values and ways of the society are so nearly universal as to be taken for granted, and the differentiation between adult and youthful society is minimal. Thus, it is entirely conceivable that the adults in such a setting would be able to limit themselves to the role of interpreters of the prevailing system and, instead of being authorities or disciplinarians, could be friends of the children. This kind of relationship seemed, indeed, to be the case.

I found no reason to doubt that this school was fairly typical of similar institutions for young people in the Soviet Union. Certainly I found much the same system and atmosphere in the public high school that I visited in Kiev. Investigation might quite likely reveal, however, some deterioration in the workings of the system in the Komsomol organizations. Young people at this age level are often relatively free of family and school restraints, are open to a broader outlook, and have reached a stage where questioning of established ways is normal. The only time I saw the Komsomols in action was when, as a preliminary to a performance at the circus, a group of them staged a celebration in honor of the youth organization's anniversary. This was full of the slogans, placards, and exaggerated, artificially induced enthusiasm that characterize Communist youth festivals. In all likelihood, many intelligent young people in Russia—like a couple of my guides—regard this sort of thing as "corny" and respond as would our youth to a Fourth-of-July oratory. I was told—more or less officially and by one of my guides—that the Komsomol organizations were highly varied: Some did good work, other were pervaded with apathy, and the rest were pretty much given over to purely social enjoyments. What goes on in them depends mainly on their leadership.

But once again, before leaving this topic, let me comment,

as have other observers, upon the great care, solicitude, and fondness that are given to children in Russia. Myrtle McGraw, after many observations of mothers and children in parks in Russia, has emphasized the apparent great harmony of mother-child relations—an absense of impatience, bawlings-out, and shakings. I saw nothing that would contradict her. On the other hand, Professor Zaporozhets, child psychologist at the Pedagogical Institute in Moscow, said he thought this picture of harmony was exaggerated. However, he then went on to remark that probably most Russian parents today had known much hardship as children and were determined that their own offspring should be well treated. The same thesis was advanced by others. The young philosopher whom I had first met at the Friends' seminar thought his wife spoiled their baby. He disapproved of her indulgence and supported the American practice of making children more independent by expecting them to do more things for themselves. The official view, of course, is that children deserve the best because they are the future of Russia. One hypothesis for this indulgence is suggested by observations I made at the institutions I visited. The parents may feel that they can afford to be easy on their children because the all-embracing harsher system of the state will insure that adequate behavior standards will be maintained.

EFFECTS OF THE RUSSIAN SYSTEM

Reliable information about the effects of the Russian system are, and will be, very difficult to obtain. I do not refer here to any "Iron-Curtain" phenomenon but, rather, to the difficulties in evaluating the results of any large-scale experiment. For example, the Russians have argued that the nursery school is as good for a child's development as a normal home. How could anyone demonstrate this claim without extensive and well-controlled follow-up studies of matched groups of individuals who have undergone one or the other of these experiences? Again, even if juvenile-delinquency rates are lower in Russia than in Western countries, how can it be demonstrated that these differences are due to upbringing and not to various other differences—such as the overall standard of living—that exist between the countries in question? It is common to link Soviet success in science with the Soviet educational system. Critics have suggested that the present generation of scientists are not products of the educational system that exists today but of the progressive educational system that prevailed during the early years of the revolution. The products of the system I have described here have still to prove themselves.

Nevertheless, it is certainly not impossible to investigate broad questions about the effects of the system. As I have pointed out, the Russians themselves are busy with research on questions in this area. Their perspective, of course, has certain limitations. But, as I have indicated, the Russians do seem to be open to a certain amount of international cooperation.

Difficulties in obtaining essential facts will not prevent me from recording some of my impressions. The children and teen-agers that I saw might be described by such adjectives as *fresh, naive, unspoiled, well behaved, modest, self-respecting,* and *responsible.* They were very much like the young people whom Americans think of as "adult oriented." I suspect that I repeatedly underestimated their age. This was dramatically brought home to me during my wife's and my one visit in a Russian home. I assumed that the daughter, who acted as hostess during her mother's temporary absence, was a schoolgirl. Happily, I discovered before revealing my error that she was a junior at the university. During the evening, she spent a long time talking on the telephone. "To a boy," her father said. "But," he added wryly, "they talk about nothing but science!"

Good Freudian doctrine indicates that wherever there is strictness in upbringing—no matter whether the control is exercised by the parents or by the social group—sexuality, just because it is naturally most guilt-laden, is the first impulse to suffer inhibition and repression. Presumably, this drive finds expression in proper circumstances later on! I might add here the incidental observation that although sex roles are not defined in terms of work in the Soviet Union, these roles are clearly defined in other areas of life from a very early age. Two-year-old girls in the nursery school I mentioned visiting earlier wore ribbons in their hair and were dressed in dainty little frocks, while the boys wore suitably masculine coveralls. Part of the freshness and attractiveness of these children, as well as of older youngsters and teen-agers, was their apparent serenity with respect to their sex identity. The female scientists, philosophers, and teachers that I met were motherly types, and although the young women who served as guides could give a pretty tough line about the "great October Socialist Revolution of 1917" and the "fascist aggressors," they were very much concerned with their appearance.

It would be interesting to investigate urban-rural differences in respect to the qualities just described. The children in the country and the small towns seemed even more uncorrupted than those of the cities. Certainly there was a difference between the shy, honest, openly curious, and friendly boys who clustered about our car whenever my wife and I stopped in the country and the more forward, but pleasant, little "city slickers" who were eager to trade buttonhole emblems for foreign coins. All spokesmen, whether from Russia or other Eastern European countries, agreed that less delinquency existed in the country than in the cities. But seemingly this can hardly be attributed to the persistence of traditional ways in the country. On the contrary, all indications were that collectivization has proceeded even further in the villages and towns than in the cities. Yet, in the country, the organizations and institutions could, as it were, keep track of everybody. The finger points, of course, to the temptations and the variety of influences, including foreign ones, that the big cities offer.

What one would like to know, of course, is what the wholesome and well-behaved Russian youngsters are like "inside." In other words, what would a searching, "depth-psychologcial" investigation of their personalities reveal? What potentials would they show? What future structures, attitudes, and behavior patterns have already been determined? I had the impression of much "openendedness." Young people seem to be psychologically normal and open to further development and change. Certainly they are prepared to become good Soviet citizens and to fall in with the policies of their government; but nothing has happened yet to make them unresponsive to liberal influences or incapable of the personal growth which could come from exposure to the truth. My argument for this position is based both on my observation that young people past high school age have a lively curiosity and an interest in freedom and on evidence that a great deal of creative activity exists in the Soviet Union.

Throughout the trip, I received some strong hints that university students and university-educated young people have both the capacity and the desire for intellectual freedom. I had not known Nicholas, one of my wife's and my guides, more than five minutes before he said that he wished I could meet the psychologist who had been one of his professors. This professor had been disciplined and almost purged for his recalcitrance during the Stalin era, but now he was something of a hero. As everyone knows today, considerable changing of the guards occurred after Stalin's death, with many people simply beginning to talk out the other side of their mouths.

As I continued to talk to Nicholas, he expressed an extraordinary variety of highly individualistic opinions. He said that after reading Jerome K. Jerome, he believed he was impervious to any kind of totalitarian ideology. He pointed out that the differences between communism and capitalism are not nearly so great as the contrasts between cultures—for example, like those between the Russians and the Chinese. The disappearance of personality into a uniform mass in China is an expression, he thought, not so much of communism as of Chinese character. He also thought the revolutionary play that we saw presented in Poltava was spoiled in the end by being turned into "a placard," and he was uneasy and somewhat contemptuous when schoolgirls in Kiev were asked by their teacher to give patriotic declamations for the benefit of their visitors.

The young man serving as guide to another American professor wanted to make an appointment with me to get some suggestions for readings in psychology. What had he been reading with such great interest and intelligence? Freud, who above all others is the object of official condemnation! I found other signs of open-mindedness and independence of thought among educated young people. Naturally, I also encountered ideological rigidity. The point I am making here is that the Soviet system of education by no means disqualifies the individual from freedom of inquiry. I suspect that Soviet youth if given the same opportunity as Americans would be just as inquiring and as creative as our own young men and women.

From what I have said so far about upbringing, one might suspect that a tendency to kick over the traces would show up when the opportunity arose. Some of my experiences among university students gave some indirect evidence of this. On a Russian train, I talked to an American of university age who had had the foresight and daring to bring with him a number of jazz recordings and a copy of Pasternak's *Dr. Zhivago*. Through a Swedish student, with whom he had become acquainted on the flight over, he had met some Russian students, and soon his room at his hotel became a "den of iniquity." The students indulged themselves in jazz, the latest American slang, of course, in the forbidden literature, and even in political heresy. They competed for the opportunity to buy the young American's records, his copy of Pasternak, his clothes, and various manufactured items that he had brought with him. He himself came away with a collection of sixteenth-century icons. (Nicholas said these were probably fakes, since the sale of these to tourists was a well-established racket.) My American friend summed up the incident by saying that the Russian students would probably not have been so interested in these Western importations were they not forbidden. Certainly there is much in this view.

In Poland I was told by university professors that the outstanding characteristics of their students—since 1956—were their honesty and their hunger for the truth. Any teacher whom they suspected of withholding information was in for a bad time. At the time of my wife's and my visit, Poland was enjoying a period of relative intellectual freedom; the Polish press even reported then a wide range of political opinions expressed by students in a survey. At a student performance that we attended one evening in Warsaw, we even had the opportunity to hear some lively political satire.

What about the Russian phenomena of "hooliganism" and "stylism"? Unfortunately, I was unable to investigate these things directly. Nicholas told us the day we left Moscow that we should have been with him the evening before at the Hotel Moscow. About seventy stylists had patiently been waiting to have their hair cut— in the stylist manner. I did see some dissipated and highly sophisticated-looking young people drinking and dancing to Western music in the hotels, but they would appear rather "square" by the standards of contemporary British and American youth. I observed no common pattern of dress or hair style.

Informants who seemed willing or able to speak frankly told me that off-beat behavior was to be found most often among the children of rich parents. (The great variations in Russian salaries have been the object of sufficient comment by various reporters.) Being relatively well-supplied with money and protected by their parents' position, these young people, they said, were able to go places and to do things that were beyond the reach of the ordinary youngster. They had developed a taste for high living, fancy clothes, and rock-and-roll; and, bolstered by their group spirit, they had convinced themselves that they were superior to their fellows and not to be bound by ordinary rules. Thus, they had been prompted to commit actual offenses, such as stealing, engaging in petty rackets, and disturbing the peace. It also seemed clear enough to me that these young people had been influenced by the West. They had the means to buy or somehow get the products of Western mass culture, and I found their taste for these things highly developed. They wanted for themselves, and at once, what they believed Western youth have. Indeed, their behavior as I observed it seemed largely an effort at imitating trends present in Western society.

But, as I have said, official spokesmen often belittled the seriousness of the problem. The group at the Institute of Philosophy, for example, took this attitude. When I pressed for their explanation of juvenile delinquency in Russia, I was told, "There's a black sheep in every family." Pressed further, they suggested that the explanation might lie in the persistence of bourgeois elements in the family. But as we continued our discussion of the individual delinquent, they cited much the same causative factors that we do—emotional disturbances in the family, bad companions, temptations, and so on. The point is, this group was by no means willing to admit that anything was wrong with the general system; but they did admit that the system might be made to work better—for example, the Komsomols should be freshly inspired, wrong behavior should be more thoroughly condemned, social pressure should be intensified. Basically, however, the reform in high school education discussed earlier was considered a corrective for unsuitable juvenile behavior, along with a return to the true socialist course.

One wonders what these officials would say today, for the reports of numerous observers indicate that disaffection and deviance among Russian youth have expanded greatly since 1958. The whole phenomenon invites comparisons with youth cultures and youth movements in other countries, particularly our own. I suspect that careful study would reveal much qualitative and quantitative variation among the Russian youth who at first glance appear nonconforming: Different ones would show varying degrees of rebellion, alienation, or idealism. Almost certainly one would find among them—if he could use the appropriate research instruments—many who resemble the "potentially creative" students described by Heist. In the Russia of 1958, such young people would have found it difficult to find approved outlets either for their emotional needs or for their creativity; in fact, some of them today may be contributing to those underground activities in painting and poetry about which we hear reports from time to time.

This brings us to the consideration that an evaluation of creativity in terms of its products must be made on the basis of what is officially supported or approved and what is subject to censorship. Efforts of Soviet officials to bring art and literature into line with socialist ideology and to support natural science and engineering in every conceivable way are, of course, well known. I might suggest that this emphasis in Soviet life reflects not only the ideology but the developmental stage of the nation. Many times during our travels in Russia, I was reminded of the horse-and-buggy days in this country; for instance, anywhere in rural areas on a market day, one could come upon a town and see a large assortment of mud-spattered wagons, carts, and buggies with the unhitched horses nearby, eating and resting after many miles of travel. This rural scene, in turn, reminded me of the history of the nineteenth and early twentieth centuries in this country when we were "building the nation," when the emphasis in higher education was on agriculture and the mechanical arts, and when men of arts and letters—almost despairing of a nation dominated by crass materialism and practicality—

looked to Europe for inspiration and an audience. In important respects, Russia is where we were fifty or sixty years ago. So great, and
so obvious, is the need to build that a downgrading of art and literature is understandable on this ground alone. At the same time,
the Soviet Union is engaged in a massive effort to bring culture to
the peasants, and her officials, practical men who lack confidence in
their own taste, are guided by what the aristocrats liked before the
revolution, much as the successful American business man at the
beginning of the century turned uncritically to Europe for standards.

This state of affairs, as well as the ideological accent on
socialist realism, may help to account for the relative barrenness of
the Russian artistic and literary scene. Yet we keep getting indications of creative potential. As the struggle for freedom receives attention from the world press, we get reports of an active underground in painting and letters, and, now and then, we see films or
read literary works that win the praise of our critics. Even when we
allow for the tendency of these critics to overestimate creative Russian endeavors today, we are led to the conclusion that should censorship be removed and should the nation be able to ease up on
building and national defense, we would probably see a considerable
flowering in literature and the arts.

In areas where there is strong official support and little or no
censorship, the Russians seem to do very well. This is true, for example, in the performing arts. Talent is recognized early and nurtured with considerable care. Nevertheless, talented youngsters are
not permitted to avoid any part of the rigorous ten-year school curriculum required of all children. The child with special talent is
encouraged to take special instruction, but he must do so on his own
time. This approach is in contrast with common practice in this
country, where many talented youngsters study the arts in special
schools. A comparison of the two systems should be instructive.

Perhaps the performing arts do not provide a good example
because the kind of creativity required is not of the highest order,
and because these arts seem to have flourished under all kinds of
autocratic governments. Natural science presents the best test of
what the Russians can do, for not only is it encouraged and supported to the fullest but, in its nature, it involves relatively little

ideological conflict. The evidence is that university examinations are successful in selecting bright students, and there is reason to believe that the brightest students often select science, thinking that this field will afford them more freedom than the other professions offer. The university student is paid during his five-year science course and he is assured of a well-paying and well-respected position as soon as he graduates. Observers agree that scientific training is highly specialized and highly rigorous. Creativity is valued, but no student is permitted to get away from a rather staggering program of set tasks; in other words, the training does not seem to be very different from that available in typical university science programs in this country.

What is the outcome? It would be interesting if someone would carry out a large-scale study in which peer ratings are used as a basis for comparing Soviet scientists with those of other countries. Meanwhile, we may note the casual reports of American scientists that in certain fields their Soviet counterparts are as good as any in the world. It used to be remarked, in the late 1940's and early 1950's, that Soviet progress on the atomic-energy front was due either to German scientists who had been imported or detained or to the stealing of secrets from the West. Whatever the truth may be, it seems obvious today that the Soviet Union could not have become the world's second industrial power without having produced large numbers of excellent scientists and engineers.

Another way to study creativity in the Soviet Union is to examine what happens in a field of inquiry when official restrictions are removed. A case in point would be the abandonment of the Lysenko dogma as the approved line in biology. When this happened, Soviet biology advanced very rapidly, revealing that the potential was there all the time—perhaps that some scientists had already done research which they had been wisely suppressing.

I would conclude, then, that a great deal of creativity does exist in the Soviet Union: at the level of personality functioning, at the level of work that does not see the light of day, and at the level of work—in accepted areas—that is freely published or otherwise displayed. We might recall in this connection that most Western observers used to say that the Russian educational system could only produce a nation of robots. One still wonders, however, whether the creativity observable in Russia somehow manages to flourish *despite* the system; if this is the case, such testimony favors the propositions that it is hard to keep people down and that in human affairs the best-laid plans often go awry. Analysis of this kind at least hints at the complexities involved here and indicates that the Russian system should be carefully studied in respect to what favors and what hampers the development of creativity.

I would hypothesize that the Russians lose nothing by protecting their children from early stimulation of their impulses, by failing to stress autonomy in the growing child, or by accepting a relatively slow rate of emotional development. We, on the other hand, may lose something through our overeagerness to "liberate" children and to hurry everything along. The Russians may gain a great deal through offering adolescents a generally approved value system, the experience of being rewarded—for good work—by their peers, the sense of being needed by their society, and a sense of identity based on membership in a nation-state they have not yet learned to criticize. Many of our adolescents today lack precisely these things, and they suffer from it—but with what general implications for their later creativity one cannot say.

In any event, if I were to undertake to educate for creativity at the college level, I would not mind starting with young people like the Russian seventeen-year-olds. As a matter of fact, our schools did start with such young people not many years ago, when unsophisticated but fundamentally sound young people from the farms and small towns of America came up to the university to have their eyes opened and to be astonished. One must insist, of course, that the above benefits of the Russian system are benefits for *adolescents*. It is the timing of events that is crucial here. Quite possibly, the Russians are learning what we already know well: Adolescents who are to develop into self-determining adults must have all their ideas challenged; and to challenge them, a college or university must permit all ideas to be examined.

How will the youth fare now in Russia? When in Russia I suggested to various Soviet professionals and officials that as the living standard in their country rose, and as long as the heavy emphasis on education continued, young people would be increasingly disaffected and deviant. (And, of course, creative, though I didn't mention this.) My hosts, however, were not impressed by this line of argument. For a few years after my trip, events seemed to be proving me right. But now, I am afraid, our influence upon Russian youth is not important. They are still interested in our music and in the creations of our youth culture, but not in our great political and social ideas, for they, like the youth in most parts of the world, are fully aware of the failings of our system: poverty in the midst of plenty, racial conflict, and a foreign policy that works to thwart the aspirations of oppressed people everywhere. One can only hope that we will soon get back on the track.

11

CURRICULAR EXPERIENCES
FOR THE CREATIVE

Paul Heist and Robert Wilson

The educational system in the United States—from the elementary
level through advanced professional training—is based on the underlying premise that formal education is good for all people and everyone is entitled to pursue a continuing learning program to the extent of his capabilities. Needless to say, the premise exists chiefly
as an ideal rather than as a reality. Accordingly, the withdrawal of
many students from schools and colleges before they have achieved
an education commensurate with their aptitude or potential is generally viewed as a minor tragedy. The "greater good" is the attainment of high grades, many credits, and the completion of a prescribed block of study denoted by some certificate—for example, a
high school diploma or an M.D. degree.

The above premise remains an ideal. Many Caucasian youth drop out of school usually after the twelfth year but long before reaching a level of education approaching their optimal potential. A much larger proportion of the nonCaucasian minorities are frequently prevented from participating in learning experiences appropriate for them and leave the "system" before ever approaching the level of higher education. This loss of American youth of varied backgrounds and abilities, at all levels of formal learning, is gradually being interpreted as more of a criticism of schools and teachers than of the students themselves and their backgrounds. However, the causes which explain why students leave school and forsake the route to better opportunities undoubtedly lie both with the schools and the dropouts.

The major concern of this book involves only a segment of this large problem. Many very capable and talented youth leave high schools and colleges even when almost all the predictions one might make about them would indicate otherwise. The specific focus of the preceding chapters has been on the education of exceptional men and women recognized as creatives, especially those with high or unusual potentialities for original and innovative contributions. The major implication which may be drawn from these chapters is that the educational institutions have failed with most of these creative students or at least can be credited with much of the responsibility for the many who leave.

In writing about education for creative students and the problems involved, the contributors to this book seemingly have subscribed to several assumptions: (1) Creativity or the potential for it, like most mental or behavioral attributes, exists in different degrees among any sample of mankind; (2) persons with high creative potential are identifiably different from average students; and (3) students of high creative potential will stay longer in college, or will be educated more adequately, if challenged and satisfied by appropriate, meaningful learning experiences. The third assumption is largely untested, at least as far as systematically gathered evidence is concerned. However, it does seem to follow from such evidence as is available.

In the past, conceptual or theoretical explorations of good

educational programs for the highly creative have been presented and discussed innumerable times, as a quick review of the literature will indicate (see Appendix B), but the many writers in this area tend to dwell on concrete and tangible recommendations only at the elementary and secondary levels. (An exception is found in several chapters in a compilation of conference papers edited by Anderson in 1959.) Specific programs or curricula for creative college youth have been subsumed largely under the general provisions for superior students, or those with high ability. Such provisions, however, have not resolved the major problems that drive out the free-thinking, imaginative, and innovative students. These problems obviously have to be seen and understood in relation to the creatives' distinguishing characteristics (presented in earlier chapters by MacKinnon, Heist, and Snyder).

The chief source for discovering the shortcomings of colleges for innovative individuals was two samples of creative students, one group who remained four years and graduated from the college they entered as freshmen (see Chapter 3) and a second group who transferred or dropped out of college entirely. As described earlier, the problem these identified creatives most frequently discussed was the rigidity of curricula and academic experiences. They reported that they were not given the opportunity to pursue their interests or to learn in the ways most advantageous to them. For example, one boy, a college junior who had accumulated extra credits, tried to register for only two courses, so that he might make an independent study of the French, Italian, and Spanish historical backgrounds for Expressionism in art and painting. His request was refused. Another boy, a sophomore and an excellent student, wanted to enroll in the spring for a full term of reading and studying in the library on his own, without registering for courses, seminars, or independent study. He had become convinced that he didn't need the guidance or interference of instructors to pursue a variety of studies of particular interest to him. His request was also refused.

Along with their concern about too little flexibility in the curriculum, these creative students also criticized the regimentation of programs, procedures, and learning experiences. They found assignments too repetitive, too large a proportion of their time devoted to drill and rote learning, and too great a demand for memorizing mere facts. Another form of rigidity or indirect regimentation that they mentioned was the consistent use of a single set of unvaried classroom procedures. The students felt that these criticisms reflected the complete negation of the value and importance of individualization by faculty members and administrative officers.

Students reported that the faculty's uninvolvement in the total teaching process expressed itself as insensitivity to their needs and interests as individuals and offered little encouragement for them to participate. As a result, students found it difficult to involve themselves or commit themselves to their work. A young science major, after speaking of the complex of teaching-learning problems on his campus, assessed the overall situation as a curtailment of students' freedom and academic rights. Because of his college's inflexible curricular structure and restrictions on social activities, this boy, who also found that most of his instruction and classwork discouraged student involvement, believed he had lost, or had never been granted, the freedom to learn.

Among the other chief complaints that these creative students most often voiced was the lack of quality and stimulation in faculty teaching. Instructors who were not adequate lecturers consistently lectured, they said. They also criticized the pressure-cooker learning climate resulting on many campuses from a combination of too much assigned reading, too many papers, too much drill-work assignments, and an unrelenting competition for grades. Numerous students were critical of traditional grading methods and grade-point averages. However, among the variety of difficulties that were stressed, more emphasis fell on the poor functioning of the system than on the structure of the instructional process as such. Thus, the front-line man in the system, the instructor, caught the largest proportion of the criticisms.

Some of the students were or had been in schools or programs which involved some form of innovation or presumed improvement of curricular experiences, such as honors programs and provisions for independent study. However, these curricular accommodations per se served neither as a boon nor as a blessing for most of the interviewees. Since both honors and independent study frequently represented only a larger dose of conventional course work —the difference being only quantitative instead of qualitative—the freedom and opportunity for creative students to express themselves in ways true to their own needs and interests seldom materialized.

THE TEACHER AND CREATIVE DEVELOPMENT

The major focus of concern among creative students apparently is centered on what faculty members do or fail to do, both directly in their interactions with students in and out of the classroom and indirectly in their roles as formulators of policy and structure. The effects of the latter roles are manifested in instructional goals, curriculum content, standards of excellence, and methods of evaluation and grading. Although the policy-formulator role represents a means of providing a plan for the proper education of creatives, the chief area of influence in the way of producing either positive or negative effects is actually to be found in student-faculty interactions, wherever they may take place.

One of the fundamental problems is that most college faculty members, while they may be professionals in their subject fields, are amateurs in their capacity as teachers. The term "amateur" describes a number of aspects of their role as teachers. They have, first of all, a limited understanding of their "clientele." Most, in fact, have only a small awareness and appreciation of the great diversity in abilities and motivations existing among their students. Many see no need to become concerned about individual aspirations, interests, and problems. In the teaching of creative students such personalization is especially important. College teachers are also generally untutored in the fundamentals of the learning process and different styles of learning.

Typically, scholastic aptitude-test scores and grade-point averages are emphasized in selecting students for admission to a college or for placement in special programs. Most faculty members assume that raising the criterion or cutoff scores on these measures leads to the selection of a generally more homogeneous group of students. But the contrary is closer to the truth; higher cutoff scores yield as great a diversity, or even a greater diversity, on other student characteristics, including the potential for creativity (Heist,

1962; Guilford and Hoepfner, 1966). In the most selective institutions, where the students' admission is largely based on ability, the faculty is often presented with the greatest variety of interests, values, and orientations. Thus, among other exceptional youth, the very creative personality too often goes unidentified in *both* selected and unselected student bodies. Pertinent and effective teaching of any special type or group can only follow identification and recognition.

The problems of teachers are, of course, complicated by factors lying beyond these kinds of awarenesses. In large classes, for example, teachers find it difficult to react to students as individuals. The student who reacts in this situation by making obviously relevant responses and good grades on examinations is more positively reinforcing to his teacher than the student who responds with remote associations, analogies, and possible irrelevancies. There is little time to explore such answers, and the average teacher may feel that it is an injustice to other members of his class if he spends more than a few minutes talking with a student of this type.

The *majority* of teachers and students are guided by the unexpressed rules of the game and make the best of what both often regard as a somewhat irritating but tolerable situation. Many students, in fact, find the safety of impersonality and formal structure protective, if not satisfying. But a minority, including many of the creatives, find the whole situation frustrating, if not intolerable, and withdraw or transfer to greener pastures.

Even in small, selective liberal-arts colleges, where large classes are not the rule, the loss of creative students (and perhaps the more creative members of the faculty) may be high (see Chapter 3). This attrition is probably due to the fact that all colleges and universities are chiefly means-end oriented. There are goals (expressed and unexpressed) which the institutions set for students; there are goals, not always similar to those of the institution, which individual teachers set for students in their classes. Institutions and teachers may then evaluate themselves and their students in terms of the degree to which the latter achieve these academic goals. Such evaluations are perhaps understandably concerned with meeting standards and achieving high grades. Nevertheless, for a great variety of students these goals and evaluations are quite unrealistic. But they persist despite the ambiguity surrounding the relationships between college grades and actual learning or the various measures of "success" in later life (see Chapters 7 and 8); they persist despite a long history of research in learning and psychotherapy that indicates the unimportance of externally set goals.

If genuine improvement is to be made in the education of creative youngsters, the college faculty must move from amateur to professional status as teachers. Standard preparation programs, such as they exist, do not result in a set of pedagogical skills, let alone in a comprehensive understanding of what good teaching entails. Comprehensive changes must be made in the graduate training of prospective college teachers; moreover, they must be given greater assistance in their beginning years as college instructors. The minority among them who show talent and interest in providing better teaching than they themselves received need encouragement and help in trying out new ideas. Most colleges, as represented through their division or department leaders, need to understand and learn what can be accomplished through internships and year-long orientation programs.

Despite our critical comments about college faculties as teachers of creative students, some causes for optimism exist. After a decade of post-Sputnik preoccupation with academic achievement and competition for grades, there are some encouraging signs of interest in a broader definition of college goals. The success of recent student activism, the search of many for greater involvement, and the sincerity of the fundamental questions of "relevance" and morality raised by students have evoked a corresponding concern among many college teachers.

Within recent years there has also been a sharp increase in the efforts of universities to provide preparation for future college teachers. Ewing and Stickler (1964) found that ninety-one universities offered courses on college teaching or other aspects of higher education. This was three times the number providing such courses twenty years earlier. Other signs of interest in better college teaching are noticeable. The rash of awards for excellence in teaching during the past few years—however controversial, however ingenuous in implementation—reflects an increasing awareness of the importance of excellent teaching. A few colleges and universities offer seminars or other types of assistance to both new and established teachers to help them improve their teaching. More recently a few centers or institutes have been created to study effective teaching and the problems of the faculty.

If all such efforts are to be successful in assisting teachers to reach creative youngsters, they must emphasize something more than the traditional approaches to classroom teaching. Faculty members must be assisted in broadening their conceptions of their teaching roles and the very means of instruction. In addition to fulfilling the expected role of expert or information-giver, they must be ready to fulfill, at times, the roles of scholarly model, counselor, facilitator, and friend. They must be given assistance in using teaching methods which promote more active involvement of students in planning and carrying out their own learning experiences.

But the greatest challenge is for faculty members to change their orientation to students and learn to respond to their interests and aspirations, in general and as individuals. No college teacher can be fully successful if he does not understand the learning process in its totality as well as in its individual—nonintellective as well as intellective—aspects. Greater success in holding and educating talented and creative youth, if the goal is to be accomplished at all, is chiefly dependent on the faculty's acceptance of the challenge. The crux of any genuine resolution is thus in the hands of the teachers.

CURRICULAR CONSIDERATIONS AND PLANNING

We have indicated that the teacher-student relationship is basic to the success or failure of helping the potentially creative become fully creative. The teacher's role is, of course, important for all students if a sound, challenging, and provocative learning situation is to be maintained. The general assumption is that the effectiveness of instruction, both for the individual teacher and for an organized program, depends on previous consideration and planning. The best teaching and the best programs are presumably related to the quality and thoroughness of planning and preparation.

What are the essential *curricular* and *program* considerations which need to be made for creative youth, whatever the skills and attitudes of the teacher? Such considerations must be seen as fundamental, since the actual instruction is in fact an *implementation* of a set of objectives and procedures; moreover, the skill and quality of instruction vary greatly among teachers. Thus, in speaking of a good or an appropriate curricular program, we are assuming that good planning and the provision of meaningful experiences are of basic importance regardless of whether the teaching is excellent or second-rate.

One recurrent theme in this book is the need to understand the student, his characteristics, and general motivation; this knowledge is fundamental for anyone who wishes to work with students effectively. If a teacher knows and understands all of his students as individuals, his methods of instruction and his forms of encouragement and evaluation would of course reflect this knowledge. Since the identifying characteristics of the potentially creative youth distinguish him from the noncreative student, whether equally bright or brighter, we have been proposing that special attention and considerations be brought to his instruction and learning experiences. This is where the concern for program planning becomes part of the picture.

A first consideration is the comprehensiveness or breadth of possible curricular experiences, whether within a single major program or across majors. The breadth of program must be analyzed, however, on the basis of the varying needs of different creatives— for example, some seek complexity and diversity of experience in numerous areas and others seek an intensive approach within a single, seemingly limited field. Different degrees of creative involvement are undoubtedly related to these two ways of satisfying a need for complexity. Experience with both types of students has shown that the former seek and experience stimulation and sensations more on a combined cognitive-emotional basis while the latter tend to limit themselves to the cognitive sphere of theorizing and abstracting.

A program, then, must be viewed from the standpoint of its extent and depth. Such breadth includes the possibilities of pursuing a topic—by reading, discussion and research—over a wide range of subject matter *or* delving intensively into a specific problem, such as the development of a theorem or some new phase of mathematics. Obviously the latter example, which may be a problem posed only for a single individual, may seem a strange way of describing breadth; but in this case the intensity and depth of experience, frequently going far beyond the bounds of what superficially appears to be a narrow focus, may result in complexities and scope not often found in a project involving a number of disciplines.

Another consideration should be mentioned under comprehensiveness of curricular experiences. Since creative individuals entering the elite and challenging academic institutions have a strong intellectual orientation, the subject matter offered to beginning students should afford rich and diversified experiences. Such experiences are necessary to meet their curiosity and to continue the "game of inquiry" they have already learned unlike most other entering students. Even more, provocative academic experiences may be needed to nourish the potential of these creative people for originality and innovation. Course work should also be designed to promote the growth of a wholesome skepticism, which later will be of value in the objective processing of fact and fiction.

Related to breadth in curricular experiences is flexibility. With breadth must go a degree of freedom which permits the creative student to opt for certain activities or experiences—such as special courses, unusual combinations of courses, or digressive reading ventures—which may be entirely unique to his immediate or future needs. Allowing for genuine flexibility in the curricula of even the first and second years will mean that creative students occasionally will be avoiding or overlooking courses prescribed for everyone else. A sincere commitment to individualization in the teaching-learning adventure will permit such deviation because the faculty realizes that a student can readily sandwich in the "rudiments" when he recognizes or finds a need for them.

To help develop flexibility and freedom of choice a recognized procedure must be used to adapt an established curriculum to the special interests and goals of talented and creative youth. This means granting some students the privilege of taking a set of courses which may not be listed in the catalog as standard sequences recommended for study. Such a policy is not indefensible in a college program. In practice it does not mean permitting students to make choices and decisions without rhyme or reason, although this extreme may appear to be the case. In other words, there is the possibility that some students may take a program of work which appears to be based on little logic or reason—at least from the perspective of some faculty members and the college registrar. To avoid such problems flexibility in a student's curriculum should be based on good counseling. What is being encouraged here is not license in the academic sphere but responsibility—to the student. This responsibility permits and encourages him to learn in a way and at a pace that is "true" to him, so that he is not tightly bound to the system's demand for expediency or the traditional. If an administrator or a professor balks at these recommendations, one might ask him whether he would prefer to discourage and drive out the creative youth or participate, instead, in minor "innovations" that will encourage them to stay.

The two curricular considerations introduced so far should, of course, not be limited to the first two years. Respect for capable and talented students should have no beginning and no end in the educational sequence. Such a view may also demand that concessions be made regarding the requirements to be completed in four years for particular majors and minors, as well as for other graduation requirements. For a certain percentage of students—regardless of whether they are identified as creatives, scholars, or brilliant political radicals—special provisions are necessary to encourage more variation in the combinations of course work that will meet college stipulations and requirements for graduation. This plea for leniency in presumed "standards" may mean that some bright young mathematician or social scientist will graduate without appreciating Shakespearean sonnets or being able to decipher Eliot's "Ash Wednesday." So be it—for thousands are currently going through traditional programs and finding themselves in the same unhonored circumstances, yet still receiving their degrees with no questions asked. Higher education in America should be at that stage of maturity in which we recognize the many existing fallacies and futilities and are ready to accept and respect the reality of diversity throughout all of the undergraduate years. At least, the uniformity resulting from our attempt to impose the same standards on all students is widely recognized.

A number of other ways and means are available for accomplishing curricular improvements and adaptations that should keep those creative students who have protested against rigidity of structure and procedure, regimentation, and limited opportunity for involvement. One simple means is to provide recognized creatives a wider range of elective course work, to accommodate those recommended greater freedom of choice along these lines. This point is obviously an extension of the demand for flexibility mentioned earlier. Although the majority of students have not desired or demanded this privilege, those who need or want a varied program—if only to maintain an intensity of academic activity or a high level of intellectual concern—could presumably be accommodated without endless debates and harangues on the "whys and wherefores."

Objections to flexibility and freedom of choice are often a form of defense mechanism at the departmental level and seldom are premised on facts about the quality or effectiveness of a particular educational program as it currently exists. Since the facts about the success of an accepted curriculum are generally not available, little time or effort is given to examining the assumptions underlying its maintenance. Such an examination might result in either changed or new curricular experiences.

An aspect of the total learning program that creative students in the sciences criticize frequently is laboratory work and assignments. This area is another one where greater flexibility and variation are desirable. Quite likely the old system of having all students run through an identical sequence of "experiments" or assignments is somewhat passé, and the cookbook method of performing them may also be a part of the past. In those colleges where major changes have yet to be made, the faculty should be strongly admonished to consider and incorporate the principle of human diversity in planning laboratory learning. The great variety of students—from average to brilliant, from unimaginative to highly original—need different experiences to grasp the more complicated and demanding aspects of course objectives. *Groups* of students certainly can learn a common body of facts, but each *individual* has an optimal level of understanding that determines his comprehension of scientific principles and the scientific method; dissimilar approaches and experiences fitting for these levels of understanding are clearly essential. The same laboratory procedures, for example, may prove to be obvious and boring operations for a few students, difficult and meaningless for another small minority, and yet, we assume, an important learning experience for the majority.

For science students the laboratories appear to be the ideal place to bring them into first-hand contact with real research and, thus, with experiences providing for creative involvement. A problem or project orientation should be used, leaving much of the work unstructured and up to the ingenuity of the student, with the laboratory assistant serving in the capacity of a resource person and consultant. For example, instead of the student's being given a dogfish and an instruction book in Zoology 1—with the method of gaining the necessary facts all laid out in sequential steps—he should be assigned only a dogfish and given three weeks to learn all he can before presenting his findings in the form of a report. Some students would go far beyond the expected objectives in this time, while others might need more time to attain a minimum level of information. But all would learn something of the methods and problems of getting information in this seek-and-find approach, which also happens to have much more carry-over value than a memory-map of the fish's entrails.

The laboratory situation would also seem a good place for the professor to introduce students to his own research interests and projects, the problems he has encountered, and their relationships to other research activity. Students may learn more from observing their teacher-scholar in the process of thinking through the solution to a problem (with all the attendant false starts and missteps) than from taking notes on a carefully presented end product, which is the orderly reconstruction of the disorderly psychological process of thinking creatively. More than that, the innovative teachers might involve some of their better students in phases or aspects of their own research. Interviewees at various colleges have complained of being kept from the excitement of research and real scientific problems. These same students realized that certain rudiments in a course must be learned and that a step-by-step process must often be followed to attain knowledge, but they insisted that many instructors pursue this process in extremely dull, "Mickey-Mouse" fashion.

Another program consideration falls in an area that is both curricular and extracurricular. As we know, creative students need varied experiences more than most students, and some of these needs are best met by the area of esthetics, whether through appreciation or direct involvement in the arts. Many institutions permit students to take courses in the arts while also encouraging participation on an extracurricular basis. However, these curricular and extracurricular activities are usually rather limited as far as the majority of students in many colleges are concerned. With the limitations in facilities and opportunities, most able and potentially creative students also never fulfill their need for either the amount or the variety of esthetic expression that they desire. Many more institutions should arrange for activities permitting creative expression in which students might participate voluntarily and spontaneously; these would provide a balance in their lives for the time and effort that they spend on much academic activity.

In summary, the potentiality of highly creative people will only be realized over the four years (assuming that we desire to have them remain for that length of time) by *special* curricular experiences and opportunities. To effect these considerations, a proportion of interested and sensitive faculty members is essential to provide for program changes and adaptations to meet the more unusual needs and interests of creative youth.

CONSIDERATIONS AMONG MAJORS

Several chapters in this book plead for respect and understanding of the wide variation among students; a similar plea seems in order for the highly creative youth. Being identified as creative, whether by ratings or measurements, does not preclude some other interesting and important distinctions among those so identified. One of the most obvious distinctions is focal areas of interest, such as the individual's academic field or future vocation. However, because of the major characteristics which a majority of creatives have in common, the differentiations along these lines occur mostly with gross subject-matter divisions. In other words, identified creatives in literature, history, and philosophy may have very similar orientations, while others in fields such as the graphic arts, education, and chemistry may have orientations that are most noteworthy for their quite obvious differences. Among those in the latter three fields, the capability for creativity or the need to be creative takes a different form of expression in that novel ideas or original verbal analyses, whether oral or written, are not the chief means of expression. The symbolization used in the arts is mostly graphic, a fact generally well known, but it may not be much better understood or appreciated by the common man than the special means of abstraction used in chemistry.

In the field of education, creativity is probably expressed in the most varied ways, including presentation of material, the personal, relational work with students, and, for many, scholastic productivity. The real creativity in the pre-college years, and probably also at the college level, is most frequently expressed in innovative and extraordinary teaching and in the dynamic and encouraging relationships that result between teacher and student. Paradoxically, this form of creativity in teaching—like the spontaneity of the jazz musician whose product is the immediate performance—doesn't result in a tangible product which testifies to the creative act, unless the "product" is registered overtime in the altered lives of the students.

The point under consideration here is the varied ways the different degrees of creative potential are *expressed,* whether the variations are nearly indistinct or very extensive. The differences in the media, mode, and style of creative expression, however extensive, cannot and should not be overlooked in an academic setting. The faculty, along with the curricula, should have enough flexibility, within and among departments, to encourage and reward creative activity and work in differential fashion. This means that, because creatives are measurably different types of human beings, those enrolled in the humanities, the social sciences, and the natural sciences will need different media, opportunities, challenges, and growth experiences provided in the curriculum.

These differences in expression among the various curricula

can be provided for in a number of ways. One major difference is in the amount of theorizing and abstracting permitted or required, especially in philosophy, mathematics, and the physical and social sciences. Within both of the major science areas, the *specific* fields vary in the amount of theorizing demanded or encouraged. A creative expression or product in these subject areas might appear, for example, in the form of a theoretical development, an improved analytical procedure, or a statistical tool for the analysis of data. Another frequent difference is found in the type and amount of symbolization required. The most frequently used types or forms of expression are verbal, numerical, graphic, and musical (both by notation and sound). Within these four major forms, specific types (for example, algebra versus calculus or poetry versus prose) lend themselves more to some disciplines than to others. For very bright creatives, competency in several forms of symbolization leads to greater opportunity of expression, but this probably represents a fairly rare need, since persons' major orientations and background experiences tend to limit them to one or two major forms of symbolization.

Another less obvious difference among disciplines in the form of creative expression, which is related to the modes of symbolization, centers in the possibility for esthetic involvement or the use of an artistic "sense." An esthetic need, perspective, or high level of appreciation is one of the common characteristics of many, if not most, creative people. The creative and performing arts, of course, abound with opportunities for such expression, but the academic disciplines show a wide variation in these opportunities. For example, fields like philosophy and mathematics often present intellectual experiences and challenges which have esthetic overtones, while in some other fields anything representative of the esthetic seems to be entirely lacking.

The disciplines and subject-matter fields also appear to vary a great deal in the amount of freedom permitted students—freedom to be participative, to become involved, to be original and creative. As a single example, a great difference exists in the freedom to become meaningfully participative in the arts as compared with that in history and psychology, at least as generally taught. Successful teaching and learning in dramatics, dance, and painting, for the most part, are premised on a freedom or need to be thoroughly involved; most academic fields do not have or cannot effect a similar freedom.

The sum and substance of this brief comparison of differences in expressive possibilities among the college-level disciplines is that the opportunities to have one's creative potential challenged or to behave creatively vary a great deal. In certain subject areas, the course content, which may lead to high degrees of structure, formalism, and regimentation, tends to prohibit the development of opportunities for rewarding students with strong faculties of imagination and original thinking. The natural implication to be drawn from the known characteristics of creative youth and from the variations in curricular provisions for creative involvement is that students with a high potential for creativity will be attracted to some disciplines and not to others. Other creative students who initially select a major which provides inadequate challenges will tend to transfer to fields which do. A second implication centers in the possibility of changing curricular offerings and learning experiences that are too limited for many creative students. However, it is far easier to suggest and recommend such changes than it is to put them into effect. An alternative view is that some disciplines demand a stability and regularity within which the innovative and creative youth proves to be too disruptive. On the whole, the high creatives or those with a strong need for creative involvement apparently choose majors in areas of academic work which are more in line with their needs, interests, and potentialities.

In summary, existing curricular fields of specialization do not provide equally challenging learning experiences for the variety of creative students. In fact, a prominent discrepancy seems to exist among major programs in the extent to which they provide opportunities and challenges for creative youth. The one saving grace here is to be found in the nonrandom distribution of students with high creative potential. Most seem to select and pursue majors (for the time that they stay in college) which are in line with their interests and needs; at least, identified creatives tend not to enroll in majors which do not provide appropriate curricular experiences.

The need for freedom for creative students is stressed in several chapters in this book. Whether faculty members can be educated to know how to provide such freedom and whether enough of them can be convinced that program modifications need to be made to accommodate more creative students remains to be seen. Indeed, the recruitment of properly qualified teachers is the chief factor in the successful education of creative students. If they are to receive exceptional scholastic experiences, their teachers must have not only classroom skills but a sensitivity to their special characteristics; or if such sensitivity is initially lacking, their teachers must be willing and able to learn about their unique needs as creative individuals. Program and subject-matter considerations are essential but secondary; in the final analysis it is the understanding and responsive instructor that is primary.

REFERENCES

Anderson, H. H. (Ed.) *Creativity and its cultivation.* New York: Harper, 1959.

Ewing, J. C., & Stickler, W. H. Progress in the development of higher education as a field of professional graduate study and research. *Journal of Teacher Education,* 1964, *15,* 397–403.

Guilford, J. P., & Hoepfner, R. Creative potential as related to measures of I.Q. and verbal comprehension. *Indian Journal of Psychology,* 1966, *41,* Part 1, 7–16.

Heist, P. Reconsiderations in the education of high-ability youth. Paper presented at the Counseling Training Institute, University of Minnesota, Summer, 1962.

CONSIDERATIONS IN THE ASSESSMENT OF CREATIVITY

Paul Heist

TESTING AND PREDICTION

The assessment of human psychological behavior is a continuing challenge to educators, therapists, and social scientists. Members of these and other professions have long sought to find ways to measure mental or behavioral characteristics in the hope that they would lead not only to a greater understanding of a person but would also provide a more adequate basis for accurately forecasting something about his future. To date, such assessment has led to greater success in enhancing *contemporary* knowledge about people than in permitting valid predictions of later behavior, but for certain characteristics and types of behavior, and under certain circumstances, prognostications have frequently proved to be amazingly successful.

However, it is usually the large number of failures, rather than the successes, that keep the science of human prediction at a level of considerable humility.

The world of higher education—to judge by the sheer amount of testing—has had the greatest need for accurate measurement of human behavior. The chief reason for so much activity has been to find measures for predicting the academic success of those that actually enroll in college. But growing out of the studies on prediction, test results have been increasingly used to help *select* students for university education, and more frequently, of late, to aid in *understanding* the students themselves.

Nevertheless, testing and personality assessment for the greater understanding of students, as well as for considering improved methods of teaching, has never been widely utilized outside of counseling and psychological service centers. In the average classroom situation, little effort is made to understand the student's motivations, interests, and aspirations. College instruction has never demanded (presumably) much knowledge about the learner, certainly not in the sense that the physician, therapist, and lawyer generally seek and obtain certain information about the individuals whom they are assisting or treating.

However, at all levels of education the measurement of mental ability has been very widely utilized. This measurement, accomplished through a variety of tests and approaches, has led to a tremendous amount of prediction and then to the evaluation of such predictions. Through the use of this one means of assessment, we have attempted to estimate the attainment and success of students in all forms of academic settings. To a certain extent we have both succeeded and failed, and at the present time, in the late Sixties, we seem to be approaching a stage at which we fully recognize the "predicament" of such predictions and also begin to understand the reasons for our limited success. This has led some authorities to struggle more valiantly with the problems of improved prediction, while others have frowned upon the latter and begun to look with a changing perspective at the education of *individuals* in modern society. The outgrowth of these two somewhat different concerns—together with the irreversible phenomenon of more extensive education for a larger proportion of the existing populace—will quite likely mean a gradual move to a more complete assessment of human variables in the attempt to effect greater individualization in the teaching-learning process. (See Chapter 7.)

In spite of a trend in recent years to hold all testing for predictive purposes in some disrepute, a concern for more adequate assessments of human characteristics, especially as related to academic activity, has been on the increase. The development in the last decade of a number of inventories and tests of a nonintellective or noncognitive nature testifies to both a continuing and changing recognition of some unresolved problems. Some of these new nonintellective tests have been constructed for use, along with old and new ability tests, on the old problems of prediction, but others have been constructed to assist with the identification, description, and greater understanding of students. A few psychological inventories have been developed expressly for research purposes, and these also accommodate problems of identification and descriptions, as well as the assessment of change on selected characteristics.

TESTING FOR CREATIVE POTENTIAL

One aspect or area of human mental behavior which has gradually been receiving more consideration—both from the standpoint of education in general and the specific developments in testing—is creativity. A concern for the *identification* of youth with different degrees of creative potential is a natural outgrowth of the increasing interest over the past two decades in the better education of creative individuals. The major emphasis of this concern for identification, however, has been in the elementary and secondary years —a fact which may partly account for the few psychological inventories that can be used to assess creativity at the post-adolescent and college level.

A few, fairly unique performance tests have been developed by psychologists specifically to assess certain traits or aspects known to be part of the complex of creative behavior. The work of Guilford (1967) is probably the major example of this type of testing, especially where adolescents or adults are concerned. In the way of objective tests, only one multiscale instrument, consisting of attitude and interest items subgrouped under several bipolar dimensions, has been constructed chiefly to assess creative personality types. This instrument, the *Myers-Briggs Type Indicator,* is included in the list of inventories to follow (1959). Other social scientists have developed single "personality" scales (composed of objective items demanding true-false responses) on concepts known to be part of the psychological complex of creativity. An example is Barron's and his colleagues' work on scales of complexity (1953) and originality (1955). One recently constructed inventory, designed particularly for admissions work and predictive studies, includes a single comprehensive scale called "Creative Personality." This measure is found in the *Opinion, Attitude, and Interest Schedule* by Fricke (1963).

Probably the most useful and valid measures of creative components are found in the clusters of established inventory scales that are contained in general personality inventories and that have been found to be highly correlated with identified creative behavior. Two examples of inventories including such correlated scales are the *California Psychological Inventory* (1957) and the *Omnibus Personality Inventory* (1968), both of which will be introduced briefly below. There is no implication that the type of objective measurements mentioned above are of a special quality or represent particularly recommended forms of assessing creativity or various aspects of it. In all fairness, creative individuals are of such a variety and complexity that attempts at a more adequate assessment will probably continue indefinitely.

For the interested reader, several examples of different types of tests and inventories of possible value in doing research on creative youth or in identifying students with some potential for original or creative expression are listed below and followed by very brief abstracts. These particular tests are all described as objective in nature and lend themselves to easy administration and scoring. Persons initiating research or evaluative studies and getting ready to decide on appropriate psychological tools would profit from reviewing the possibilities with trained professional personnel on their campuses. The choice of the instruments included below is as much a matter of the frequency of their use in studies of students in recent years as it is of quality. However, the list is chiefly illustrative and not intended as a representative sampling of what may be currently available. The tests are listed alphabetically according to the name of the author(s).

1. Allport, G. W., Vernon, P. E., & Lindzey, G. *Study of Values*. (3rd ed.) Boston: Houghton Mifflin, 1960.

This instrument is an inventory of six prominent values or interest areas: theoretical, economic, aesthetic, social, political, and religious. It lends itself to fairly brief administration and permits inferences about some of the directional motivations of individuals. A wealth of comparative data is available on numerous student groups. One or two patterns of mean scores across the six scales have been shown to be typical of creative personalities.

Although it can also be of real help in differentiating among students on factors assessing the degree of intellectual commitment vs. a practical, utilitarian orientation, there are some limitations inherent in its use owing to the moderate reliability of some scales, the structured lack of independence among scales, and the problems of meaningful longitudinal or change measurement consequent upon the first two points.

2. Edwards, A. L. *Edwards' Personal Preference Schedule*. New York: Psychological Corporation, 1957.

This instrument provides numerous interrelated scales based on the need concepts of Henry Murray. A number of the scales would presumably be fairly close correlates of creative behavior. The items are presented in forced-choice form to reduce the operation of the response sets of those taking the inventory. From a research standpoint, the paired-comparisons approach to every response is both a strength and a weakness. It has been used for a variety of research purposes among college and professional students.

3. Gough, H. G. *The California Psychological Inventory*. Palo Alto, Calif.: Consulting Psychologists Press, 1957.

The CPI is widely used as an instrument on high school and college youth, and it appears to be particularly relevant where research on the social and emotional aspects of normal student behavior is of interest. Several scales have been included to assess academic motivation and intellectual concerns. A number of the scales also have been found to be correlates of creativity. Although a comprehensive inventory, encompassing eighteen scales of fair to good reliability, the CPI is short enough to be administered within an hour and a half to two hours' time.

4. Heist, P., McConnell, T. R., Webster, H., & Yonge, G. *The Omnibus Personality Inventory.* Berkeley: Center for Research and Development in Higher Education, University of California, 1961. (Revised version, 1968.)

This is a research instrument consisting of fourteen scales developed chiefly within the context of several longitudinal projects on student change and development. Reviewers have called attention to the high reliability across most of the scales and the particular relevance of most of the scales to research in an academic context. Different composites of scales assess the following behavioral areas or syndromes: intellectual orientation, nonauthoritarian thinking, social-emotional adjustment, and an other-directed orientation. A pattern of mean scores on seven of the scales has been found to be a strong correlate of creative potential or behavior.

5. Myers, Isabel B., & Briggs, Katherine C. *The Myers-Briggs Type Indicator.* Princeton: Educational Testing Service, 1957.

This is an attitude item inventory based on Jungian theory and concepts. It has had considerable use in distinguishing among individuals presenting varied cognitive and perceptual approaches to the environment. The composite of eight major scores purportedly have value for identifying the potentially creative from the noncreative.

6. Strong, E. H. *The Vocational Interest Blank for Men.* (Rev.) Palo Alto, Calif.: Stanford University Press, 1951.

This instrument is a major counseling inventory that has become a valuable research tool. The inventory measures the degree to which a student's interests resemble those of people successful in over forty different occupations. New developments coming from several different sources have led to utilization of profiles (based on major *patterns* of scale scores) for categorization of students. One such approach results in a distribution of categories based on fairly precise assessment of a student's "intellectual disposition." Certain not frequently seen profile patterns tend to be related to or indicators of creative potential.

COMMENTARY ON THE STUDY OF VALUES AND THE
OMNIBUS PERSONALITY INVENTORY

Since use is made of data from the A-V-L *Study of Values* and the *Omnibus Personality Inventory* in two or more chapters in this book, brief explanatory commentaries are presented to supplement the limited information included there.

The A-V-L Study of Values (AVL): The Study of Values was devised and constructed to assess six values viewed as important throughout much of Western culture. These scales are titled as follows: *Theoretical, Economic, Aesthetic, Social, Political,* and *Religious.* The single-word titles are not adequate to conveying the full meaning of the actual value or concept measured by the particular items. Definitions of the values (or scales), drawn from the *Manual,* are stated at the end of this section.

This inventory of values has a special assessment strength derived from the fact that the items or statements function in two or more directions. That is, replying in the *positive* to a specific question or attitude will add to the score for one value but at the same time subtract from the score on another value. Thus, the six scales are not structurally independent from each other. This form of scoring leads to a special strength, and simultaneously to a possible difficulty, in interpreting the results.

For example, when a person scores very high on the Theoretical value, one has good reason to believe that this score is a valid indicator of genuine theoretical interests. But if a person's theoretical orientation in his thinking is stronger than any other value, his responses to the items which indicate this on the scale in turn lower scores on scales such as the Economic and Religious. While the Theoretical score may be an indication of true strength, one has to ask if the score on the Religious value would actually be higher if measured independently from the other scales.

The *strength* of this form of scoring, however, derives also from this interdependent scale structure. The two values which are highest and the two which are lowest—that is, farthest from the midpoint (a score of 40)—give the researcher the *major* strengths and weaknesses of a person, or the predominant and nondominant value commitments. Thus, one can usually rely on the "story" represented in the two highest and two lowest value scores, but, as indicated above, one may begin to ask which (the lows or the highs) are possibly the products of the other. There are still the two other scales to interpret, in which the scores have been "forced" to be closer to the mean as a result of the total interrelationship. And, again, one wants to ask where these scores of the fifth and sixth scale would really fall if not influenced or determined by the responses made on certain items but in another direction.

Along with a presentation of these facts about the AVL, it is important to add that the "strength" of this inventory rests on the fact that the test has real value in differentiating among types of students and in giving considerable insight into some relatively important aspects of individual persons. More than that, the real advantage of the test comes from analyzing the *pattern* of scores (for example, the two highest scales versus the two lowest), but analysis of this point will be left to the discussion on the assessment of creativity. Other positive points, very much in favor of the AVL, are the brevity of the test and the short time it takes to administer, as well as the ease of scoring. It is a quick and easy means to gain some important understanding of a student body or an incoming class.

How can the *Study of Values* be used to assess a creative orientation or to identify potentially creative persons? The total history of such a use of the AVL cannot be presented here, except to mention that shortly after the middle Fifties the staffs at the Institute for Personality Assessment and Research and the Center for Research and Development in Higher Education discovered the test's value for assessing creative types. At the Center, the AVL was first used in a study of National Merit Scholars, and by the second year it became apparent that a couple of rather rare profile patterns on the AVL served to identify extraordinary types of students. In this early period, some uncertainty and confusion existed about the meaning of the patterns, including whether they denoted intellectualism, scholarship, or creativity—or all three.

At a spring conference in 1959, MacKinnon (1959) reported some corroborative and clarifying findings from his and his colleagues' studies of creative research scientists, mathematicians, and architects at the Institute for Personality Assessment and Research. The mean-score profiles on the AVL obtained for these recognized creatives were very similar to the profiles of the exceptional young students discovered in the National Merit Scholar project. The MacKinnon results resolved some of the uncertainty of the findings obtained at the Center for Research and Development in Higher Education. The bright and talented youth could be viewed as being at least as creative as they were scholarly. And as the data on the National Merit Scholars continued to come in over the years, the substantiating evidence for the earlier findings gradually became available. But, as with many problems of identification, we learned that the distinction between profiles for creatives and scholars was not always clear-cut, especially when the subjects were all students of very high ability.

Later, in a second project at the Berkeley Center, in a study on the men at Caltech, the same profile pattern was identified in about 18 per cent of the persons in one entering class. Of special interest, as later determined, the majority of these particular students did not return to Caltech for their third year.

This AVL profile *pattern,* very much like the one graphed in Chapter 3, and *shared by all the groups mentioned,* consists of very high scores on the Theoretical and Aesthetic scales and low scores on the Economic, Religious, and Social scales. The pattern for the combined average scores across several of the available creative profiles of potentially creative groups, as identified by peers and faculty, is as follows (N = 118; both sexes), shown below.

This pattern has come to be respected by the staff at the Center as indicative of atypical, unusual persons in which the high Aesthetic score is probably the most significant characteristic, adding the "spice and honey," the specialness, to the combination of a high Theoretical and Aesthetic pattern. The low scores on both the Economic and Religious values mean an absence of pragmatic, utilitarian, and dogmatic thinking and an openness to a wealth of envi-

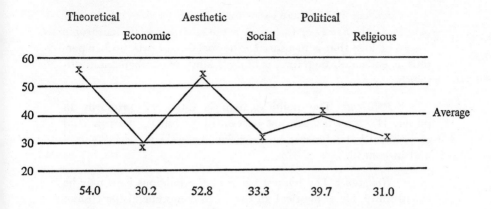

ronmental stimulation. This combined factor "releases" the person to play and experiment in the world of ideas and the world of art.

The *definitions* for six *Study of Values* scales, as stated in the *Manual,* are as follows:

> *Theoretical:* The dominant interest of the theoretical man is the discovery of truth. In the pursuit of this goal he characteristically takes a "cognitive" attitude, one that looks for identities and differences; one that divests itself of judgments regarding the beauty or utility of objects and seeks only to observe and to reason.

> *Economic:* The economic man is characteristically interested in what is useful and practical. Based originally upon the satisfaction of bodily needs (self-preservation), the interest in utilities develops to embrace the practical affairs of the business world—the production, marketing, and consumption of goods, the elaboration of credit, and the accumulation of tangible wealth.

> *Aesthetic:* The aesthetic man sees his highest value in form and harmony and judges each single experience from the standpoint of grace, symmetry, or fitness. He regards life as a procession of events, enjoying each single impression for its own sake. He need not be a creative artist, nor need he be effete; he is aesthetic if he but finds his chief interest in the artistic aspects of life.

Social: The highest value for this type of person is love of people. In the *Study of Values,* it is the altruistic or philanthropic aspect of love that is measured. The social man prizes other persons as ends and, therefore, is himself kind, sympathetic, and unselfish.

Political: The political man is interested primarily in power. His activities are not necessarily within the narrow field of politics; but whatever his vocation, he seeks to be influential and in control.

Religious: The highest value of the religious man may be called unity. He is mystical and seeks to comprehend the cosmos as a whole in order to relate himself to its embracing totality. The religious man may be described as one whose mental structure is permanently directed to the creation of the highest and absolutely satisfying value experience.

The *Omnibus Personality Inventory* (*OPI*): The OPI was constructed and revised over a period of ten years to serve as one of several major instruments for research on college students. The particular research and the development of the present instrument (OPI–F) was done under the auspices of the Center for Research and Development in Higher Education at Berkeley. The major purpose for constructing a new personality inventory was to provide a set of psychological dimensions which were especially relevant to describing and understanding important aspects of students' lives and behavior in an academic context. The underlying concerns included the students' involvements in both the academic and social-relational spheres of campus life and activity.

The chief approach to assessment in an inventory of this type is based on the assumptions that all or most persons in a particular society or culture acquire or develop a number of psychological characteristics in common, but that the diversity of genetic contributors and environmental experiences lead to great variation in the development of these characteristics. Since this is the case, it is also assumed that scales (measuring devices) can be constructed, with satisfactory validity, to tap the different degrees to which a characteristic exists. The measured characteristics, sometimes referred to as personality dimensions, are represented in ways or styles of thinking, in general orientations to things, events or persons in the environment, in feelings or emotional expressions, and in perceptions about oneself. These ways of thinking or perceiving are verbally expressed in the form of attitudinal statements, opinions, preferences, and interests to which a person is asked to respond, indicating whether or not they describe or typify him in these respects. A specific scale is composed of a related set of such statements (twenty or more items in the case of the OPI) which are focused on a measurable characteristic, such as religious orientation or feelings of introversion. Each statement or item in a scale serves as a sample of behavior or an indicator of the overall characteristic. The number of statements responded to, according to the keyed scoring, serve as a measure of the degree of intensity to which the characteristic exists in comparison with the average score obtained on a large, representative sample of students. Thus, any score represents a relative and not an absolute measurement.

The OPI was designed to measure several syndromes in the cognitive and affective spheres of behavior (Heist and Yonge, 1968). One scale or a cluster of two or more scales assess the following syndromes or complexes: intellectual orientation, nonauthoritarian thinking, social-emotional adjustment, pragmatic-applied orientation, other-directed orientation, and masculinity versus femininity. The first syndrome, intellectual orientation, is measured at two levels—by four scales measuring several primary dimensions *and* these same four plus two more that measure the degree of readiness to learn and to examine the new and the different.

The assessment of creativity or possible correlates of creativity were another consideration in the construction and development of the OPI. Later opportunities in several different research projects permitted the assessment of a variety of persons who exhibited creative behavior through different media and in different contexts (see Chapter 3). Over a period of time, this collection of data produced some interesting findings regarding a number of characteristics which these identified creative people had in common. These groups of creatives—whether in college contexts or in the adult world (artists and social scientists)—scored above the mean on the following scales (with most of the scores falling at the eighty-fourth percentile or higher): Thinking Introversion, Theoretical Orientation, Estheticism, Complexity, Autonomy, Religious Orientation, and Impulse Expression. For most of these people, the scores on the Personal Integration scale were between the thirtieth and fourtieth percentile, indicating varying degrees of anxiety, self-concern, introspection, and need or willingness to disaffiliate from others.

More important, perhaps, than the actual mean scores for the identified creatives was the very similar *profile pattern* obtained for all groups. The chief consistency across the several patterns was the high level of the scores on the Estheticism, Complexity, Autonomy, and Thinking Introversion scales, with the first two generally falling above the last two. The greatest fluctuation, contingent upon several factors such as the religion and ability of the individuals, was on the Theoretical Orientation and Religious Orientation scales. The common characteristics or correlates found among the creative groups have been combined and used as criteria, in the form of a profile pattern, for identifying other students who presumably possess a greater degree of creative *potential* than those students whose scores do not approach, match, or exceed this particular pattern of scores.

OPI scale definitions: Brief definitions for all the OPI scales are stated below:

> *Thinking Introversion (TI)*: Persons scoring high on this measure exhibit a liking for reflective thought, particularly of an abstract nature. They express interests in areas such as literature, philosophy, and history. Their thinking tends to be less dominated by objective conditions and generally accepted ideas than that of low scorers. The latter—extroverts—tend to evaluate ideas on the basis of their immediate practical application.

> *Theoretical Orientation (TO)*: This scale assesses the degree of interest in using scientific methods in thinking, including interest in science as such and in scientific activities. High scor-

ers are generally more logical, rational, and critical in their approach to problems than those whose scores are average or below.

Estheticism (Es) : High scorers endorse statements indicating diverse interests in artistic matters and activities. The content of the statements extends beyond painting, sculpture, and music and includes interests in literature and dramatics.

Complexity (Co) : This measure reflects an experimental orientation rather than a fixed way of viewing and organizing phenomena. High scorers are tolerant of ambiguities and uncertainties, are fond of novel situations and ideas, and are frequently aware of subtle variations in their environment. Most persons with very high scores on this dimension *prefer* to deal with complexity, as opposed to simplicity, and seem disposed to seek out and enjoy diversity and ambiguity.

Autonomy (Au) : The characteristic measured is composed of nonauthoritarian thinking and a need for independence. High scorers are sufficiently independent of authority, as traditionally imposed through social institutions, to opposed infringements on the rights of individuals. They tend to be nonjudgmental and realistic.

Religious Liberalism (RL) : The high scorers are skeptical of religious beliefs and practices and tend to reject most of them, especially those that are orthodox or fundamentalistic. Persons scoring around the mean and lower indicate various degrees of belief in general and their subscription to specific tenets and dogma.

Impulse Expression (IE) : This scale assesses the degree to which one is generally ready to express impulses and to seek gratification either in conscious thought or overt action. The high scorers value sensations, have an active imagination, and their thinking often is dominated by feelings and fantasies.

Schizoid Functioning (SF) : High scorers (above 70) exhibit some attitudes and behavior that characterize socially alienated persons. Along with frequent feelings of isolation, loneliness, and rejection, they may intentionally avoid most others and experience feelings of hostility and aggression.

Social Introversion (SI): High scorers withdraw from social contacts and responsibilities. They display little interest in people or in being with them. The social extroverts (low scorers), on the other hand, seek social contacts and gain satisfaction from them.

Lack of Anxiety (LA): Persons scoring high on this measure indicate that they have few feelings or symptoms of anxiety and do not admit to being unduly nervous or worried. Low scorers admit to a variety of these kinds of symptoms and complaints.

Masculinity-Femininity (MF): This scale reflects some of the differences in attitudes and interests between college men and women. High scorers (masculine) deny interest in esthetic matters and admit to few feelings of anxiety and personal inadequacy. They also tend to be less socially oriented than low scorers and more interested in scientific matters.

Response Bias (RB): High scorers respond to a majority of the statements in this scale in a way which is typical of experimental subjects who are asked to make a good impression. The responses of low scorers are similar to those of subjects instructed to make a poor impression. Scores between 40 and 60 denote valid scores on other scales.

REFERENCES

Barron, F. Complexity-simplicity as a personality dimension. *Journal of Abnormal and Social Psychology*, 1953, *48*, 163–172.

Barron, F. The disposition toward originality. *Journal of Abnormal and Social Psychology*, 1955, *51*, 478–485.

Fricke, B. *Opinion, Attitude and Interest Survey, OAIS Handbook: A Guide to Personality and Interest Measurement*. Ann Arbor: Evaluation and Examinations Division, University of Michigan, 1963.

Gough, H. G. *The California Psychological Inventory*. Palo Alto, Calif.: Consulting Psychologists Press, 1957.

Guilford, J. P. *The Nature of Human Intelligence*. New York: McGraw-Hill, 1967.

Heist, P., & Yonge, G. *Manual for the Omnibus Personality Inventory—Form F,* 1968.

MacKinnon, D. W. Identifying and developing creativity. *Selection and Educational Differentiation.* Berkeley: Field Service Center and Center for Research and Development in Higher Education, University of California, 1959.

Myers, I. B., & Briggs, N. C. *The Myers-Briggs Type Indicator.* Princeton: Educational Testing Service, 1959.

SELECTED BIBLIOGRAPHY

Paul Heist and Janet Tallman

This bibliography represents a selection of the available writing and research reports on the topic of creativity, its nature and nurture. The selections were limited, with a few exceptions, to the period following 1950, with major attention directed to the years from 1958.

The abstracted or summarized publications were selected in part because of their actual or possible relevance to education for creativity in college and also as chief examples of the variety of recent pertinent literature. The abstracted publications review what is known about creative young people and the problems of educating them.

225

ANNOTATED OR SUMMARIZED REFERENCES

Some of the brief abstracts that follow were taken from *Psychological Abstracts* (indicated by *) and from *Creativity and the Individual* (indicated by †) by Stein and Heinze.

Barron, F. *Creativity and psychological health: Origins of personal vitality and creative freedom.* Princeton: Van Nostrand, 1963.

This book summarizes ten years of research on recognizing and fostering creativity in ourselves and others. The research, involving more than 5,000 men and women, is concerned with personal change and growth through psychotherapy, religious beliefs and philosophies of life as bases for action, the paradox of freedom and necessity, transcendental experience, and personal creativeness. The book also discusses the relationship between artistic creation and religious belief and self-renewal and conflict in creative change. The book analyzes the relation between psychological health and the ability to be free, original, and expressive. The author superimposes realistic individuals on statistical profiles, discusses the philosophical questions of sanity and society, and evolves to some extent an idea (rather than a description) of a creative, healthy individual.

Burkhart, R. C. *Spontaneous and deliberate ways of learning.* Scranton, Penna.: International Textbook, 1962.

This book is a sophisticated teachers' manual. The work is based on research of the author and other research-oriented teachers, and it follows the work of V. Lowenfeld. The main focus is on the pupil's creative growth as an individual as seen in his work and progress in art. The author distinguishes between spontaneous and deliberate creators, and discusses their personalities, relationships to productive teachers, experiences during the creative process, and the influence of instructions on these two kinds of students. Personality analyses are made on the bases of student reports, judgments of the students' art, observation of their methods, and psychological tests.

De Mille, R. The creativity boom. *Teachers College Record*, 1963, *65*, 199–209.*

Three discernible components of creative productivity—temperament, motivation, and intellect—are discussed. Intellectual abilities tend to be associated with creativity, although they are not highly correlated at all levels. The author also discusses the development of creativity in the classroom.

Dentler, R. A., & Mackler, B. Originality: Some social and personal determinants. *Behavioral Science,* 1964, *9,* 1–7.

This study defines originality as the degree to which uncommon responses are given to a task. The subjects were university undergraduates with high academic achievement. Sex and individual level of anxiety were controlled. The study aimed to identify some social conditions under which the production of novel, statistically uncommon, or infrequent responses to a problem increased. Social and interpersonal situations can affect the quantity and quality of novel responses. The study also explores the association between originality and certain individual personality characteristics viewed as affecting interpersonal behavior. Anxiety acts as a depressant; the more anxious were less original.

Drews, Elizabeth M. The development of talent. *Teachers College Record,* 1963, *65,* 210–219.*

There appear to be marked similarities between the cultivation of creativity and the process by which psychologists say that mental health is achieved. The article examines two of the most important environmental conditions, freedom and an unconditional psychological acceptance.

Feibleman, J. K. The genius versus the American university. *Journal of Higher Education,* 1960, *31,* 139–142.

This author believes that "U.S. educators have made a mistake in imitating the model of American business. Universities should have an atmosphere of contemplation, not hustle and bustle. . . . The genius is not *pro*duced but *in*duced. . . . If we are to have our share of geniuses, we must learn how to leave people alone. Perhaps we should not place so much emphasis on degree requirement. . . ."

Flescher, I. Anxiety and achievement of intellectually gifted and creatively gifted children. *Journal of Psychology,* 1963, *56,* 251–268.

> The author states as the purpose of his study: "Explanations regarding complex cognitive functioning inevitably lead to the search for intervening variables. The Getzels and Jackson study revealed that achievement motivation was not a distinguishing factor. In seeking clarification of the intelligence-creativity-achievement relationship, the present investigation was designed to determine to what extent the personality variable of anxiety is a mediating influence.
>
> "The results showed the significant role of intelligence in academic performance. Creativity was not determined to be related to academic success. The extent of general and test anxiety were also assessed and found to be unrelated to intellectual ability or productive thinking."

Getzels, J. W., & Jackson, P. W. *Creativity and intelligence: Explorations with gifted students.* New York: Wiley, 1962.

> This book reports intensive research on a selected sample of students, using specific instruments designed to provide relevant data. "The primary purpose of the study was to explore certain neglected issues regarding gifted cognitive and psychosocial functioning. The criterion at each point in our exploration was not whether this step would provide an unalterable datum but if it would lead to an observation that is heuristic. Our work with children is itself an extension and partial replication of work with adults done by F. Barron, J. P. Guilford, D. W. MacKinnon, M. I. Stein, and others."
>
> The authors worked with high school students of high intelligence (average IQ, 132) in a special school. They focused on creative potential among their subjects, as well as intelligence measures. They tried to outline such things as personality characteristics, family background, etc. The report discusses the educational implications of the findings, and suggests revisions to accommodate the highly creative as well as the highly intelligent. It also includes descriptions and examples of the measures used.

Golann, S. E. Psychological study of creativity. *Psychological Bulletin,* 1963, *60,* 548–565.

> This review of the literature covers much the same material M. Stein and S. Heinze reviewed a year earlier. Golann discusses four areas of emphasis, one of which usually appears in all studies of creativity. These include the use of products as criteria for creativity, the creative process itself, the devising or adapting of tests as measures of creativity (and the relationship of intelligence to creativity), and personality. Golann subdivides the latter area into studies of the motivation of creative behavior and personality characteristics or life styles of creative individuals.

Gruber, H., Terrell, G., & Wertheimer, M. (Eds.) *Contemporary approaches to creative thinking: A symposium held at the University of Colorado.* New York: Atherton Press, 1963.

> This book contains articles by J. Bruner, M. Henle, A. Newell, R. S. Crutchfield, R. McClelland, and R. B. McCloud. Each approaches somewhat differently the problem of defining and discussing the nature of creativity. The approaches include analogies to computers, statistical analyses, intuitive reports of creativity, and others. Contributors attempt to define creativity and identify the personality correlates of creativity.

Holland, J. L. Creative and academic performance among talented adolescents. *Journal of Educational Psychology,* 1961, *52,* 136–147.*

> The relationships among criteria of academic and creative performance and seventy-two personal, demographic, and parental variables were studied in a sampling of talented adolescents. The results showed that creative performance at the high school level occurs more frequently among students who are independent, intellectual, expressive, asocial, consciously original, and who have high aspirations for future achievement. Students who are persevering, sociable, responsible, and whose parents hold somewhat authoritarian attitudes and values are more frequently academic achievers.

Levy, N. J. Notes on the creative process and the creative person. *Psychiatric Quarterly,* 1961, *35,* 66–77,*

This article reviews twenty-one references on creativity. The creative potential exists in varying degrees in everyone. Psychological studies reveal that creative people often seek and live with tension and conflict and are more in contact with the unconscious than are other people. The creative potential is directly related to the periods of psychic freedom a person experiences. Inner conflicts may lead to emotional constriction, fears, compulsive behavior, and other neurotic solutions. Each individual responds to the creative urge in his own way.

Lowenfeld, V. *Creative and mental growth*. New York: Macmillan, 1957.

This book is written for art teachers who want to understand the mental and emotional development of children. The author attempts to show how the child's general growth is related to his creative development and vice versa. The child's creative expression during specific stages in his mental and emotional growth can be understood and appreciated only if the general causal interdependence between creation and growth is understood. The author also attempts to show methods of approaches to art education based upon psychological relations between creation and creator at the different age levels. Students' progress should be considered on an individual basis, with consideration of the students' developmental stages, rather than on a rigid, planned, generalized class basis.

Lowry, W. M. The university and the creative arts. *Educational Theatre Journal*, 1962, *14*, 99–112.

The author points out that universities have almost put out of business music conservatories and fine-arts colleges, yet do not provide adequate training for talented students.

MacKinnon, D. W. Fostering creativity in students of engineering. *Journal of Engineering Education*, 1961, *52*, 129–142.

In this article, the author discusses how to foster creativity in students. Although his work has been with mature creative people, the characteristics of these people are seen in students with creative potential. Creativity, he suggests, is a process which involves originality, adaptiveness, and realization. The creative person is less interested in small details and more concerned with meanings and implications. He also is more flexible cognitively and is characterized by verbal skills and interests as well as accuracy in communication with others. He values the theoretical and the esthetic, is intuitive-perception oriented rather than sense-perception oriented, and is inclined toward introversion. In school, he is not necessarily an honor student, sometimes as a result of rebelliousness or lack of interest. He is more in touch with his unconscious psychic processes.

As creativity is not necessarily correlated with intelligence, selecting and rewarding students on the basis of grades may rule out highly creative people. In teaching creative students, MacKinnon suggests "not that we slight acute and accurate sense perception, but that we use that to build upon, leading the student always toward an intuitive understanding of what he experiences." He also suggests giving creative students maximum freedom in attaining their academic objectives and advises setting the goals high enough to challenge the student and involve him in overcoming obstacles. The author stresses the importance of the college community which, if stimulating, can contribute to nourishing creativity. Finally, he warns the teachers he is addressing that they may not always like their creative students because of the students' attitudes toward themselves and the world around them.

MacKinnon, D. W. The nature and nurture of creative talent. *American Psychologist,* 1962, *17,* 484–495.

MacKinnon emphasizes his work with architects in this article. He discusses personality characteristics of the creative person. This person generally has a good opinion of himself, has a good intellect, shows a complexity and richness of personality, a general lack of defensiveness, and a candor in self-description. In other words, he shows an openness to experience both outside and inside himself. He has a wide range of interests (including those which are considered feminine), is more often introverted, shows a preference for feeling and perception rather than thought and judgment. He often has a lack of intense closeness with one or both parents. Many of the creative people in MacKinnon's study had autonomous mothers, and their families moved frequently. Discipline was consistent and predictable. The author cautions parents and teachers in setting limits for creative people, yet points out that some discipline and self-control are necessary. He also gives suggestions on how to train creative people to be intuitive.

McClelland, D. C., Baldwin, A. L., Bronfenbrenner, U., & Strodtbeck, F. L. *Talent and society.* Princeton: Van Nostrand, 1958.

Two chapters give a general treatment of the whole field of creativity. The remaining chapters are reports of completed research projects. The studies are searches for noncognitive factors that will facilitate the identification and development of talent. McClelland sees a need for research on (1) the stability of traits over time, (2) the functional characteristics of various performance situations, and (3) the stability of relationships between characteristics over time. He discusses the criteria of talent. Criteria will vary with the social and cultural milieu in which they are judged. Another determinant is subculture membership and values associated with it.

Baldwin considers ability as "a characteristic of the person which permits him to behave adaptively" and discusses it as such. The authors' recommendations for further study include (1) continued study of the expressive characteristics of the person—values, motives, etc., (2) study of the social situation in which performance occurs, and (3) study of ways of modifying stable characteristics of persons and situations. Their research shows that offering scholarships is not enough to encourage talent. Research should be strengthened in talent identification and development.

McDaniel, E. D. (Ed.) *Creativity and college teaching.* (Conference proceedings.) *Bulletin of the Bureau of School Services,* June 1963, *35,* (4). Lexington: College of Education, University of Kentucky.

This book contains contributions from D. W. MacKinnon, D. W. Taylor, R. L. Mooney, H. A. Thelen, M. J. M. Aschner, and R. W. Tyler. The introduction to the collection states: "MacKinnon's report of his investigation of the backgrounds of creative people suggests that creative individuals exhibit personality traits which distinguish them from people in general. MacKinnon goes on to examine some of the implications of his findings for nurturing the creative potential of students. . . . Taylor approaches the problem of creativity through analysis of the thinking process. A productive approach to understanding this process, he feels, is that of utilizing computers to simulate human thinking. . . . The teacher might well concentrate on identifying and teaching the heuristics most applicable to his discipline. . . . Mooney, in his presentation, sees the act of creating as analogous to the biological phenomena of life. He suggests that the creative person, like all living systems, is selectively taking in elements from the environment, integrating them, and testing the evolving internal system for fit with the environment. Mooney would ask of teachers and educational systems that they establish conditions which facilitate this process. . . .

"Thelen sees creativity as emerging from the process of inquiry. He constructs a conceptual model of the imperatives generated in the sequence of inquiry in the classroom. Students move from problem confrontation toward solutions, from formlessness toward structure, from preconscious toward conscious ideas, from private hunches toward public statements of position. These transitions are viewed as steps in the process of creating, and teaching becomes a matter of maximizing these qualities of experience. . . . Aschner's report of work in progress is an illustration of the empirical studies which ultimately must be made to test hypotheses relative to the development of creative thinking. . . . Tyler directs attention to the ways in which teachers may evaluate their efforts to develop creativity in students. . . . As a group these papers point to problem areas which are in need of further investigation: The background and personality of the student, the dynamics of the instructional group, and the strategy and tactics of the teacher."

McElvain, J. L., Fretwell, L. N., & Lewis, R. B. Relationship between creativity and teacher variability. *Psychological Reports,* 1963, *13,* 186.

The authors drew several conclusions from creativity test

scores of 209 teachers. Differences were unrelated to sex, education, experience, and teaching level and were negatively correlated with age. "Results suggest that for the selected adult population, creativity may be a fairly stable trait, since all variables but age were nonsignificant and correlated so closely to O. The evidence reported here, that school administrators tend to give lower ratings to the highly creative teacher, gives direction to other topics for research. There may be inherent within creativity, as it is measured, personality characteristics that are not valued in teachers."

McKellar, P. *Imagination and thinking: A psychological analysis.* New York: Basic Books, 1957.†

The author analyzes the psychological bases of thinking, imagination, originality, creativity. He distinguishes between thought products which are reality adjusted and those which are artistic. Originality consists in connection, rearrangement, and fusion of perceptions in a new way. Any human thought can be analyzed from the aspect of motivation and content. The book deals primarily with content and relies heavily on the associationist tradition. The author asserts that the type of imagery and imagination experiences of creative individuals might go far in explaining their works.

Conditions for creativity include a suitable and worthwhile *field* for its exercise. The most profitable fields are those in which criticism leads to the refinement and extension of ideas; a critical attitude also is favorable to creativity. A period of incubation, involving inactivity or a change of activity, is also conducive to creativity. Overlearning may lead to either creativity or mental rigidity. The latter is found in those people who become dependent on either primary or secondary perceptions. Creativity requires interaction of the primary and secondary perceptions. Understanding, which enables one to criticize and reformulate in alternate ways, would serve as a criterion of learning that is favorable to creativity. Works of art as thought products are dealt with extensively. Scientific reasoning is also analyzed and contrasted to art. Art is both artistic and reality-adjusted thinking. Scientific reasoning consists primarily of the latter.

Schaefer-Simmern, H. *The unfolding of artistic activity*: *Its basis, processes, and implications*. Berkeley and Los Angeles: University of California Press, 1948.

This book presents the results of an experiment undertaken ". . . for the purpose of showing by actual case histories the development of the creative potentialities in men and women in business and the professions, and in institutionalized delinquents and mental defectives—that is, persons not devoted to the arts. New directions in art education are essential to meet the need for creative experience, and they must be based on the natural unfolding and development of artistic abilities. Art teaching now is too systematic and detailed. Yet this contradicts the nature of man and of creativity which should grow out of the artist as a total process. The goal of art education is 'the natural cultivation of growing mental powers as they operate scientifically and interfunctionally within the process of artistic 'configuration.' "

The author sees as one of the main obstacles to development of creativity the common attitude that gives credit only to talent. He believes that the cultural decline which he sees in America and Europe can be stopped only if everyone learns to develop his own creativity. Creativity should be developed through organically conceived educational processes.

Simons, J. H. Scientific research in the university. *American Scientist*, 1960, *48*, 80–90.*

The author suggests that teaching creative scholarship and training creative scholars could be accomplished by exposing the student to the stimulation and example of a mature scholar of demonstrated creative ability through intimate contact.

Stein, M. *Survey of the psychological literature in the area of creativity with a view toward needed research*. New York: Research Center for Human Relations, New York University, 1962.

The research which Stein sees as necessary includes setting up ultimate criteria of creativity, with factors spelled out so comparative research can be done. Also, researchers should come to agreement about systematic sets of personality characteristics and sets of variables in the structural aspects of the field of creative endeavor. Another subject needing investigation is the types of individuals who are and are not creative, perhaps to establish constellations of personality characteristics. Finally, he sees a need for predictive studies.

In general, the author asks for coordinated and cooperative research efforts among problem-oriented researchers. He suggests that a group of investigators be established from several fields to select groups of individuals for study in a variety of areas. They would use a core battery of tests on subjects, plus more specialized tests from each investigator. They would pool results. Coordination is needed between lab studies of subjects chosen from psychometric data and studies of individuals proven to be creative by their production. The author advocates using a wider range of theories and speculations on creativity, for example, psychoanalytic, rather than only the empirical methods which are emphasized to date.

Street, W. P. (Ed.) *Creativity in its classroom context.* (Conference proceedings.) *Bulletin of the Bureau of School Services,* 1964, *36,* (4). Lexington: College of Education, University of Kentucky.

This book includes presentations by the following: N. Sanford, K. Keniston, H. A. Thelen, J. W. McKeachie, and P. Dressel. The papers were delivered at a conference held at Carnaham Hill, University of Kentucky, in 1964.

The introduction states: "Sanford's analysis of American college youth emphasizes the adjustment each student must make when he finds himself catapulted into a totally new environment. . . . The student substitutes a new social order— the student culture—for the previous moral authority. The power of this social milieu in changing the student is perhaps one of the major forces operating in the student during the college experience. Sanford would encourage faculty to be more cognizant of this subtle but substantial force. . . . Keniston . . . discusses values and perceptions which depart in significant ways from the values underlying the adult culture of the faculty members. . . .

"Thelen speaks out against the use of the class primarily as an instrument of 'socialization rather than education.' He follows with a discussion of classroom activity organized around the results of research in group dynamics. Central to his argument is the interpersonal support for the intellectual venture provided by classroom groups. Two types of groups operating in the classroom are discussed: the *psyche* group, based on voluntary associations mainly for the purpose of ego satisfaction, and the *socio* group, formed to accomplish work. The relation of these groups to teaching . . . is the major theme of Thelen's contribution. . . . McKeachie, in a comprehensive review of research on teaching, provides excellent coverage on the range of techniques usually encountered in the classroom. While the research is often inconclusive and contradictory, he concludes that the effective teacher tends to be a listener rather than a talker, a questioner rather than an answerer, a moderator rather than a dictator, a clarifier rather than an evaluator, and a stimulator rather than a performer. . . . Dressel, after reviewing what he sees as the six major functions of instruction, notes two points at which teaching may be evaluated: the process of instruction itself and the results of the instruction. Dressel identifies testing as a critical component in determining the kind of learning behavior in which students are actually engaged."

Taylor, C. W., & Barron, F. (Eds.) *Scientific creativity: Its recognition and development.* New York: Wiley, 1963.

This book includes selected papers from the proceedings of the first, second, and third University of Utah Conferences on the Identification of Creative Scientific Talent. The papers are arranged according to criteria; intellectual, personality, and motivational characteristics; environmental conditions and specific situational determinants; and theoretical analyses of process. Includes a 400-item bibliography.

Thorndike, R. L. The measurement of creativity. *Teachers College Record,* 1963, *64,* 422–424.

The author's discussion takes off from 1962 publications by Getzels and Jackson, IPAR, and Torrance, plus the 1954 article by Wilson, Guilford, *et al.* All agree on the low correlation between creativity and what is measured by IQ and scholastic aptitude tests. On creativity tests, the examinee must produce answers, not select one. He usually must produce multiple responses. The overlap between subtypes of creativity is less than that between cognitive subabilities. This fact has received little attention from those who have used creativity tests. The major suggestion of the article is that researchers give each so-called creativity test a more specific name.

Torrance, E. P. Must creative development be left to chance? *Gifted Child Quarterly,* 1962, 6, 41–44.*

Certain teaching techniques increase original thinking. Evidence adduced from investigation in Samoa links the decline in creativity to the low value placed on adventurousness and curiosity and the high value placed on promptness and competitiveness. Associated with cultural "discontinuities," however, is a rise in creativity.

PUBLISHED ARTICLES AND CHAPTERS IN BOOKS

Arnold, J. E. Useful creative techniques. In S. J. Parnes & H. F. Harding (Eds.), *A sourcebook for creative thinking.* New York: Scribners, 1962, 251–268.

Barron, F. Some personality correlates of independence of judgment. *Journal of Personality,* 1953, 21, 287–297.

Barron, F. Originality in relation to personality and intellect. *Journal of Personality,* 1957, 25, 730–742.

Barron, F. The psychology of imagination. *Scientific American,* 1958, 150–166.

Barron, F. Creative vision and expression. In A. Frazer (Ed.), *New insights and the curriculum. Yearbook 1963, Association for Supervision and Curriculum Development,* 1963, 285–305.

Barron, F. Diffusion, integration, and enduring attention in the creative process. In R. W. White (Ed.), *The study of lives: Essays on personality in honor of Henry A. Murray.* New York: Atherton Press, 1963, 234–248.

Barron, F. The needs for order and for disorder as motives in creative activity. In C. W. Taylor & F. Barron (Eds.), *Scientific creativity: Its recognition and development.* New York: Wiley, 1963, 153–160.

Bedrosian, A., & Jackson, B. Intellectual conformity: Not the answer. *Journal of Higher Education,* 1958, *29* (7), 381–385.

Beittel, K. R. (Ed.) Creativity, education, and art: Interpretations. Research issue, *Eastern Arts Association Bulletin,* 1962, *19* (4).

Beittel, K. R., & Burkhart, R. C. Strategies of spontaneous, divergent, and academic art students. *Studies in Art Education,* 1963, *5,* 20–41.

Berlin, T. N. Aspects of creativity and the learning process. *American Image,* 1960, *17,* 83–99.

Birney, R. C., & Houston, J. P. The effects of creativity, norm distance, and instructions on social influence. *Journal of Personality,* 1961, *29* (3), 294–302.

Brittain, W. L. Do we develop creative people? *Art Education Bulletin,* 1961, *18,* 22–36.

Brittain, W. L., & Beittel, K. R. Analyses of levels of creative performance in the visual arts. *Journal of Aesthetics and Art Criticism,* 1960, *19* (1), 83–90.

Buel, W. D., & Bachner, V. M. The assessment of creativity in a research setting. *Journal of Applied Psychology,* 1961, *45* (6), 353–358.

Burgart, H. J. Art in higher education: The relationship of art experience to personality, general creativity, and esthetic performance. *Studies in Art Education,* 1961, *2,* 14–35.

Cristensen, P. R., Guilford, J. P., & Wilson, R. C. Relations of creative responses to working time and instructions. *Journal of Experimental Psychology,* 1957, *53,* 82–89.

Clark, W. H. A study of some of the factors leading to achievement and creativity, with special reference to religious skepticism and belief. *Journal of Social Psychology,* 1955, *41,* 57–69.

Crutchfield, R. S. Independent thought in a conformist world. In S. M. Farber & R. H. L. Wilson (Eds.). *Conflict and creativity: Control of the mind, Part 2.* New York: McGraw-Hill, 1963, 208–228.

Dense, T. C., & Burns, H. W. Knowledge and creativity. *Proceedings of the 1962 invitational conference on testing problems.* Princeton: Educational Testing Service, 1963, 13–30.

Drevdahl, J. E. Factors of importance for creativity. *Journal of Clinical Psychology,* 1956, *12,* 21–26.

Drevdahl, J. E., & Cattell, R. B. Personality and creativity in artists and writers. *Journal of Clinical Psychology,* 1958, *14,* 107–111.

Dunkel, H. B. Creativity and education. *Educational Theory,* 1961, *11,* 209–216.

Eiduson, B. T. Artist and non-artist: A comparative study. *Journal of Personality,* 1958, *26,* 13–28.

Forslund, J. E. An inquiry into the nature of creative teaching. *Journal of Education,* 1961, *143,* 72–82.

Franklin, A. (Chr.), Henry, J., *et al.* The teacher's role in creativity. Symposium, 1958. *American Journal of Orthopsychiatry,* 1959 (April), *29,* 266–297.

Freedman, J. L. Increasing creativity by free-association training. *Journal of Experimental Psychology,* 1965, *69* (1), 89–91.

Garwood, D. S. Personality factors related to creativity in young scientists. *Journal of Abnormal and Social Psychology,* 1964, *68* (4), 413–419.

Getzels, J. W., & Jackson, P. W. Family environment and cognitive style: A study of the sources of highly intelligent and highly creative adolescents. *American Sociology Review,* 1961, *26,* 351–359.

Getzels, J. W., Jackson, P. W., & Burt, C. Psychology of creative ability: Review of creativity and intelligence. *British Journal of Educational Psychology,* 1962, *32,* 292–298.

Gezi, K. I., & Nygreen, G. T. Is creativity within the academic community compatible with operational efficiency? *Journal of Higher Education,* 1964, *35,* 224–225.

Givens, P. R. Identifying and encouraging creative processes. *Journal of Higher Education,* 1962, *33,* 295–301.

Gjesdahl, M. S. Education for creativity in engineering. *Journal of Engineering Education,* 1955, *45,* 766–769.

Ghiselin, B. Ultimate criteria for two levels of creativity. In C. W.

Taylor & F. Barron (Eds.), *Scientific creativity: Its recognition and development.* New York: Wiley, 1963, 30–43.

Gruen, W. The utilization of creative potential in our society. *Journal of Counseling Psychology,* 1962, *9,* 79–83.

Guilford, J. P. Can creativity be developed? *Art Education,* 1956, *11,* 14–18.

Guilford, J. P. Creative abilities in the arts. *Psychological Review,* 1957, *64,* 110–118.

Guilford, J. P. Creativity: Its measurement and development. In S. J. Parnes & H. F. Harding (Eds.), *A sourcebook for creative thinking.* New York: Scribners, 1962, 151–168.

Guilford, J. P. Factors that aid and hinder creativity. *Teachers College Record,* 1962, *63,* 380–392.

Hallman, R. J. Can creativity be taught? *Educational Theory,* 1964, *14,* 15–23.

Harlow, H. F., Miller, J. G., & Newcomb, T. M. Identifying creative talent in psychology. *American Psychologist,* 1962, *17* (10), 679–683.

Harris, D. H. The development and validation of a test of creativity in engineering. *Journal of Applied Psychology,* 1960, *44,* 254–257.

Hitt, W. D., & Stock, J. R. The relation between psychological characteristics and creative behavior. *Psychological Record,* 1965, *15* (1), 133–140.

Holland, J. L., & Astin, A. W. The prediction of the academic, artistic, scientific, and social achievement of undergraduates of superior scholastic aptitude. *Journal of Educational Psychology,* 1962, *53,* 132–143.

Hopkins, L. T. Classroom climate can promote creativeness. *Educational Leadership,* 1956, *13,* 279–282.

Houston, J. P., & Mednick, S. A. Creativity and the need for novelty. *Journal of Abnormal and Social Psychology,* 1963, *66* (2), 137–141.

Israeli, N. Creative processes in painting. *Journal of General Psychology,* 1962, *67* (2), 251–263.

Leuba, C. A new look at curiosity and creativity. *Journal of Higher Education,* 1958, *29,* 132–140.

Lovelace, W. B. Profile of the creative student. *Superior Student,* 1963, *5,* 31–34.

Lowenfeld, V. Creativity and art education. *School Arts,* 1959, *59,* 5–15.

Lowenfeld, V., & Beittel, K. R. Interdisciplinary criteria of creativity in the arts and sciences: A progress report. *Research in Art Education,* 9th Yearbook of the NAEA, 1959, 35–44.

MacKinnon, D. W. Identifying and developing creativity. In *Selection and educational differentiation.* Berkeley: Field Service Center and Center for the Study of Higher Education, University of California, 1960, 75–89.

MacKinnon, D. W. Characteristics of the creative person: Implications for the teaching-learning process. *Current Issues in Higher Education.* Washington, D.C.: National Education Association, 1961, 89–92.

MacKinnon, D. W. Creativity and images of the self. In R. W. White (Ed.), *The study of lives: Essays on personality in honor of H. A. Murray.* New York: Atherton Press, 1963, 250–278.

MacKinnon, D. W. Identifying and developing creativity. *Journal of Secondary Education,* 1963, *38,* 166–174.

MacKinnon, D. W. The characteristics of creative architects and further reflections on their implications for architectural education. In M. Whiffen (Ed.), *The teaching of architecture: Papers from the 1963 AIA-ACSA teacher seminar.* Washington, D.C.: American Institute of Architects, Office of Educational Programs, 1964, 73–93.

MacKinnon, D. W. Conditions for effective personality change. In A. H. Passow (Ed.), *Nurturing individual potential: Papers and reports from the ASCD seventh curriculum research institute.* Washington, D.C.: Association for Supervision and Curriculum Development, 1964, 12–27.

MacKinnon, D. W. Personality and the realization of creative potential. *American Psychologist,* 1965, *20,* 273–281.

Maslow, A. H. Emotional blocks to creativity. *Humanist,* 1958, *18,* 325–332.

Maw, W., & Maw, E. W. Establishing criterion groups for evaluating measures of curiosity. *Journal of Experimental Education,* 1961, *29,* 299–305.

Mednick, S. A. Development of admissions criteria for colleges and universities that will not eliminate such applicants as the bright and non-conformist, the underchallenged, and the individual with highly specialized abilities. *Current Issues in Higher Education.* Washington, D.C.: National Education Association, 1961, 86–88.

Mednick, S. A. The associative basis of the creative process. *Psychological Review,* 1962, *69* (3), 220–232.

Mednick, M. T. Research creativity in psychology graduate students. *Journal of Consulting Psychology,* 1963, *27* (3), 265–266.

Mednick, M. T., Mednick, S. A., & Mednick, E. V. Incubation of creative performance and specific associative priming. *Journal of Abnormal and Social Psychology,* 1964, *69* (1), 84–88.

Meer, B., & Stein, M. I. Measures of intelligence and creativity. *Journal of Psychology,* 1955, *39,* 117–126.

Mooney, R. L. Cultural blocks and creative possibilities. *Educational Leadership,* 1956, *13,* 273–278.

Myers, R. E., & Torrance, E. P. Can teachers encourage creative thinking? *Education Leadership,* 1961, *19,* 156–159.

Nyder, J. Creativity and psychotherapy. *Psychoanalytic Review,* 1962, *49,* 29–33.

Orowan, E. Our universities and scientific creativity. *Bulletin of Atomic Scientists,* 1959, *6,* 236–239.

Parnes, S. J. Effects of extended effort in creative problem solving. *Journal of Educational Psychology,* 1961, *52* (3), 117–122.

Parnes, S. J. Education and creativity. *Teachers College Record,* 1963, *64,* 331–339.

Piers, E. V., Daniels, J. M., & Quackenbush, J. F. The identification of creativity in adolescents. *Journal of Educational Psychology,* 1960, *51,* 346–516.

Phillips, G. D. Education through creative expression. *Journal of Education,* 1963, *145,* 3–66.

Rees, M. E., & Goldman, M. Some relationships between creativity and personality. *Journal of General Psychology,* 1961, *65,* 145–161.

Ripple, R. E., & May, F. B. Caution in comparing creativity and IQ. *Psychological Reports,* 1962, *10,* 229–230.

Rubin, L. J. Creativeness in the classroom. *Education Digest,* 1963, *29,* 49–51.

Sanford, N., Webster, H., & Freedman, M. Impulse expression as a variable of personality. *Psychological Monographs,* 1957, *71* (Whole No. 440).

Snyder, B. R., & Tessman, L. H. Gifted students and scientists. In H. H. Anderson (Ed.), *Creativity in childhood and adolescence.* Palo Alto, Calif.: Science and Behavior Books, 1965, 20–33.

Sommers, W. S. The influence of selected teaching methods on the development of creative thinking. Doctoral dissertation, University of Minnesota, 1961.

Stein, M. I. Toward developing more imaginative creativity in students. In R. M. Cooper (Ed.), *The two ends of the log.* Minneapolis: University of Minnesota Press, 1959, 69–75.

Sullivan, A. J. Right to fail: Creativity vs. conservatism. *Journal of Higher Education,* 1963, *34,* 191–195.

Taylor, C. W. Effects of instructional media on creativity: A look at possible positive and negative effects. *Educational Leadership,* 1962, *19* (7), 453–458.

Taylor, C. W., & Holland, J. L. Development and application of tests of creativity. *Review of Educational Research,* 1962, *32* (1), 91–102.

Terman, L. M. The discovery and encouragement of exceptional talent. *American Psychologist,* 1954, *9,* 221–230.

Thistlethwaite, D. L. College environments and the development of talent. *Science,* 1959, *130,* 71–76.

Torrance, E. P. Cultural discontinuities and the development of originality of thinking. *Exceptional Children,* 1962, *29,* 2–13.

Torrance, E. P. Testing and creative talent. *Education Leadership,* 1962, *20,* 7–104.

Torrance, E. P. Multiphasic study of creativity. *Contemporary Psychology,* 1964, *9,* 277–278.

Torrance, E. P. Scientific views on creativity and its development. *Daedalus, Summer,* 1965, 663–681.

Torrance, E. P., & Henrickson, P. R. Some implications for art education from the Minnesota studies of creative thinking. *Studies in Art Education,* 1961, *2,* 36–44.

Vernon, P. C. Creativity and intelligence. *Educational Research,* 1964, *6,* 163–169.

Walcott, F. G. The climate for creative learning. *University of Michigan School of Education Bulletin,* 1959, *31,* 33–56.

Weisberg, P. S., & Springer, K. J. Environmental factors in creative function. *Archives of General Psychiatry,* 1961, *5,* 554–564.

Wenkart, A. Creativity and freedom. *American Journal of Psychoanalysis,* 1963, *23,* 195–204.

Wilson, R. C., Guilford, J. P., *et al.* A factor-analytic study of creative thinking abilities. *Psychometrika,* 1954, *19,* 297–311.

Wilson, R. C., Guilford, J. P., & Christensen, P. R. The measurement of individual differences in originality. In W. B. Barbe (Ed.), *Psychology and education of the gifted.* New York: Appleton-Century-Crofts, 1965, 161–171.

Witty, P. A. Gifted and creative students. *School & Society,* 1964, *92,* 183–184.

Yamamoto, K. Creativity and sociometric choice among adolescents. *Journal of Social Psychology,* 1964, *64* (2), 249–261.

Yamamoto, K. Threshold of intelligence in academic achievement of highly creative students. *Journal of Experimental Education,* 1964, *32,* 401–405.

BOOKS, MONOGRAPHS, AND BULLETINS

Anderson, H. H. (Ed.) *Creativity and its cultivation.* New York: Harper, 1959.

Anderson, H. H. Creativity and education. *College and University Bulletin,* 1961, *13.*

Anderson, H. H. (Ed.) *Creativity in childhood and adolescence: A diversity of approaches.* Palo Alto, Calif.: Science and Behavior Books, 1965.

Andrews, M. L. (Ed.) *Creativity and psychological health.* Syracuse, N. Y.: Syracuse University Press, 1961.

Aschner, M. J., & Bish, C. E. (Eds.) *Productive thinking in education*. Washington, D.C.: National Education Association, 1965.

Benton, M. Creativity in research and invention in the physical sciences: An annotated bibliography. *USN Research Laboratory Report,* 1961, Bibliography No. 19.

Block, H. M. (Ed.) *The creative vision: Modern European writers on their art.* New York: Grove Press, 1960.

Brandwein, P. F. *The gifted student as future scientist.* New York: Harcourt, 1955.

Creativity of gifted and talented children. Addresses by P. Witty, J. B. Conant, & R. Strang. New York: American Association for Gifted Children, Bureau of Publications, Columbia University Teachers College, 1959.

Farber, S. M., & Wilson, R. H. (Eds.) *Conflict and creativity: Control of the mind, Part 2.* New York: McGraw-Hill, 1963.

Frank, L. K., *et al. Imagination in education.* New York: Bank Street College of Education, 1956.

Gardner, J. W. *Self-renewal: The individual and the innovative society.* New York: Harper, 1964.

Gordon, W. J. J. *Synectics: The development of creative capacity.* New York: Harper, 1961.

Hammer, E. F. *Creativity: An exploratory investigation of the personalities of gifted adolescent artists.* New York: Random House, 1961.

Koestler, A. *The act of creation.* New York: Macmillan, 1964.

Kubie, L. S. *Neurotic distortion of the creative process.* New York: Noonday Press, 1961.

Maltzman, I., Simon, S., Raskin, D., & Licht, L. *Experimental studies in the training of originality.* Washington, D.C.: American Psychological Association, 1960.

Marshall, G. O. (Ed.) *Creativity and the arts.* Athens, Ga.: Center for Continuing Education, University of Georgia, 1961.

Mearns, H. *Creative power: The education of youth in the creative arts.* New York: Dover, 1958.

Myden, W. Interpretation and evaluation of certain personality characteristics involved in creative production. *Perceptual and Motor Skills,* 1959, *9,* 139–158. Monograph Supplement No. 3.

Parnes, S. J., & Harding, H. I. (Eds.) *A sourcebook for creative thinking.* New York: Scribners, 1962.

Razik, T. A. *Bibliography of creative studies and related areas.* Buffalo, N.Y.: University of Buffalo Foundation, 1965.

Rugg, H. *Imagination.* New York: Harper, 1963.

Smith, P. (Ed.) *Creativity: An examination of the creative process.* New York: Hastings House, 1959.

Stein, M., & Heinze, S. *Creativity and the individual: Summaries of selected literature in psychology and psychiatry.* Glencoe, Ill.: Free Press, 1960.

Summerfield, J. D., & Thatcher, L. (Eds.) *The creative mind and method. Exploring the nature of creativeness in American arts, sciences, and professions.* Austin: University of Texas Press, 1960.

Taylor, C. W. (Ed.) *The 1955 University of Utah research conference on the identification of creative scientific talent.* Salt Lake City: University of Utah Press, 1956.

Taylor, C. W. (Ed.) *The second (1957) University of Utah research conference on the identification of creative scientific talent.* Salt Lake City: University of Utah Press, 1958.

Taylor, C. W. (Ed.) *The third (1959) University of Utah research conference on the identification of creative scientific talent.* Salt Lake City: University of Utah Press, 1959.

Taylor, C. W. (Ed.) *Widening horizons in creativity.* New York: Wiley, 1960.

Taylor, C. W. (Ed.) *Creativity: Progress and potential.* New York: McGraw-Hill, 1964.

Torrance, E. P. (Ed.) *New educational ideas: Third Minnesota conference on gifted children.* Minneapolis: University of Minnesota Press, 1961.

Torrance, E. P. *Guiding creative talent.* Englewood Cliffs, N.J.: Prentice-Hall, 1962.

Torrance, E. P. *Education and the creative potential.* Minneapolis: University of Minnesota Press, 1963.

INDEX

249